Assessment

DEC Recommended Practices Monograph Series

Assessment

Recommended Practices for Young Children and Families

DEC Recommended Practices Monograph Series

Division for
Early
Childhood

of the Council for Exceptional Children

Washington, DC

Disclaimer

The opinions and information contained in the articles of this monograph are those of the authors of the respective articles and not necessarily those of the Division for Early Childhood (DEC) of the Council for Exceptional Children. Accordingly, DEC assumes no liability or risk that may be incurred as a consequence, directly or indirectly, or the use and application of any of the contents of this monograph.

Published and Distributed by:

E-mail: dec@dec-sped.org
Website: http://www.dec-sped.org/

The Division for Early Childhood (DEC), a division of the Council for Exceptional Children, is an international membership organization for individuals who work with or on behalf of young children with disabilities and other special needs. Founded in 1973, DEC's mission is to promote policies and advance evidence-based practices that support families and enhance the optimal development of young children who have or are at risk for developmental delays and disabilities. Information about membership and other resources available can be found at www.dec-sped.org

Editors: Mary McLean, *University of Florida*, Rashida Banerjee, *University of Denver*, Jane Squires, *University of Oregon*, and Kathleen Hebbeler, *SRI International*

Copy editing and cover and interior design: Kevin Dolan
Indexer: Jean Jesensky, *Endswell Indexing*
Typeset in Warnock Pro, Myriad Pro, and Calibri
All photos provided by iStock except on Page 125

Suggested Citation

McLean, M., Banerjee, R., Squires, J., & Hebbeler, K. (Eds.). (2020). *Assessment: Recommended practices for young children and families* (DEC Recommended Practices Monograph Series No. 7). Washington, DC: Division for Early Childhood.

TABLE OF CONTENTS

Division for
Early
Childhood
of the Council for Exceptional Children

Download the DEC Recommended Practices
www.dec-sped.org/
dec-recommended-practices

Assessment
Introduction and Overview

Mary McLean
University of Florida

Rashida Banerjee
University of Denver

Jane Squires
University of Oregon

Kathleen Hebbeler
SRI International

F OR YOUNG CHILDREN WITH OR AT RISK FOR DEVELOPMENTAL DELAYS or disabilities and their families, assessment is an ongoing and important component of early intervention and early childhood special education services that can serve a variety of purposes. Assessment is a generic term for the process of gathering information to make informed decisions. The purpose of any assessment activity must be clear to all involved because the purpose should determine what is assessed, how it is assessed, and how the results of the assessment are used. Families of young children with or at risk for disabilities can expect that their child's skills or behaviors will be assessed frequently for a number of different purposes. Practitioners in early intervention/early childhood special education (EI/ECSE) can expect that they will be responsible for assessing child skills or behaviors for a number of different purposes, sharing the resulting information with families, and using the collected information appropriately in teaching and intervention. Administrators of EI/ECSE programs can expect that they will be responsible for guiding assessment instrument and strategy selection, training assessors appropriately, using gathered assessment information appropriately, and designing and implementing a team-based, family-centered approach to assessment.

The purposes of assessment in EI/ECSE have traditionally been identified as:
- screening,
- determining eligibility for special education services,
- program planning,
- monitoring child progress, and
- program evaluation and accountability.

Screening, as a purpose of assessment, refers to the administration of a brief instrument or procedure to identify children who may need further assessment to verify developmental and/or health risks. *Developmental screening*, as mandated by the Individuals With Disabilities Education Act (IDEA, 2004), is part of a broader system of child identification that should be completed on a regular, periodic basis as well as when families have questions about their child's development. The primary result of a developmental screener is a decision about whether a child should be referred for further evaluation to determine the need for EI/ECSE services.

Universal screening, as used in the field of education, is defined in relation to a tiered model of intervention and refers to screening of all children in a program on a regular basis throughout the year. Universal screening results in decisions relative to the delivery of additional instruction within the classroom or setting the child is already in. If a child has a positive screen, the child would be offered additional support within the setting and monitored to see if this additional help results in improved child functioning.

Assessment to determine eligibility for services results in a determination of whether the child qualifies to receive EI/ECSE services. This assessment typically considers general developmental functioning, medical conditions, sensory and motor functioning, and adaptive behavior. The outcome may lead to the identification of a specific condition or category of disability or to the identification of a developmental delay that qualifies the child for services offered under IDEA.

Assessment for program planning refers to assessment for the purpose of guiding instruction in the general curriculum or guiding development or implementation of IFSP or IEP outcomes and goals.

Assessment for monitoring child progress typically takes place on an ongoing basis and may include assessment of progress in the general education curriculum relative to intervention strategies established within a tiered model of instruction or relative to outcomes and goals from the IFSP or IEP. Child progress must be monitored on an ongoing basis to determine whether adjustments should be made to instructional targets or strategies.

Assessment for program evaluation refers to assessment that includes the collection, analysis, and use of information to evaluate the intervention or educational program. This may include an evaluation of overall child progress and/or parent satisfaction as a measure of the quality of the program. *Program accountability* refers to the collection, analysis, and use of assessment information to hold programs responsible for the quality of the service system and the outcomes achieved.

The DEC Recommended Practices are based on empirical evidence as well as the wisdom and experience of the field and, as such, serve as a guide for practitioners, families, and administrators as they work together to provide the best possible services for young children and their families. The Assessment recommended practices were developed to provide guidance about effective practices for implementing assessment with young children. There are 11 Assessment recommended practices, which can be found at the end of this introduction.

The 12 articles included in this monograph illustrate the implementation of the Assessment recommended practices for children from birth through age 5 who are at risk for or have identified developmental delays or disabilities. Each article describes the use of assessment strategies that are based on two or more of the Assessment recommended practices. The articles have been organized according to the purpose of assessment that is addressed. The first two articles (Wackerle-Hollman & Durán; Hojnoski & Missal) focus on screening. Eligibility determination is the topic of the next four articles (DeAnda, Larson, & Cycyk; Hill, Childress, Terry, & Brager; Acar, Silva, & Brown; Blanchard, Acar, Hurley, Cummings, & Durán). Four articles (Rush, Everhart, Sexton, & Shelden; Blasco & Acar; McWilliam & Stevenson; Peck & Neeper) then focus on assessment for program planning. The final two articles (Bishop, Shannon, & Harrington; Ridgley) address the topic of progress monitoring.

Wackerle-Hollman and Durán focus on understanding how dual language learners (DLLs) develop language and early literacy skills in both of their languages as a result of differentiated instruction. They describe a method for screening and progress monitoring with DLLs using the Spanish and English Individual Growth and Development Indicators (IGDIs). A comparative score rubric helps early educators consider children's performance in both languages in home and classroom language environments. DEC Recommended Practice A10, which relates to using assessment tools with sufficient sensitivity to detect child progress, is part of the IGDIs process, as is A5, conducting assessments in the child's dominant language. Through the assessment process, information is obtained about the child's skills in daily activities and routines (A7), and ongoing assessment is conducted to identify learning targets, plan activities, and monitor child progress (A9).

Hojnoski and Missall describe a multiple-gate assessment process that can be used to systematically screen and monitor preschoolers' social-emotional development. The approach considers a child's behavior over time in natural settings and requires input from teacher and caregiver ratings as well as classroom observation before specialized instruction or referral. Through this process, practitioners work as a team with the family to gather assessment information using a variety of methods, including observation and interviews (A2, A6). Also, a multiple-gate approach can be used for ongoing assessment to identify learning targets, plan activities, and monitor child progress (A9). An overview of how one preschool implemented a multiple-gate approach for screening of social-emotional development is provided.

De Anda, Larson, and Cycyk focus on evaluation and assessment of communication for Latinx infants and toddlers. Four steps are recommended for evaluating communication as part of eligibility determinations for early intervention. Step 1 focuses on preparing for the evaluation, which includes working with the family to identify preferences for assessment processes (A1). Step 2 addresses gathering background information by working with the family and other professionals (A2), using observation and interviews to obtain information about the child's skills in daily routines and activities (A6 and A7), and conducting an ethnographic interview and language background questionnaire. Step 3 focuses on measuring child language ability and experience in the child's dominant language and additional languages (A5) in ways that are appropriate for the child's cultural, linguistic, and social characteristics (A3) and in ways that have

DEC Recommended Practices Commissioners

Mary McLean, chair
Rashida Banerjee
Erin Barton
Angel Fettig
Chelsea Guillen
Kathleen Hebbeler
Anne Larson
Hailey Love
Jose Martinez
Lori Erbrederis Meyer
Michelle Ogorek
Brian Reichow
Beth Rous
Susan Sandall
Kristen Schraml-Block
Sheila Self
Patricia Snyder
Judy Swett

Past Commissioners

Barbara J. Smith, past chair
Judy Carta
Tricia Catalino
Mary Louise Hemmeter
Tara McLaughlin
Pam Winton

sufficient sensitivity to detect child progress (A10). Step 3 also includes caregiver report, dynamic assessment, direct observation, language sampling, and the use of norm- and criterion-referenced tools. Step 4 addresses eligibility determination by using clinical reasoning in addition to assessment results (A8) as well as reporting assessment results so they are understandable and useful to families (A11). This article provides information about the selection of evaluation team members, respectful information-gathering from a child's family, and appropriate use of formal and informal measures to determine child language skills in all languages to which the child has been exposed.

Hill, Childress, Terry, and Brager describe a comprehensive early intervention assessment process from eligibility determination to program planning to ongoing progress monitoring using the Assessment recommended practices. Nine of the Assessment recommended practices (A1–A9) are addressed, with practical definitions of each phase and accompanied by strategies for practitioners. As an illustration, the Assessment recommended practices are cross-walked with assessment procedures from the state of Virginia, including vignettes illustrating each of the assessment practices. This assessment process emphasizes getting to know families and what is important to them, as well as providing supports that are meaningful, functional, and authentic.

Acar, Silva, and Brown provide guidelines for communicating and presenting assessment findings consistent with the Assessment recommended practices. They specifically address recommended practices A2 and A11 when collecting assessment data, building collaborative relationships with families, and sharing results. The authors propose working with families as active team members in a data-collection process by seeking families' help to complete observation forms and asking open-ended questions about their child's development. They suggest several steps to make communication with parents more meaningful and functional. One such strategy discussed is "LAFF don't CRY," which provides a flexible framework that EI/ECSE practitioners can use to demonstrate empathy and respect during the assessment process.

Blanchard, Acar, Hurley, Cummings, and Durán focus on understanding developmental levels in young children who are refugees. Often faced with a lack of program resources to conduct assessments in a child's native language, lack of available measures, and challenges with understanding the full impact and possible trauma of being a refugee, many programs must rely on supplemental strategies to ensure family-centered assessment practices. This article presents an overview of ways to solve some of these challenges by applying the Assessment recommended practices for a family-centered approach. The authors illustrate their assessment approach with an example of a team focused on considering the development of a young child whose family is from Bhutan. The importance of building systematic collaborative relationships with families as well as important stakeholders, including cultural liaisons, interpreters, and extended family members, is illustrated. Four Assessment recommended practices are specifically targeted, including using assessment materials and strategies that are appropriate for the child's age and level of development and accommodating specific characteristics throughout the process (A3); conducting all assessments in the child's dominant language (A5); using a variety of methods including observation and interviews to gather information from a variety of sources (A6); and using clinical reasoning in addition to assessment results to identify the child's current level of functioning, eligibility, and plan for instruction (A8).

Rush, Everhart, Sexton, and Shelden describe a tool, entitled Roadmap for Assessing Meaningful Participation (RAMP), to assist practitioners with gathering and documenting information, conducting a functional assessment, and writing meaningful, participation-based outcomes. The tool also includes roadmaps to guide practitioners' use of a coaching interaction style with families. In Part I of the RAMP process, practitioners work with families to identify family preferences and collect assessment information in all areas of development (A1, A2, A4). In Part II, the participation-based assessment, practitioners observe the family or other caregivers and the child within the context of a typical activity related to one of the family priorities to analyze what works and what does not and why, and to develop alternative strategies (A6, A7). Finally, Part III focuses on developing the IFSP outcomes and next steps in the service delivery and intervention process.

Blasco and Acar focus on the assessment of executive function (EF) skills in early childhood through parent reports and observation of child behavior during daily routines and across environments with a focus on A2, practitioners work as a team with the family and other professionals to gather assessment information; A6, practitioners use a variety of methods, including observation and interviews, to gather assessment information from multiple sources; and A9, practitioners implement systematic ongoing assessment to identify learning targets, plan activities, and monitor the child's progress to revise instruction as needed. The authors define executive function as central processes in the brain that link and categorize information and which can be observed in the cognitive, motor, and behavioral responses of young children. A rationale is provided for the importance of assessing executive functioning in young children. They review two parent-report instruments and two performance-based instruments that can be used to assess executive functioning in young children for intervention planning purposes. Ongoing assessment strategies for monitoring child progress relative to EF skills are also presented for emotional control, self-regulation, inhibitory control, working memory, cognitive flexibility, and organization and planning.

McWilliam and Stevenson describe the process of conducting a needs assessment and planning process using a routines-based interview. Conducting a semistructured interview with parents, developing an ecomap, and identifying participation-based outcomes/goals are specifically described as part of the routines-based interview (RBI) process. The relation between RBI and Assessment recommended practices is also described. Highlighted recommended practices include working as a team with families to gather assessment information (A2) and conducting comprehensive assessments in developmental areas (A4) while using a variety of methods to gather information (A6). The RBI process also includes obtaining information about child's skills (A7) and conducting ongoing assessment to identify learning targets, plan activities, and monitor child progress (A9). A brief discussion of how to conduct an RBI is summarized, including what practitioners can do until they are trained on the RBI to fidelity.

Peck and Neeper align all 11 Assessment recommended practices to an assessment process of asking questions, collecting and analyzing data, and taking action within the context of assistive technology (AT). Recognizing that not all teams have ready access to an AT specialist, they provide strategies to build the assessment team's capacity by increasing access to quality AT assessment resources that may support children's and families' opportunities for early adoption of AT. They discuss potential barriers to AT implementation and provide a compilation of free online resources to support teams in their work through the AT assessment process.

Bishop, Shannon, and Harrington focus on assessment for the purpose of progress monitoring within an embedded instruction approach. Embedded instruction is an evidence-based and recommended naturalistic instructional approach that involves the use of contextualized assessment procedures. Highlighted recommended practices include A7, obtaining information about child skills in daily activities; A9, implementing systematic ongoing assessment to identify learning targets and monitor child progress; and A11, reporting assessment results so they are understandable and useful to families. This article begins by explaining contextualized instruction and assessment followed by an explanation and example of developing priority learning targets (PLTs) that are aligned with IEP goals and early learning foundations and are the basis for progress monitoring in embedded instruction. PLTs are instrumental in determining what data to collect (frequency, rate, accuracy, level of support) for each child throughout the day. Decisions about what data to collect as well as who will collect it and when are facilitated by the use of a data-planning matrix. A final focus of this article is on the use of collected data to determine whether to continue instruction, modify instruction, or move to the next step with the development of a new PLT.

In the final article of this monograph, Ridgely argues that home visits may not provide practitioners with enough information about a child's current skills. Thus, strategies are provided for helping families find meaningful, authentic, and family-centered approaches for engaging in regular, ongoing data collection that informs the work of early intervention or other home-based supports for young children. Ridgley begins by suggesting strategies to get the family "onboard" with documenting observations, then recommends steps and strategies for how to include families in data collection for the purpose of progress monitoring. This article focuses on eight assessment recommended practices (A1, A2, A3, A4, A6, A7, A9, and A10) and is based on Family recommended practices as well.

Assessment is a vital and foundational component of services for young children with disabilities and their families. It is also complex in that there are a variety of functions of assessment in EI/ECSE that require different ways of gathering and interpreting assessment results for a population of very young children and their families. The 12 articles included in this monograph are representative of the impressive research and intervention being conducted in the area of assessment. As such, these articles exemplify the application of the Assessment recommended practices (DEC, 2014) and facilitate their understanding. We are hopeful the field will continue to engage in and study the application of evidence-informed practices relative to the various functions of assessment so that all young children and their families will benefit from the application of the highest quality of assessment results to intervention.

References

Division for Early Childhood. (2014). *DEC recommended practices in early intervention/early childhood special education 2014*. Retrieved from https://www.dec-sped.org/dec-recommended-practices

Individuals With Disabilities Education Act, 20 U.S.C. § 1400 (2004).

Assessment

Assessment is the process of gathering information to make decisions. Assessment informs intervention and, as a result, is a critical component of services for young children who have or are at risk for developmental delays/disabilities and their families. In early intervention and early childhood special education, assessment is conducted for the purposes of screening, determining eligibility for services, individualized planning, monitoring child progress, and measuring child outcomes. Not all of the practices that follow apply to all purposes of assessment. For example, practice A9 focuses on monitoring child progress but does not relate to assessment for eligibility.

We recommend the following assessment practices to guide practitioners:

A1. Practitioners work with the family to identify family preferences for assessment processes.

A2. Practitioners work as a team with the family and other professionals to gather assessment information.

A3. Practitioners use assessment materials and strategies that are appropriate for the child's age and level of development and accommodate the child's sensory, physical, communication, cultural, linguistic, social, and emotional characteristics.

A4. Practitioners conduct assessments that include all areas of development and behavior to learn about the child's strengths, needs, preferences, and interests.

A5. Practitioners conduct assessments in the child's dominant language and in additional languages if the child is learning more than one language.

A6. Practitioners use a variety of methods, including observation and interviews, to gather assessment information from multiple sources, including the child's family and other significant individuals in the child's life.

A7. Practitioners obtain information about the child's skills in daily activities, routines, and environments such as home, center, and community.

For Your Reference

The Assessment recommended practices are presented here as a reference while you read these articles. We encourage you to access the entire set of DEC Recommended Practices at …

www.dec-sped.org/dec-recommended-practices

A8. Practitioners use clinical reasoning in addition to assessment results to identify the child's current levels of functioning and to determine the child's eligibility and plan for instruction.

A9. Practitioners implement systematic ongoing assessment to identify learning targets, plan activities, and monitor the child's progress to revise instruction as needed.

A10. Practitioners use assessment tools with sufficient sensitivity to detect child progress, especially for the child with significant support needs.

A11. Practitioners report assessment results so that they are understandable and useful to families.

Screening and Progress Monitoring Language and Early Literacy Skills in Spanish-Speaking Dual Language Learners With Disabilities

Alisha Wackerle-Hollman
University of Minnesota

Lillian Durán
University of Oregon

Shari is a 5-year-old student with developmental disabilities who speaks Spanish at home. Although Shari was born in the United States, her parents were born and raised in Guatemala, and they exclusively speak Spanish at home. Shari recently began attending a Head Start preschool classroom where her early childhood special education (ECSE) and Head Start teachers and specialists speak only English; however, one of the teaching assistants is a native Spanish speaker. Shari's teaching team is struggling to determine how best to support her early language and literacy skills. They feel uninformed about her instructional levels in each language without assessments and guidance to understand her language and early literacy skills in both Spanish and English. Shari is in an inclusive setting and is exposed to early literacy instruction. However, the results of her diagnostic testing to establish her eligibility for special education provide little information to the team about her instructional levels. In this case a different type of assessment is needed to help guide the level of early literacy instruction she is provided.

Shari represents one of the nearly 250,000 Spanish-speaking dual language learners (DLLs) in preschool programs across the United States (Friedman-Krauss et al., 2018). Numerous policy reports and research briefs have noted that DLLs are the fastest growing subgroup of children and are expected to surpass 25% of all early childhood classrooms by 2020 (Friedman-Krauss et al., 2018). The increases in this population provide the fields of early childhood education and special education (ECE/ECSE) an important opportunity to improve practices with children who speak languages other than English and to make strides in improving their long-term outcomes through the provision of effective early intervention services. Improving practices is critically important as evidence also suggests DLLs are more likely to live in poverty and are more likely to experience social and economic risk factors than their native English-speaking peers (Child Trends, 2019).

Even for those DLLs enrolled in an early education program, there are often limitations in practice that jeopardize the potential benefits of early intervention. ECE/ECSE professionals must recognize the funds of knowledge these children bring to the classroom and how to build on their prior knowledge to target instruction and accelerate learning. Too often young DLLs enter English-only settings with little support to access the curriculum and benefit from instruction in a language that they are in fact still in the process of acquiring (National Academy of Sciences, Engineering, and Medicine, 2017). An important first step in improving how we plan instruction for DLLs is to accurately measure their language and early literacy ability in both Spanish and English.

For children who have been exposed primarily to Spanish in their homes, measuring Spanish language development becomes an important window into their general language learning ability (Castilla, Restrepo, & Perez-Leroux, 2009). In the United States, however, Spanish-speaking children are also exposed to English. Therefore, it is also important to measure children in English because it is generally the language of instruction, and teachers also need to understand how to more effectively scaffold their English instruction. Current evidence-based clinical recommendations also indicate that assessing children in both Spanish and English yields the most accurate estimates of their overall language ability (Hoff & Core, 2015).

A significant challenge to implementing a dual language assessment approach that is directly linked to instruction rather than diagnostic decision-making is that very few psychometrically sound measures are available to screen and progress monitor preschool language and early literacy skills in Spanish and English. There are diagnostic assessments in both languages that can support the identification of children with significant language delays and impairments, such as the *Bilingual English Spanish Assessment* (Peña, Gutiérrez-Clellen, Iglesias, Goldstein, & Bedore, 2018), the *Clinical Evaluation of Language Fundamentals–Preschool-2* (Wiig, Secord, & Semel, 2009), and the *Preschool Language Scales* (Zimmerman, Steiner, & Pond, 2011). However, language and early literacy measures that directly relate to instructional planning in English and Spanish are largely missing from practice. One type of measure designed to be used by teachers to determine whether children are meeting benchmark levels of performance and whether they are making adequate progress are general outcome measures

(GOMs), which are designed to guide instruction of generalized skills and to identify children in need of additional instructional supports (Fuchs & Fuchs, 2006). GOMs are different than diagnostic measures in that they do not identify delay or disability. Rather, they can be used to identify children who are not yet successfully developing important prerequisite language and early literacy skills that are predictive of later reading outcomes, as well as to monitor progress of those students as they develop skills toward the goal of meeting an identified benchmark.

Administering GOMs emphasizes the importance of intervening early and preventing a reading disability from emerging, particularly disabilities that may in large part be attributable to a lack of high-quality, targeted, and effective language and literacy instruction. GOMs are designed specifically for teachers to use to improve data-based decision-making and inform instructional practices. One GOM designed to support this type of decision-making in preschool with children with disabilities, those at-risk, and typically developing children is the Individual Growth and Development Indicators (IGDIs; McConnell, Wackerle-Hollman, & Rodriguez, 2012; McConnell, Wackerle-Hollman, Roloff, & Rodriguez, 2014; Wackerle-Hollman, Durán, & Rodriguez, 2016; Wackerle-Hollman et al., 2018).

IGDIs and IGDIs-Español are two complementary assessments designed for use in screening and progress monitoring of language and early literacy performance in 4- and 5-year-old preschoolers. IGDIs have evidence of technical adequacy, demonstrating their capacity to accurately estimate growth in children with disabilities and those at-risk (see Bradfield et al., 2014; McConnell et al., 2014; Wackerle-Hollman et al., 2018; Wackerle-Hollman, Schmitt, Bradfield, Rodriguez, & McConnell, 2015, for information on technical characteristics). Further, IGDIs achieve sufficient sensitivity to be used as a progress monitoring tool, which meets Assessment recommended practice A10, that practitioners should "use assessment tools with sufficient sensitivity to detect child progress, especially for the child with significant support needs" (Division for Early Childhood [DEC], 2014, p. 8).

> An important first step in improving how we plan instruction for DLLs is to accurately measure their language and early literacy ability in both Spanish and English.

Individual Growth and Development Indicators

The IGDIs (McConnell et al., 2012) can be used with all preschool-age children; however, for the purposes of this article, we focus on their use with children with disabilities and those at-risk of lower language and literacy performance. The English IGDIs include a suite of five measures across three domains. Oral language is measured by Picture Naming, phonological awareness is measured by Rhyming and First Sounds, alphabet knowledge is measured by Sound Identification, and early comprehension is measured by Which One Doesn't Belong (WODB). Each measure is administered via two tablet devices connected via Bluetooth in a one-on-one setting. The administrator uses the adult format to provide instructions and scoring prompts depicted for each item. The child uses the child format to view images and select images via touch on receptive measures. Each measure is preceded by up to four sample items. The first two sample items (1 and 2) demonstrate the required task and the second two sample items (3 and 4) provide scaffolded feedback to the child's response as a learning trial. If the child cannot successfully respond to items 3 and 4 after a scaffolded directive about the correct answer, the child discontinues the measure. For all measures, testing paradigms are untimed, student responses are scored dichotomously, and correct responses are listed on the adult tablet device. In expressive measures, students are required to state their response verbally; for all receptive measures, students can state their response verbally or touch their response on the tablet device.

Picture Naming is an expressive task in which the student views an everyday image of an object and is asked "what's that?" Rhyming is a receptive task in which the student views a target image paired with three choices. The administrator labels each image and asks the child to select the image that rhymes with the target image (e.g., bear, house, foot, chair, which two rhyme? Is it bear, house; bear, foot; or bear, chair?). First Sounds is a receptive task with three images in which the administrator labels each image and a prerecorded prompt asks the child to identify the image that begins with the target sound (e.g., mitten, pumpkin, dragon, which one starts with /d/?). Sound Identification is a receptive task in which three or four letters are presented and a recorded prompt asks the child to select the letter that corresponds with the target sound (e.g., given images of R/T/B/M, which letter makes the sound /m/?). WODB is a receptive task in which three or four images are presented and labeled and the child is asked which image doesn't belong to the depicted category (e.g., banana, apple, airplane, "which one doesn't belong?"; see Appendix A for examples of each measure).

IGDIs-Español are a set of companion measures designed by studying how Spanish language and early literacy develops separate from English (Durán et al., 2019, Wackerle-Hollman et al., 2019). As a result, the measures are not direct translations, nor are they equated. Spanish and English have different lexical and syntactic structures and therefore different items and tasks may be more meaningful to measure in each language (Antovich & Graf Estes, 2018; Peña, Kester, & Sheng, 2012).

IGDIs-Español include five measures in three domains: Oral language is captured by Identificación de los Dibujos and Verbos (Expresivo), phonological awareness is captured by Primeros Sonidos, and alphabet knowledge is captured by Identificación de las Letras and Identificación de los Sonidos. The measures feature the same administrative characteristics as English measures. They are untimed, images are presented in the same arrangements, prompts are standardized, assessors follow the same format for sample items, and scoring occurs in the same dichotomous model. However, with the exception of Verbos (Expresivo), where items are presented on a tablet to show brief videos, as of late 2019, IGDIs-Español are only available in paper/pencil format.

Identificación de los Dibujos requires children to name images of common objects, animals, and foods after hearing the prompt "Qué es?" Verbos (Expresivo) is an expressive measure in which the administrator presents a brief video that depicts an action, asking the child, "¿Qué está pasando?" (What is happening?) Primeros Sonidos is a phonological awareness measure designed to detect a child's ability to identify initial sounds (both syllables and phonemes) of words independent of meaning. Identificación de las Letras measures a child's ability to select the letter that corresponds to the letter spoken by the administrator.

> It is important for teachers to attend to language and early literacy growth for children with disabilities and those at-risk in Spanish and English.

Identificación de los Sonidos is designed to measure a child's ability to match the sound of a target letter with the written form of that letter. (See Appendix A for a sample of the measures.)

All IGDIs can be purchased in print or for digital administration through their dissemination partner, MyIGDIs by Renaissance Learning (www.myigdis. com). Training is required to achieve initial fidelity, but the design of the measures makes this process easy and seamless.

Understanding assessment results. Both the English IGDIs and IGDIs-Español are meant to be administered to children who speak English and Spanish to identify language and early literacy instructional levels in each language through screening and progress monitoring. For example, ECE/ECSE teachers can use IGDIs to gather more information about a child's language and literacy development in phonological awareness, oral language, and alphabet knowledge domains, including information about which domains may require additional support or intervention. The universal screening version of the IGDIs is designed to be administered seasonally in fall, winter, and spring; scores are reported relative to a tier-level designation with color coding (Tier 1, Tier M, Tier 2/3). If a child needs additional instruction or intervention, the child's score will fall into the Tier 2/3 designation. More recently, the progress monitoring version of IGDIs were completed (available in English and Spanish). These versions include additional items to produce a more robust estimate of student ability, and the measures are designed to be administered once a month. Evidence from psychometric IGDI studies suggests assessment at a one-month frequency reliably estimates student performance and detects meaningful growth over the course of an academic year (Wackerle-Hollman & Durán, 2018b).

In a recent study, children with identified disabilities and those who were identified as at-risk by scoring below fall screening benchmarks on Spanish and English IGDIs were found to have higher growth rates in Spanish IGDI alphabet knowledge measures and similar growth rates in Spanish phonological awareness measures than typically developing peers (Wackerle-Hollman et al., 2018). These findings provide evidence that it is important for teachers to attend to language and early literacy growth for children with disabilities and those at-risk in Spanish and English. Even if children are scoring below benchmark, their growth may be more indicative of their ability to master these skills over time than their tier designation.

When teachers use IGDIs, they perform the assessment and immediately receive an automated score for English IGDIs and can quickly and easily score IGDIs-Español. Scores are reported by domain and evaluated against benchmarks for screening and are evaluated against prior performance and growth expectations for progress monitoring. It is the domain-specific scores relative to each language that provide the framework for modifying instruction.

Shari has developmental disabilities, and she scored at the Tier 2/3 range in English and Spanish across domains. Given these results, teachers can immediately recognize Shari needs support in both languages to be successful. They can plan to adjust instructional dosage and then use the progress monitoring IGDIs in both languages to track Shari's growth in phonological awareness, alphabet knowledge, and oral language. As Shari's teachers consider strategies to support instruction, they must attend to the importance of her home language profile in Spanish. Specifically, in an English-only setting, teachers should be careful to attend to the level of English used in instruction and in conversation to ensure comprehension as her English skills are still emerging. Teachers should adapt lessons to include preteaching of key vocabulary, using many visuals and real items during lessons, acting out stories, and embedding repetition and practice opportunities (Baker et al., 2014). Teachers should select books with concrete images and gradually expand the number of words per page to scaffold the child's English-language development.

Given that there is a bilingual teaching assistant, Shari should also receive high-quality instruction in Spanish, particularly in the areas of language and early literacy to support her continued development of Spanish. Activities such as dialogic book reading, practicing early phonological awareness skills such as identifying words that start with the same sound, and playfully segmenting words into syllables are important in Spanish. Teaching Shari letter names and sounds in Spanish is also an important strategy to build her alphabet knowledge in her more dominant language. A solid foundation in Spanish will support her English-language and literacy acquisition, and many early literacy skills have been found to transfer from Spanish to English (Melby-Lervåg & Lervåg, 2011). Further, language and early literacy skills in Spanish have been found to predict English reading fluency (Solari, Petscher, & Folsom, 2014). Teachers should also reach out to Shari's family to help them continue to engage in rich conversations during daily routines in Spanish and include book reading and/or storytelling in Spanish at home.

Comparative score rubric. Another important consideration for teachers is how to interpret performance in English and Spanish and to make data-based instructional decisions in each language. To understand English and Spanish performance and to support teachers in understanding how to take a child's home language background and the language of instruction in the classroom environment into consideration, we developed a comparative score rubric (CSR; see Figure 1). The goal of the CSR is to support teachers in interpreting IGDI scores in English and Spanish as a total language profile. This supports data-based decision-making to scaffold differentiated instruction through recommended evidence-based practices in both languages. Bilingual children will have varying levels of proficiency in each of their languages, and attention to their level of exposure to each language across home and school environments should also guide intervention in each language. When using the CSR, the following

Bilingual children will have varying levels of proficiency in each of their languages, and attention to their level of exposure to each language across home and school environments should also guide intervention in each language.

Figure 1
Comparative Score Rubric for an Example Domain

IGDIs-Español score	English IGDI score	Home language profile	Classroom language of instruction	Intervention recommendation
Tier 1 score OR Tier M score OR Tier 2/3 score	Tier 1	Spanish	English	Evidence-Based Practice
			Spanish	Evidence-Based Practice
			Bilingual	Evidence-Based Practice
		English	English	Evidence-Based Practice
			Spanish	Evidence-Based Practice
			Bilingual	Evidence-Based Practice
		Balanced bilingual	English	Evidence-Based Practice
			Spanish	Evidence-Based Practice
			Bilingual	Evidence-Based Practice

Note. Repeat the same procedure for Tier M and Tier 2/3 English IGDI scores.

recommendations have been developed based on four sources of information: a student's score on IGDIs-Español, their score on English IGDIs, a teacher survey about the classroom instructional language, and a survey about the student's home language profile, called the Language and Literacy Exposure Evaluation Report (LLEER; Durán & Wackerle-Hollman, 2016). These are used together to generate practical recommendations linked to evidence-based practices.

Home language exposure. To determine language exposure, families can complete the LLEER. The LLEER requires caregivers to indicate what languages children hear and speak within a weekly time-block matrix. Caregivers indicate whether children hear and speak Spanish, English, or both for each time block. The CSR guides practitioners in computing whether a child is Spanish dominant, English dominant, or balanced bilingual. Using a cluster analysis of LLEER data in relation to IGDI data, the strongest indicators of language group membership are what children speak from waking to bedtime on the weekend, and from 4 p.m. to bedtime on the weekdays (Durán & Wackerle-Hollman, 2016; Wackerle-Hollman et al., 2018). These response windows are used to determine the child's dominant language.

Classroom language exposure. To determine classroom language use, teachers are encouraged to complete the IGDI Classroom Survey (Wackerle-Hollman & Durán, 2018a). Classroom language environments will vary, and each teacher should document which languages are used throughout the day and during which activities each language is more likely to be used. For some, English will clearly be the only language, but for others there may be a mix of

Spanish and English used throughout the day. Teachers should use this information when interpreting the child's performance over the year. Children's language and early literacy skills may develop at different rates in each language based on the quality and quantity of exposure and use in each language. The Classroom Language Survey can help classify classroom language as predominantly Spanish-language instruction (SLI, 80% or more in Spanish), bilingual instruction (BI, about 50/50 English and Spanish), or English-language instruction (ELI, 80% or more in English). Taken in context with IGDI scores, the CSR uses these four pieces of data to support instructional recommendations. These recommendations were crafted by engaging in a comprehensive literature review, including content reviews of the What Works Clearinghouse to produce summaries of evidence-based practices educators can integrate into daily activities. Let's revisit Shari's case and see how the CSR can support more effective and accurate data-based decision-making.

Based on Shari's profile, Shari's teachers are uncertain about where to start their instruction and how to best support her. By using Spanish and English IGDIs, Shari's teachers can quickly and efficiently determine in which domains and in which language she is on track. Shari clearly comes from a Spanish-dominant household and has limited access to Spanish when she is at school. Even though scores on the IGDIs-Español will be a more accurate measure of Shari's language and early literacy ability, it is important to know what English skills she may have for instructional planning. Most instruction in her classroom is in English, with limited support from a bilingual teaching assistant.

Once the team has scores in English and Spanish, they should consider her home language profile (Spanish dominant) and classroom language of instruction (English) to determine how best to support her. Specifically, given that Shari is in a predominantly English classroom environment, teachers should consider how her performance in each language might change over the year based on the rapid increase in exposure to English. Because this is her first year in preschool and her first formal exposure to English, it is likely that she will make significant gains on the English measures. Her performance in Spanish may possibly plateau or even decline while her English begins to increase. Therefore, it is important to not only use the seasonal screening IGDIs but also the progress monitoring IGDIs to evaluate her growth over the year, even if she is initially below benchmark in all areas in the fall.

Discussion

Teaching young DLLs with disabilities and those at risk necessitates special attention to assessment in both languages. Once children are evaluated and qualify for special education services, home language assessment should not simply end there. Too often, once children qualify for special education, their ongoing assessment is only conducted in English. DLLs should continue to benefit from dual language assessment that can accurately capture their overall language and early literacy growth and guide intervention and differentiated instruction.

Criterion-referenced assessments such as the Assessment and Evaluation Programming System for Infants and Children (AEPS; Bricker & Pretti-Frontczak, 1996) and Hawaii Early Learning Profile (HELP; Furuno et al., 2005) are often used in ECE/ECSE settings to document children's growth in all developmental areas over the year. On many survey-level assessments, such as the HELP and AEPS, the checklist criteria are intended to be reviewed as criterion-referenced developmental milestones. However, few of these tools have engaged in psychometric studies that evaluate their capacity to measure progress or inform instruction in meaningful ways. These tools are useful for documenting whether children have a particular skill or not, and this can guide IEP development through curriculum-based mastery monitoring (Stockall, Dennis, & Rueter, 2014). However, for critical skills that are predictive of later reading and academic success, it is also important to include measures that provide more accurate estimates of a child's ability level with benchmarks that can inform teachers whether a child's performance is on track or falling behind as it relates to later reading performance. The IGDIs are specifically designed to accurately estimate children's ability levels and growth in phonological awareness, oral language, and alphabet knowledge in English and Spanish. Using IGDIs, teachers can empirically answer important questions about the efficacy of their instruction and evaluate children's progress during intervention in Spanish and English.

Early educators have limited access to psychometrically robust tools that attend to nuances of bilingual development and resources to support interpretations of those scores for differentiating instruction. Spanish and English IGDIs were designed to meet this need and specifically support ECE/ECSE teachers serving young children with disabilities in making data-based decisions. Using IGDIs directly aligns with the Assessment recommended practices. Specifically, the IGDIs align with A5, which recommends practitioners "conduct assessments in the child's dominant language and in additional languages if the child is learning more than one language" (DEC, 2014, p. 8). The IGDI comparative score rubric is a contribution to an important shift in early childhood assessment by focusing on how teachers can use IGDI scores in English and Spanish to inform instructional practices. The use of the CSR facilitates data-based decision-making, which aligns with A7, that practitioners should "obtain information about the child's skills in daily activities, routines, and environments such as home, center, and community" (DEC, 2014, p. 8) when parents are asked to report on their child's language use at home and teachers are asked to document the language of instruction in their classrooms. ECE/ECSE teachers often have to make effective instructional decisions based on intuition and professional development

Using IGDIs, teachers can empirically answer important questions about the efficacy of their instruction and evaluate children's progress during intervention in Spanish and English.

alone when sound assessment instruments do not exist. The IGDIs and the CSR support data-based decision-making and implementation of A9, that "practitioners implement systematic ongoing assessment to identify learning targets, plan activities, and monitor the child's progress to revise instruction as needed" (DEC, 2014, p. 8).

In sum, IGDIs provide a set of psychometrically sound screening and progress monitoring measures that can be used with children with disabilities and those at risk for later reading failure. There is support built into the assessment to interpret a child's performance in both English and Spanish while considering their home language environments and the classroom language of instruction. This innovation facilitates ECE/ECSE teachers' use of data in Spanish and English to adjust their instructional decisions and gather accurate data about a child's ability level. Ultimately the goal of general outcome measurement is to effectively target instruction, monitor the response of children to intervention, and document their progress with the goal of improving long-term language and literacy outcomes.

Authors' Note

This work was supported by the Institute of Education Sciences, Grant No. R305A160077. All statements offered in this article are the opinion of the authors, and official endorsement by IES should not be inferred. The authors gratefully acknowledge assistance in conducting this research from the various early childhood programs across the United States that participated in the measurement studies as well as the meaningful contributions of Stephanie Brunner, José Palma, Theresa Kohlmeier, and Chase Callard.

References

Antovich, D. M., & Graf Estes, K. (2018). Learning across languages: Bilingual experience supports dual language statistical word segmentation. *Developmental Science, 21*(2), e12548. doi:10.1111/desc.12548

Baker, S., Lesaux, N., Jayanthi, M., Dimino, J., Proctor, C. P., Morris, J., . . . Newman-Gonchar, R. (2014, April). *Teaching academic content and literacy to English learners in elementary and middle school.* Washington, DC: Institute of Educational Sciences.

Bradfield, T. A., Besner, A. C., Wackerle-Hollman, A. K., Albano, A. D., Rodriguez, M. C., & McConnell, S. R. (2014). Redefining individual growth and development indicators: Oral language. *Assessment for Effective Intervention, 39*, 233–244. doi:10.1177/1534508413496837

Bricker, D., & Pretti-Frontczak, K. (1996). *AEPS measurement for three to six years: Assessment, evaluation, and programming system for infants and children* (Vol. 3). Baltimore, MD: Paul H. Brookes.

Castilla, A. P., Restrepo, M. A., & Perez-Leroux, A. T. (2009). Individual differences and language interdependence: A study of sequential bilingual development in Spanish-English preschool children. *International Journal of Bilingual Education and Bilingualism, 12*, 565–580. doi:10.1080/13670050802357795

Child Trends. (2019). Dual language learners. Retrieved from https://www.childtrends.org/indicators/dual-language-learners

Division for Early Childhood. (2014). *DEC recommended practices in early intervention/early childhood special education 2014*. Retrieved from https://www.dec-sped.org/dec-recommended-practices

Durán, L., & Wackerle-Hollman, A. K. (2016). *Language exposure evaluation report*. Unpublished assessment, University of Minnesota, Minneapolis.

Durán, L. K., Wackerle-Hollman, A. K., Kohlmeier, T. L., Brunner, S. K., Palma, J., & Callard, C. H. (2019). Individual Growth and Development Indicators-Español: Innovation in the development of Spanish oral language general outcome measures. *Early Childhood Research Quarterly, 48*, 155–172. doi:10.1016/j.ecresq.2019.02.001

Friedman-Krauss, A. H., Barnett, W. S., Weisenfeld, G. G., Kasmin, R., DiCrecchio, N., & Horowitz, M. (2018). *The state of preschool 2017: State preschool yearbook*. New Brunswick, NJ: National Institute for Early Education Research.

Fuchs, D., & Fuchs, L. S. (2006). Introduction to response to intervention: What, why, and how valid is it? *Reading Research Quarterly, 41*, 93–99. doi:10.1598/RRQ.41.1.4

Furuno, S., O'Reilly, K. A., Hosaka, C. M., Inatsuka, T. T., Allman, T. L., & Zeisloft, B. (2005). *Hawaii early learning profile*. Palo Alto, CA: Vort.

Hoff, E., & Core, C. (2015). What clinicians need to know about bilingual development. *Seminars in Speech and Language, 36*, 89–99. doi:10.1055/s-0035-1549104

McConnell, S., Wackerle-Hollman, A., & Rodriguez M. (2012). *Individual growth and development indicators screening and progress monitoring measures*. St. Paul, MN: Early Learning Labs.

McConnell, S. R., Wackerle-Hollman, A. K., Roloff, T. A., & Rodriguez, M. (2014). Designing a measurement framework for response to intervention in early childhood programs. *Journal of Early Intervention, 36*, 263–280. doi:10.1177/1053815115578559

Melby-Lervåg, M., & Lervåg, A. (2011). Cross-linguistic transfer of oral language, decoding, phonological awareness and reading comprehension: A meta-analysis of the correlational evidence. *Journal of Research in Reading, 34*, 114–135. doi:10.1111/j.1467-9817.2010.01477.x

National Academies of Sciences, Engineering, and Medicine. (2017). *Promoting the educational success of children and youth learning English: Promising futures*. Washington, DC: The National Academies Press.

Peña, E. D., Gutiérrez-Clellen, V. F., Iglesias, A., Goldstein, B. A., & Bedore, L. M. (2018). *Bilingual English Spanish assessment (BESA) manual*. Baltimore, MD: Paul H. Brookes.

Peña, E. D., Kester, E. S., & Sheng, L. (2012). Semantic development in Spanish-English bilinguals: Theory, assessment, and intervention. In B. A. Goldstein (Ed.), *Bilingual language development and disorders in Spanish-English speakers* (2nd ed., pp. 131–152). Baltimore, MD: Paul H. Brookes.

Solari, E. J., Petscher, Y., & Folsom, J. S. (2014). Differentiating literacy growth of ELL students with LD from other high-risk subgroups and general education peers: Evidence from grades 3–10. *Journal of Learning Disabilities, 47,* 329–348. doi:10.1177/0022219412463435

Stockall, N., Dennis, L. R., & Rueter, J. A. (2014). Developing a progress monitoring portfolio for children in early childhood special education programs. *Teaching Exceptional Children, 46*(3), 32–40. doi:10.1177/004005991404600304

Wackerle-Hollman, A., & Durán, L. (2018a). *IGDI classroom survey.* Unpublished assessment, University of Minnesota, Minneapolis.

Wackerle-Hollman, A., & Durán, L. (2018b). *Preschool Spanish-English dual language learner growth trajectories for at-risk students.* Paper presented at the Division for Early Childhood Conference, Orlando, FL.

Wackerle-Hollman, A., Durán, L., Brunner, S., Palma, J., Kohlmeier, T., & Rodriguez, M. C. (2019). Developing a measure of Spanish phonological awareness for preschool age children: Spanish individual growth and development indicators. *Educational Assessment, 24,* 33–56. doi:10.1080/10627197.2018.1545570

Wackerle-Hollman, A., Durán, L., Raikes, A., Brunner, S., Palma, J., & Rodriguez, M. (2018). *Understanding preschool Spanish language and early literacy skills in the context of bilingual language exposure profiles.* Manuscript submitted for publication.

Wackerle-Hollman, A., Durán, L., & Rodriguez, M. (2016). *Spanish individual growth and development indicators.* Wisconsin Rapids, WI: Renaissance Learning.

Wackerle-Hollman, A. K., Schmitt, B. A., Bradfield, T. A., Rodriguez, M. C., & McConnell, S. R. (2015). Redefining individual growth and development indicators: Phonological awareness. *Journal of Learning Disabilities, 48,* 495–510. doi:10.1177/0022219413510181

Wiig, E. H., Secord, W. A., & Semel, E. (2009). *Clinical evaluation of language fundamentals – preschool–2* [Spanish edition]. New York, NY: Pearson.

Zimmerman, I. L., Steiner, V. G., & Pond, R. E. (2011). *Preschool language scales* (5th ed.). New York, NY: Pearson.

Appendix A
English IGDIs

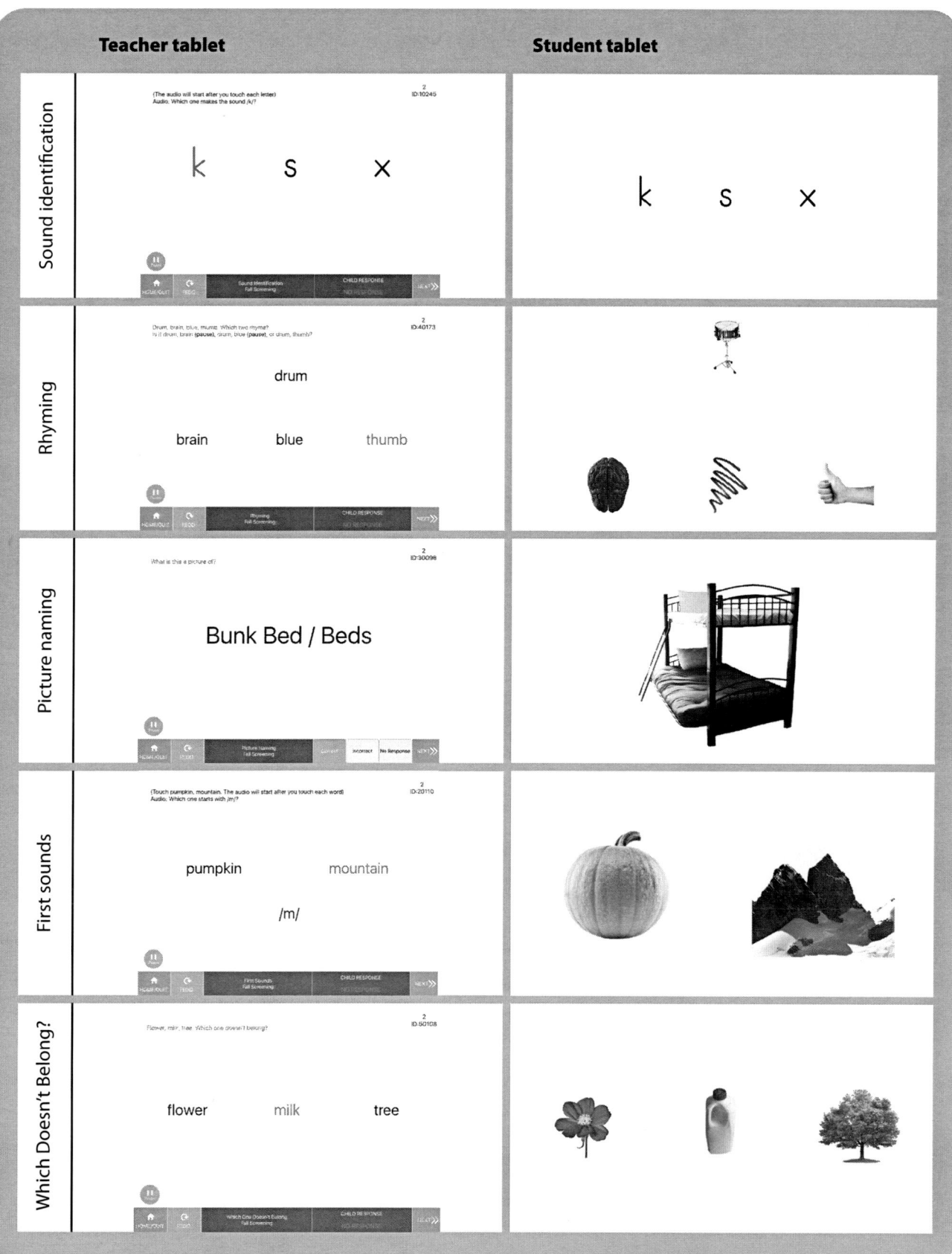

Appendix B
IGDIs-Español

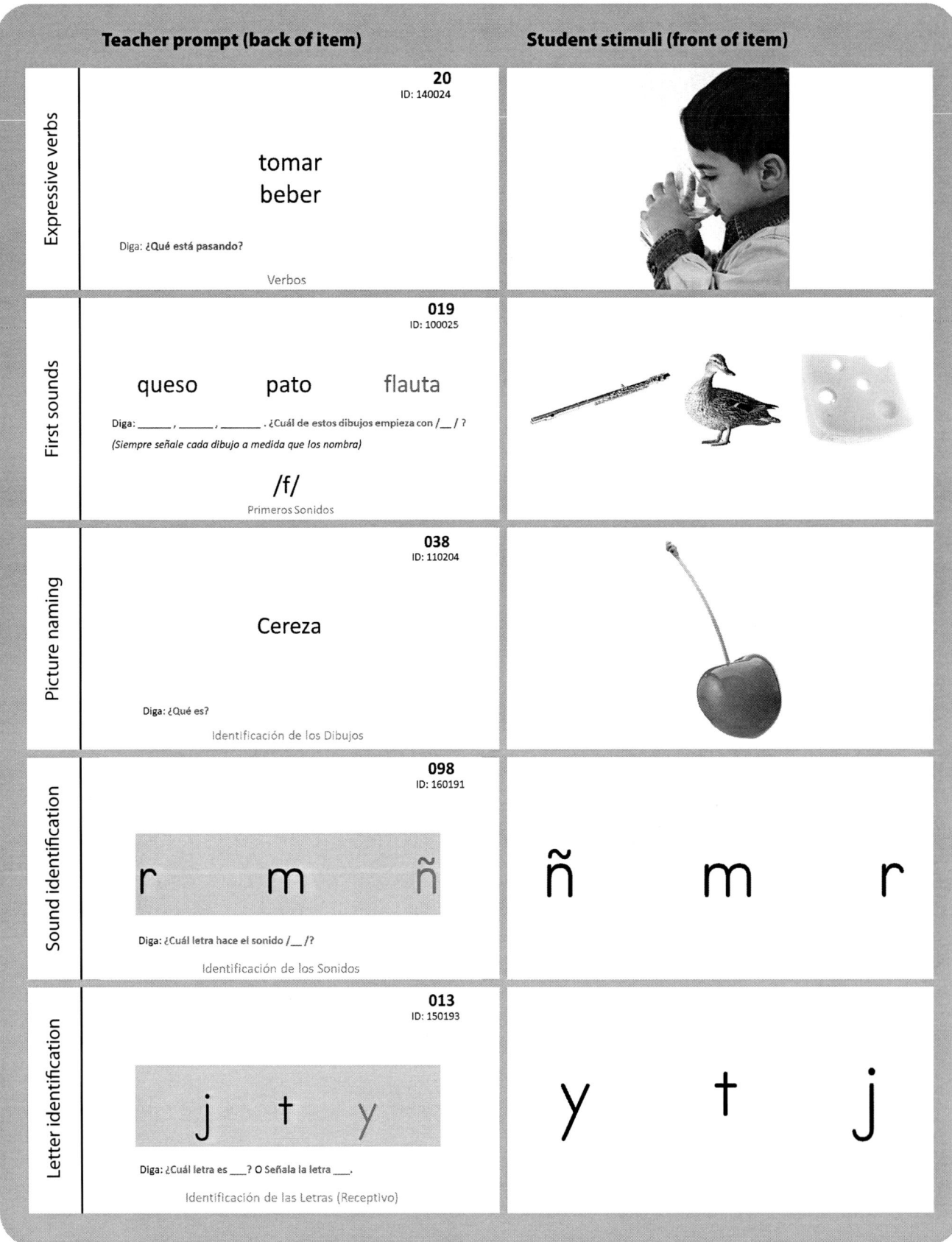

	Teacher prompt (back of item)	Student stimuli (front of item)
Expressive verbs	**20** ID: 140024 — tomar beber — Diga: ¿Qué está pasando? — Verbos	
First sounds	**019** ID: 100025 — queso pato flauta — Diga: _____, _____, _____ . ¿Cuál de estos dibujos empieza con /__/ ? (Siempre señale cada dibujo a medida que los nombra) — /f/ — Primeros Sonidos	
Picture naming	**038** ID: 110204 — Cereza — Diga: ¿Qué es? — Identificación de los Dibujos	
Sound identification	**098** ID: 160191 — r m ñ — Diga: ¿Cuál letra hace el sonido /__/? — Identificación de los Sonidos	ñ m r
Letter identification	**013** ID: 150193 — j t y — Diga: ¿Cuál letra es ___? O Señala la letra ___. — Identificación de las Letras (Receptivo)	y t j

2

Using a Multiple-Gate Assessment Approach to Support the Social-Emotional Development of Preschoolers

ROBIN L. HOJNOSKI
Lehigh University

KRISTEN N. MISSALL
University of Washington

Mrs. Jones is the principal of an inclusive public early education center that serves children between the ages of 3 and 5. The center has eight mixed-age preschool classrooms, which are each composed of up to 18 children with diverse backgrounds and needs. All classrooms include at least five children with an identified disability. Additionally, a number of children who are dual language learners (DLL) are enrolled in the program. Classrooms are staffed by one lead teacher and two teacher assistants. Recently, Mrs. Jones attended a conference about the importance of universal screening for social-emotional development. The center conducts targeted universal screening for key early language and literacy skills as part of their multitiered systems of support (MTSS; Carta & Young, 2019) framework. Mrs. Jones is wondering about the feasibility and usefulness of expanding screening to include assessment of social-emotional skills. Currently, the children who come to her attention for social-emotional issues are those who demonstrate challenging behaviors or external and acting-out behavior. Mrs. Jones is concerned that there may be children who are dealing with internalizing difficulties, such as excessive sadness or worry, and that these children are not identified as readily.

Why Focus on Social-Emotional Skills?

Research indicates a significant proportion of young children exhibit externalizing, or acting out, behavior as well as internalizing behaviors such as excessive sadness or worry (Egger & Angold, 2006), and children living with environmental risk are even more likely to lack necessary social-emotional skills (Brown, Copeland, Sucharew, & Kahn, 2012; Weitzman, Edmonds, Davagnino,

& Briggs-Gowan, 2014). A lack of social-emotional skills is a major challenge to developing social and academic competence because these skills provide a foundation for successful functioning (Denham et al., 2002; S. M. Jones & Bouffard, 2012). Young children who have challenges interacting with adults (e.g., noncompliance, lack of initiation and response) and peers (e.g., limited cooperative play, aggressive behavior) or engaging in learning and play activities may have difficulty functioning in the classroom, and ultimately, may face exclusion from early education settings (Brown et al., 2012; Gilliam, 2005). Data from the 2016 National Survey of Children's Health indicated approximately 17,000 preschoolers have been expelled from their early education setting with another 50,000 children experiencing suspension (Malik, 2017).

> Early childhood presents a critical time for ensuring young children have access to supports to develop critical social-emotional skills.

Children who are excluded miss opportunities to develop important early learning skills, engage in peer socialization, and participate in early intervention efforts for behavioral concerns. Specifically, in preschool, young children acquire social-emotional skills in three key areas (Edwards, 2018): (1) interpersonal social skills for peer and adult relationships (e.g., positive engagement and effectiveness in interactions; Denham & Brown, 2010), (2) social-emotional competence (e.g., emotion knowledge, emotion regulation; Curby, Brown, Bassett, & Denham, 2015), and (3) learning-related social skills (e.g., task persistence, following directions; McClelland & Morrison, 2003; McClelland, Tominey, Schmitt, & Duncan, 2017). Difficulties in these areas often manifest as externalizing or internalizing behaviors. Thus, early childhood presents a critical time for ensuring young children have access to supports to develop critical social-emotional skills. Effective assessment is essential to identifying children who may benefit from those supports.

Why Universal Screening?

Universal screening is the process of systematically collecting information from all the individuals in a defined group (e.g., classroom, center, school) on a target outcome (e.g., health outcome, language skills, early reading skills) that is related to short- and long-term functioning. Universal screening is distinct from developmental screening. Developmental screening focuses on providing basic information for developmental milestones across several areas (e.g., cognition, communication, motor, adaptive, social-emotional) to determine whether more information is needed with targeted assessment. Universal screening is conducted in key skill areas (e.g., language, literacy, social development) known to be important for children's ongoing school success to provide targeted instruction and intervention as needed, and often as part of an MTSS framework. For example, early social-emotional development is predictive of adjustment to school, relationship quality, and later school success (D. E. Jones, Greenberg, & Crowley, 2015).

The purpose of universal screening of social-emotional development in early education, specifically, is to identify young children who may need additional support to develop key social-emotional skills necessary for school success. Because universal screening by definition is intended to be used with an entire population (e.g., all children enrolled in a program), assessment procedures include all children regardless of disability status, income background, prior concerns, and home language. Engaging in systematic, ongoing, universal screening minimizes bias that can creep into concerns, referrals, and interventions when a systematic process is not used. For example, some adults may assume that children with identified disabilities inherently have fewer social-emotional skills and, thus, may be more likely to refer those children for intervention. Similarly, children with challenging behaviors are more likely to be referred for intervention than children with withdrawn behaviors because of the intensity of their behavior (Edwards, 2018). Universal screening requires adults to consider all children in the assessment process and systematically evaluate a full range of concerns. This promotes data-based decision-making and the use of formative data collection to evaluate children's growth and development.

Universal screening is consistent with the Assessment recommended practice A9: "Practitioners implement systematic ongoing assessment to identify learning targets, plan activities, and monitor the child's progress to revise instruction as needed" (Division for Early Childhood [DEC], 2014, p. 8). Although universal screening data do not explicitly and directly link to learning targets and instructional activities, universal screening is a systematic process to identify individual children who are in need of more in-depth assessment that will directly inform instruction and learning supports.

Universal screening in educational settings targets behaviors and skills that are important to successful functioning in that setting; that is, targets are relevant and socially valid. Academically, universal screening often focuses on reading and mathematics whereas in the social-emotional domain universal screening focuses on social skills and self-regulation. These targets are consistent with and reflective of common educational goals for children and youth.

In early childhood settings, universal screening efforts have been informed by a general outcome measurement approach to designing instructionally relevant assessments (e.g., Individual Growth and Development Indicators; Greenwood, Carta, & McConnell, 2011). Further, because universal screening in educational settings is conducted periodically, changes in child behavior can be monitored at a broad level of risk; for example, if children remain at-risk after interventions and supports have been implemented, interventions are revised (Parisi, Ihlo, & Glover, 2014). Finally, universal screening can be viewed as the first step in a systematic assessment process to ensure that all children receive the supports necessary within an MTSS framework (Snyder, Wixson, Talapatra, & Roach, 2008).

With universal screening data, Mrs. Jones will be able to evaluate systematically the social-emotional development of all children enrolled in the center. Mrs. Jones discusses universal screening for social-emotional behavior at a staff meeting, drawing on what they already know based on their experiences with screening for early learning. The teachers agree on the benefits of universal screening for social-emotional behavior and express concern that many of the children in their classrooms live in high-risk environments that stress their functioning. Mrs. Jones invites four teachers and the school psychologist who supports the program to form a planning and implementation team. What tools are available? Which are most appropriate for their needs? How are data collected? How should children with social-emotional challenges be identified? How are families involved in the screening process?

It is important to differentiate universal screening within a multiple-gate approach from other universal screening approaches.

Multiple-Gate Approach to Assessment

One challenge to universal screening of social-emotional development in pre-school is the limited availability of assessment tools that are easy to use, are efficient to administer, are appropriate at the individual and classroom levels, and are linked to important social-emotional outcomes. The most common tools are rating scales completed by teachers and caregivers (e.g., Ages and Stages Questionnaire: Social-Emotional [ASQ:SE-2; Squires, Bricker, & Twombly, 2015], Social Skills Improvement System [SSiS; Elliott & Gresham, 2008], Preschool and Kindergarten Behavior Scales [PKBS-2; Merrell, 2002]) and classroom observations that are typically informal in nature and based on everyday interactions. Although these assessment methods can be used independently, a multiple-gate approach blends them efficiently and effectively by using a series of steps, or gates, to collect specific information and make decisions about what to do next (Severson, Walker, Doolittle, Kratochwill, & Gresham, 2007; Walker et al., 1998). Research suggests that using multiple-gate procedures to first rate the extent to which individual children meet behavioral expectations and then follow up with children ranked as "at-risk" with more intensive assessment procedures, such as direct observation (Lane, Menzies, Oakes, & Kalberg, 2012), is an efficient and comprehensive approach for students most in need of intervention. A multiple-gate approach to assessment is designed to be time and cost efficient, as well as systematic and comprehensive across children, and to help save resources for where and whom they are needed.

It is important to differentiate universal screening within a multiple-gate approach from other universal screening approaches. In general, universal screening instruments use items that are designed to sort individuals into two groups—simply speaking, those at-risk and those not at-risk, or those in need of additional assessment and those who do not need additional assessment. In a multiple-gate approach, universal screening serves as the first gate; essentially, children are sorted and those children considered at-risk and in need of more assessment move through the first gate to the second gate, which consists of additional assessment to better understand the nature of the risk, or the child's social-emotional challenges.

Figure 1 provides an example of a multiple-gate approach. In this example,

Figure 1
Multiple-Gate Process

Gate 1	Universal screening with teacher rating using standardized, norm-referenced assessment of social-emotional development that examines children's externalizing and internalizing behaviors. Teacher rates each child individually before examining scores. Scores should be evaluated using norms and teacher judgment about child's needs and life experience. Teachers evaluate individual scores and classroom scores to determine effectiveness of classwide social-emotional supports and instruction. Directors consider classroom scores individually and in comparison to evaluate effectiveness of schoolwide social-emotional supports and instruction.
⬇	Children with elevated risk scores in one or both areas of external and internal behavior concerns move to Gate 2.
Gate 2	Teachers plan for additional data collection with children with elevated risk scores. Teachers complete additional rating scale, and request caregiver rating form, request formal classroom observations of specific skills. Teachers consider additional child information that may influence classroom behavior (e.g., disability status, language learning) for determining whether targeted instruction or intervention is appropriate. Directors consider whether numbers of children identified with risk are appropriate for targeted intervention and whether changes need to be made at the universal classroom level for all children.
⬇	For children who move past Gate 2, provide individual and small group evidence-based supports for social-emotional learning needs as needed. Consider referral to outside agencies and special education as needed.

Gate 1 consists of a brief norm-referenced standardized rating scale (e.g., Behavior Assessment System for Children-3 Behavioral and Emotional Screening System [basc-3 bess]; Reynolds & Kamphaus, 2015) that teachers complete for each child based on their informal observations over a recent period. At Gate 1, teachers consider all children's development across a range of social skills, including externalizing (e.g., "gets into trouble") and internalizing concerns (e.g., "is sad") that relate to both interpersonal social skills (e.g., "gets along well with others") and learning-related social skills (e.g., "follows instructions"). Teachers then rate the extent to which a child demonstrates these skills on a continuum (e.g., never, sometimes, often, almost always). Summative ratings are used to determine whether a child is considered "at-risk" compared with a nationally representative sample of same-age children or a norm group. Risk status is also determined separately for externalizing and internalizing behaviors. bess scores at preschool have strong relations with important indicators of school success, including kindergarten readiness, receptive vocabulary, and social-emotional development (Dowdy, Chin, & Quirk, 2013).

Norm-referenced standardized screening instruments offer an advantage over other tools in that they are typically developed with attention to reliability (e.g., the extent to which scores are stable over time) and validity (e.g., the extent to which a tool adequately measures what it purports to measure). In addition, tools for screening typically have been evaluated for sensitivity and specificity. Briefly, sensitivity is the likelihood that a screening assessment will accurately identify a child for whom there are social-emotional concerns whereas specificity is the likelihood that a screening test will accurately not identify a child for whom there are no social-emotional concerns. However, it is important to consider whether norm-referenced standardized screening assessments are appropriate for diverse populations. For example, because Mrs. Jones' program is an inclusive program that enrolls a high number of children with identified disabilities and

children who are DLL, it is critical for the team to consider the unique characteristics of these children in evaluating their performance against a normative group, which leads to the importance of Gate 2 in a multiple-gate approach.

On the BESS, for example, children identified with "elevated risk" or "extremely elevated risk" at Gate 1 generally move to Gate 2 for further consideration. However, there may be cases in which a child rated with risk at Gate 1 is not considered at Gate 2 because additional teacher information indicates that monitoring without additional assessment is most appropriate. At Gate 2, teachers are asked to provide more information about a child's skills in context, and additional rating scales are completed by the child's caregiver to evaluate whether concerns are setting-specific (e.g., only at school) or pervasive across settings (e.g., at home and school). Most rating scales for social-emotional development include parent forms in addition to teacher forms. Rating scales should be supplemented with caregiver interviews to highlight child strengths and understand the family's perspective. Involving families in the assessment process is consistent with A2: "Practitioners work as a team with the family and other professionals to gather assessment information" (DEC, 2014, p. 8).

Formal observations may also be considered at Gate 2 to better understand a child's social-emotional behavior in context (see Gischlar, Hojnoski, & Missall, 2009; Hojnoski, Gischlar, & Missall, 2009a, 2009b for discussion on collecting, graphing, and interpreting data). The use of observation in assessment with young children can inform understanding about child behavior in natural settings (Brassard & Boehm, 2007). Formal observations produce measured, systematic, standardized data that can be compared across time and settings and tend to require time-based (e.g., interval sampling, momentary time sampling) or event-based sampling (e.g., frequency or latency measurement). With these types of structured observations, it is helpful to include observations of a peer for comparison. Observations should be conducted at different times of day and in different contexts to provide a more comprehensive understanding of social-emotional concerns. Observations should also attend to contextual variables that may contribute to a child's social-emotional difficulties. For example, observations may indicate that other children seldom initiate interactions with a child with withdrawn behavior or that a consistent picture schedule is not used, which may contribute to a child's externalizing behaviors during transitions among activities.

Gathering additional information is critical in determining the extent to which the child is truly at-risk or whether there are other factors to consider. For example, young children with disabilities and children who are DLL may be rated lower than their typically developing, monolingual peers and thus be nominated as "at-risk" compared with the normative group. However, additional information from teachers, caregivers, and observations may suggest a child's social-emotional difficulties are not interfering with access to the classroom experiences and that appropriate supports are in place. At Gate 2, the team considers all of the data collected and identifies areas of convergence and divergence in determining how best to move forward in developing social-emotional supports to meet children's needs.

In addition to using teacher ratings at Gate 1 to identify children for whom additional assessment might be warranted, universal screening data can also be used at the classroom and program level to evaluate the effectiveness of universal strategies to support targeted social-emotional skills. For example, Mrs. Jones and the team can review the percentage of children identified as at-risk at the program level. If these percentages are high, the program might want to increase its efforts at the universal level before proceeding to more in-depth assessment and more intensive intervention at the individual child level. The Teaching Pyramid (Hemmeter, Snyder, Fox, & Algina, 2016) provides a strong framework for considering tiered levels of instructional and environmental supports for young children's social-emotional development. Universal screening and follow-up data can be used in conjunction with the Pyramid framework for a comprehensive approach to assessment and intervention.

The team decides on a multiple-gate assessment model that will allow them to efficiently screen all children at Gate 1 and then gather additional information about children identified as at-risk at Gate 2. At Gate 1, the team decides to use the BESS preschool teacher rating form. The school district uses the BESS for K–12, and teachers are typically given time during a professional development day to complete the rating scales. Because the preschool teachers attend these meetings, this will be an efficient use of their time. Additionally, Mrs. Jones hopes that using a linked assessment system will facilitate planning discussions as preschoolers transition to kindergarten.

Consistent with A6, that "practitioners use a variety of methods, including observation and interviews, to gather assessment information from multiple sources,

Gathering additional information is critical in determining the extent to which the child is truly at-risk or whether there are other factors to consider.

including the child's family and other significant individuals in the child's life"
(DEC, 2014, p. 8), the team decides to gather additional teacher input via inter-
views at Gate 2 and, if necessary, caregiver input via interviews and the BESS
preschool parent rating. The school psychologist has agreed to conduct formal
classroom observations as well. In planning for implementation and data review,
the team expresses concern about the potential for over-identifying children from
certain subgroups (e.g., on the basis of ability, language status). They agree to look
at their center as a whole and then to look at results for subgroups of children to
ensure that all children evaluated are carefully, sensitively, and equally represent-
ed in discussions about concerns.

Conclusion

A multiple-gate assessment process can be used to systematically screen and
monitor preschoolers' social-emotional development. Because the multi-gate
process is evidence-based, multistep, repeatable over time, and can be designed
to be inclusive of school and home perspectives, it offers an innovative approach
for universally screening and monitoring young children's social-emotional development. In turn, effective assessment and early identification of children with
social-emotional challenges promotes data-based decision-making in providing
targeted instruction and support as needed. This is critical given that a child's
social-emotional development contributes to their overall school experience, and
when a child's social-emotional development goes unchecked, outcomes are less
positive. In addition to supporting the social-emotional development of individual children, data from universal screening can be used to inform program-level
and classroom-level changes. Instructional changes, environmental arrangements, and additional professional development can be considered among other
strategies to address group-level needs and ensure all children are developing a
strong social-emotional foundation.

Mrs. Jones recognized that her early education center could adopt a multiple-gate
approach with relative ease and that such a process would complement the uni-
versal screening for early learning that teachers already used. Additionally, Mrs.
Jones and the teachers used the data from the multiple-gate assessment approach
in communicating with families about the importance of positive social-emotional
development. Teachers reported the data were meaningful and easy to interpret,
and both teachers and families agreed that the process contributed to improving
outcomes for children's social-emotional development over time.

References

Brassard, M. R., & Boehm, A. E. (2007). *Preschool assessment: Principles and*
practices. New York, NY: The Guilford Press.

Brown, C. M., Copeland, K. A., Sucharew, H., & Kahn, R. S. (2012). Social-emotional problems in preschool-aged children: Opportunities for prevention
and early intervention. *Archives of Pediatrics and Adolescent Medicine, 166,*
926–932. doi:10.1001/archpediatrics.2012.793

Carta, J. J., & Young, R. M. (Eds.). (2019). *Multi-tiered systems of support for young children: Driving change in early education.* Baltimore, MD: Paul H. Brookes.

Curby, T. W., Brown, C. A., Bassett, H. H., & Denham, S. A. (2015). Associations between preschoolers' social-emotional competence and preliteracy skills. *Infant and Child Development, 24,* 549–570. doi:10.1002/icd.1899

Denham, S. A., & Brown, C. (2010). "Plays nice with others": Social-emotional learning and academic success. *Early Education and Development, 21,* 652–680. doi:10.1080/10409289.2010.497450

Denham, S. A., Caverly, S., Schmidt, M., Blair, K., DeMulder, E., Caal, S., . . . Mason, T. (2002). Preschool understanding of emotions: Contributions to classroom anger and aggression. *Journal of Child Psychology and Psychiatry, 43,* 901–916. doi:10.1111/1469-7610.00139

Division for Early Childhood. (2014). *DEC recommended practices in early intervention/early childhood special education 2014.* Retrieved from https://www.dec-sped.org/dec-recommended-practices

Dowdy, E., Chin, J. K., & Quirk, M. P. (2013). Preschool screening: An examination of the behavioral and emotional screening system preschool teacher form. *Journal of Psychoeducational Assessment, 31,* 578–584. doi:10.1177/0734282913475779

Edwards, N. M. (2018). *Early social-emotional development: Your guide to promoting children's positive behavior.* Baltimore, MD: Paul H. Brookes.

Egger, H. L., & Angold, A. (2006). Common emotional and behavioral disorders in preschool children: Presentation, nosology, and epidemiology. *Journal of Child Psychology and Psychiatry, 47,* 313–337. doi:10.1111/j.1469-7610.2006.01618.x

Elliott, S. N., & Gresham, F. M. (2008). *Social skills improvement system.* New York, NY: Pearson.

Gilliam, W. S. (2005). *Prekindergarteners left behind: Expulsion rates in state prekindergarten systems.* New York, NY: Foundation for Child Development.

Gischlar, K. L., Hojnoski, R. L., & Missall, K. N. (2009). Improving child outcomes with data-based decision making: Interpreting and using data. *Young Exceptional Children, 13*(1), 2–18. doi:10.1177/1096250609346249

Greenwood, C. R., Carta, J. J., & McConnell, S. (2011). Advances in measurement for universal screening and individual progress monitoring of young children. *Journal of Early Intervention, 33,* 254–267. doi:10.1177/1053815111428467

Hemmeter, M. L., Snyder, P. A., Fox, L., & Algina, J. (2016). Evaluating the implementation of the pyramid model for promoting social-emotional competence in early childhood classrooms. *Topics in Early Childhood Special Education, 36,* 133–146. doi:10.1177/0271121416653386

Hojnoski, R. L., Gischlar, K. L., & Missall, K. N. (2009a). Improving child outcomes with data-based decision making: Collecting data. *Young Exceptional Children, 12*(3), 32–44. doi:10.1177/1096250609333025

Hojnoski, R. L., Gischlar, K., L., & Missall, K. N. (2009b). Improving child outcomes with data-based decision making: Graphing data. *Young Exceptional Children, 12*(4), 15–30. doi:10.1177/1096250609337696

Jones, D. E., Greenberg, M., & Crowley, M. (2015). Early social-emotional functioning and public health: The relationship between kindergarten social competence and future wellness. *American Journal of Public Health, 105,* 2283–2290. doi:10.2105/AJPH.2015.302630

Jones, S. M., & Bouffard, S. M. (2012). Social and emotional learning in schools: From programs to strategies and commentaries. *Social Policy Report, 26*(4).

Lane, K. L., Menzies, H. M., Oakes, W. P., & Kalberg, J. R. (2012). *Systematic screenings of behavior to support instruction: From preschool to high school.* New York, NY: The Guilford Press.

Malik, R. (2017). New data reveal 250 preschoolers are suspended or expelled every day. Retrieved from https://www.americanprogress.org/issues/early-childhood/news/2017/11/06/442280/new-data-reveal-250-preschoolers-suspended-expelled-every-day/

McClelland, M. M., & Morrison, F. J. (2003). The emergence of learning-related social skills in preschool children. *Early Childhood Research Quarterly, 18,* 206–224. doi:10.1016/S0885-2006(03)00026-7

McClelland, M. M., Tominey, S. L., Schmitt, S. A., & Duncan, R. (2017). SEL interventions in early childhood. *The Future of Children, 27*(1), 33–47.

Merrell, K. M. (2002). *Preschool and kindergarten behavior scales* (2nd ed.). Austin, TX: Pro-Ed.

Parisi, D. M., Ihlo, T., & Glover, T. A. (2014). Screening within a multitiered early prevention model: Using assessment to inform instruction and promote students' response to intervention. In R. J. Kettler, T. A. Glover, C. A. Albers, & K. A. Feeney-Kettler (Eds.), *Universal screening in educational settings: Evidence-based decision making for schools* (pp. 19–46). Washington, DC: American Psychological Association.

Reynolds, C. R., & Kamphaus, R. W. (2015). *Behavior assessment system for children* (3rd ed.). New York, NY: Pearson.

Severson, H. H., Walker, H. M., Doolittle, J. H., Kratochwill, T. R., & Gresham, F. M. (2007). Proactive, early screening to detect behaviorally at-risk students: Issues, approaches, emerging innovations, and professional practices. *Journal of School Psychology, 45,* 193–223. doi:10.1016/j.jsp.2006.11.003

Snyder, P. A., Wixson, C. S., Talapatra, D., & Roach, A. T. (2008). Assessment in early childhood: Instruction-focused strategies to support response-to-intervention frameworks. *Assessment for Effective Intervention, 34,* 25–34. doi:10.1177/1534508408314112

Squires, J., Bricker, D., & Twombly, E. (2015). *Ages and stages questionnaires: Social-emotional* (2nd ed.). Baltimore, MD: Paul H. Brookes.

Walker, H. M., Kavanagh, K., Stiller, B., Golly, A., Severson, H. H., & Feil, E. G. (1998). First step to success: An early intervention approach for preventing school antisocial behavior. *Journal of Emotional and Behavioral Disorders, 6,* 66–80. doi:10.1177/106342669800600201

Weitzman, C., Edmonds, D., Davagnino, J., & Briggs-Gowan, M. J. (2014). Young child socioemotional/behavioral problems and cumulative psychosocial risk. *Infant Mental Health Journal, 35,* 1–9. doi:10.1002/imhj.21421

3

Communication Evaluation and Assessment for Latinx Infants and Toddlers
A Guide for Practitioners

Stephanie De Anda
University of Oregon

Anne L. Larson
Utah State University

Lauren M. Cycyk
University of Oregon

COMMUNICATION-RELATED DISABILITIES ARE THE MOST FREQUENT reason that children receive early intervention (EI) services with estimates of more than 40% of children qualifying because of a communication delay (Hebbeler, Spiker, Morrison, & Mallik, 2008). Increasingly, children assessed for early communication development come from culturally and linguistically diverse backgrounds, the largest proportion of whom are considered Hispanic or Latino (27% of all children served in 2017–2018; U.S. Department of Education, 2018). Many Latinx[1] children are exposed to Spanish in their homes and communities and have varied exposure to English. Some Latinx children may also be exposed to other languages, including indigenous languages (e.g., Mixtec, Mam). Moreover, children from this background are often growing and learning in more than one culture in that they experience the traditional beliefs, values, and practices of Latinx communities simultaneously with those of the (non-Latinx) majority culture of the United States (Hammer, Rodriguez, Lawrence, & Miccio, 2007). This varied exposure to multiple languages and cultures influences early communication development (Goldstein, 2012).

Unfortunately, disparities have been identified in the access to equitable EI services for children who are Latinx, including those with identified communication needs (Kraemer & Fabiano-Smith, 2017). Providers' lack of adequate training in how to best consider the child and family's cultural and linguistic backgrounds in EI likely contributes to these disparities. The Division for Early Childhood (DEC, 2014) recommends that children's language(s), culture(s), and family context be integrated into the assessment process. In this article, we present a step-wise approach in applying the DEC Recommended Practices to communication assessment of children birth to age 3 from Latinx backgrounds. Although many of these recommendations may be applied elsewhere, we tailor our recommendations specifically to children and families who are Latinx to best address the unique cultural and linguistic context of this population. Further, these recommendations allow for flexibility in considering the diversity *across* Latinx children, as illustrated in the application of these principles in two diverse cases:

Debbie is a monolingual English-speaking service provider in EI. She recently received referrals for two young children from Latinx backgrounds. A referral from Sophia's (22 months old) pediatrician indicated that her family speaks Spanish at home. A referral from Mateo's (26 months old) parents reported that both parents speak English. Debbie asked her program's trained interpreter to schedule a visit with Sofia's family and called Mateo's family directly.

Ethnographic interviews allow the family to openly share information related to child communication development and also give practitioners the opportunity to build rapport.

A Process for Evaluating and Assessing Communication in Young Latinx Children

The following steps (see Appendix A) are recommended for evaluating the communication of Latinx infants and toddlers to determine eligibility for EI. Practitioners may adjust the sequence of steps to account for the particular procedures of their agency and/or state.

Step 1: Preparing for the Evaluation

Following the receipt of a referral for EI, practitioners should first assemble the evaluation team. Parents should be contacted ahead of the evaluation for several purposes. Specifically, practitioners should ask about the inclusion of other family members and family language preferences (A1, that "practitioners work with the family to identify family preferences for assessment processes"; DEC, 2014, p. 8) as well as ensure the family's understanding of the eligibility process. With respect to family involvement, extended family members commonly live close to the child (often in the same home) and provide consistent child care within many Latinx families (Sarkisian, Gerena, & Gerstel, 2007). Any consistent caregivers should be involved in the evaluation process early on. Practitioners should also review the referral information and discuss the family's preferred language(s) for phone contact, in-person conversations, and written material. Practitioners can then determine which caregiver(s) to include in the evaluation process and assess the need for interpreters.

Practitioners should also determine the family's knowledge of the special education system in the United States and describe the purpose of the evaluation, the process, and the expectations for family involvement (e.g., "Tell me about your experience with early intervention or special education services"). Latinx families in the United States have expressed a need for more information about the evaluation process but noted that personal connections with practitioners helped to overcome these challenges (Hardin, Mereoiu, Hung, & Roach-Scott,

2009). Thus, this initial contact can support a successful evaluation about which the family is well-informed.

When working with Latinx children and families who speak a language other than English, it is best to recruit a practitioner with training in dual language development and disorders within Latinx populations, as well as someone who is proficient in the language(s) and culture(s) of the child's caregivers (e.g., bilingual speech-language pathologist). Professionals with this background and training can assist the evaluation team in distinguishing between a language difference and a true delay or disorder (see Step 4) and may also serve as a trusted contact for the family. If the evaluation will be completed with the aid of an interpreter, the early interventionist must ensure that the interpreter is trained on EI processes and procedures (see Acar & Blasco, 2018, for guidelines). Lack of adequate interpretation services may present a substantial barrier for accessing services and participating in the evaluation (Hardin et al., 2009).

Step 2: Gathering Background Information

After developing the evaluation team and preparing the family, practitioners should gather background information relevant to early communication evaluation and future instructional planning as in A2, that "practitioners work as

a team with the family and other professionals to gather assessment information" (DEC, 2014, p. 8). The initial evaluation must include (among other components) taking the child's history through a family interview, gathering information about the child's unique strengths and needs, and reviewing records. This ensures that the evaluation follows practice A7, that "practitioners obtain information about the child's skills in daily activities, routines, and environments such as home, center, and community" (DEC, 2014, p. 8). When evaluating Latinx children with early communication concerns, we recommend beginning with an ethnographic interview of the child's primary caregiver(s), as recommended in A6, that "practitioners use a variety of methods . . . to gather assessment information from multiple sources, including the child's family and other significant individuals in the child's life"; DEC, 2014, p. 8), followed by a language background questionnaire to capture child exposure and use of multiple languages.

Ethnographic interview. In contrast to close-ended developmental checklists and record reviews that provide fact-based information about the child's developmental history, ethnographic interviews allow the family to openly share information related to child communication development (for a review of this

Table 1
Examples of Ethnographic Interview Questions for Latinx Caregivers

Construct	Example questions about communication development
Beliefs	How do children learn to talk in one and two languages?
	What have you heard about teaching your child to speak a second language, or any language other than English?
	What might cause a child to have difficulties communicating? What would help them improve?
Values	What goals do you have for your child at this age?
	How important is it to you that your child learns to speak your home language(s)?
Practices	In which activities do you or your family talk to your child the most?
	Who is involved, and what language(s) do they use?

Note. Some questions adapted from Hammer (1998) and Cycyk and Hammer (2018). These questions may be added to other family interview formats. These questions do not cover facts that should otherwise be discussed in a case history/review of records.

topic, see Hyter & Salas-Provance, 2018) and also give practitioners the opportunity to build rapport. Specific interview questions can target the family's (a) beliefs about early communication development and disability, (b) values regarding communication and child development, and (c) practices related to support of child communication development, home and English language and use, and the child's participation in family routines and activities (see Table 1 for a list of example questions).

Information from the ethnographic interview informs next steps in the eligibility process as well as the presentation of eligibility results (Hammer, 1998; Peredo, 2016). Latinx families may share that adult-child dyadic play practices and a focus on early academic skills are less common in their homes than multiparty interactions with young children and child-rearing among older siblings (Cycyk & Hammer, 2018). In this case, providers may choose to assess communication in contexts that are relevant to the family (e.g., helping with family chores) and consider including older siblings on the evaluation team. Ethnographic interviews can also help identify misconceptions about dual language learning. For example, families may have been misinformed that exposure to two languages contributes to delay or disorder despite significant evidence to the contrary. This myth can be dispelled when discussing eligibility.

Language background questionnaire. To more fully understand the family's language practices and the child's language environment, EI providers should capture the relative amount of all languages to which the child is exposed and uses. Indeed, assessing the child's language *output* requires understanding sources of language *input*. Several tools (e.g., the Language Exposure Assessment Tool

[LEAT]; De Anda, Bosch, Poulin-Dubois, Zesiger, & Friend, 2016) provide guidance on assessing the relative amount of input provided by each of the child's communication partners (e.g., 40% Spanish, 30% Mixtec, and 30% English) and can be supplemented with reports of the child's comprehension and use of each language. Practitioners can use this information to determine which communicative interaction(s), and in which language(s), should be observed during the evaluation process. Such information can also be used to interpret assessment results and discern why a child may perform differently in one language compared with others. In addition, understanding the child's language background facilitates selection of assessment tools. For children hearing multiple languages, assessments should consider allowing them to demonstrate knowledge across languages (e.g., conceptual scoring) because capturing both languages (rather than one) offers greater classification accuracy of communication disorders (Peña, Bedore, & Kester, 2016). For children who are exposed to only one language (i.e., English or Spanish), the assessment should be delivered in that language.

Debbie learned that Sofia's family recently emigrated to the United States from Mexico. They shared the pediatrician's concerns about Sophia's development but did not previously know about EI services in the United States. Sofia hears only Spanish from her parents. They are also very interested in supporting her English skills to prepare her for an English-dominant school setting. Although Mateo's mother and father speak English fluently, Mateo is also cared for by his maternal grandmother, who is from the Dominican Republic and speaks only Spanish. The family worries Mateo is not speaking English, but Debbie wonders whether this is due to lack of English exposure or a true language disorder. Mateo's family would like to support him in becoming bilingual, but they are unsure of how to do so. Debbie recognized that both children are growing and learning in two cultures and with exposure to two languages. She contacted the bilingual speech-language pathologist to determine the best method for evaluating each child's language skills across both English and Spanish. Because both sets of caregivers were unfamiliar with EI and expectations for bilingual development, Debbie also made sure to plan time to provide educational resources.

Step 3: Measuring Child Language Ability and Experience

Typical child language development (including dual language development) in the birth-to-3 period ranges from production of communicative gestures and early vocalizations to consistent combinations of three-word phrases (Goldstein, 2012). Note that (assuming typical development) general language milestones (i.e., stages of babbling, age of production of first words, complexity of speech sounds, and two-word combinations) are the same for monolingual and bilingual children. This is particularly the case for simultaneous bilinguals who are developing language skills in two languages from birth (Goldstein, 2012). In measuring child language ability and experience, practitioners should consider the instruments to be used in appraising the skills of Latinx children and ensure that they include *multiple* culturally and linguistically responsive measures (A5, that

In measuring child language ability and experience, practitioners should consider the instruments to be used in appraising the skills of Latinx children and ensure that they include *multiple* culturally and linguistically responsive measures.

"practitioners conduct assessments in the child's dominant language and in additional languages if the child is learning more than one language"; DEC, 2014, p. 8). Although comprehensive standardized and norm-referenced assessments are used in many EI programs to evaluate child communication, culturally and linguistically responsive options are presently limited and many are inappropriate for children from Latinx backgrounds in the United States (Macy, Bagnato, Macy, & Salaway, 2015). Indeed, eligibility evaluations must include a range of tools; therefore, we recommend that evaluations of early communication of children from Latinx backgrounds prioritize caregiver report, dynamic assessment, and direct observation (including language sampling).

Caregiver report. Caregiver report is an integral part of communication evaluations given that Latinx children are more likely to be deemed eligible for services if their family expresses concern (Restrepo, 1998). However, the lack of caregiver concern does not rule out the presence of a disorder (García, Méndez Pérez, & Ortiz, 2000), and care must be taken to ask families to describe their children's communication abilities, such as: "In comparison with other children of the same age, do you think that your child has a problem expressing him/herself or being understood? Can you understand everything your child says to you? Can others?" (Restrepo, 1998, p. 1410). Practitioners should also ask about family history of language and/or learning difficulties because positive family history is a further indicator of communication concerns in young Latinx children (e.g., "Have any family members experienced difficulty with communication and/or learning?" [Restrepo, 1998, p. 1410]).

Dynamic assessment. Communication evaluations should also prioritize dynamic assessment (A10, that "practitioners use assessment tools with sufficient sensitivity to detect child progress, especially for the child with significant support needs"; DEC, 2014, p. 8). Dynamic assessments offer a culturally responsive and unbiased evaluation by informing how well and how quickly the child can acquire a new communicative skill given a supportive learning context. This approach also allows the practitioner to observe the child's underlying language learning abilities and skills, which we expect to be intact in the absence of a communication disorder (for a review of this topic specific to language disorders, see Orellana, Wada, & Gillam, 2019). Although research-based dynamic assessment practices are not readily available for children between birth and age 3, practices established for preschool-aged children are likely to be developmentally appropriate for some younger children as well. For example, in a test-teach-retest task, children who fail to quickly learn words after an adequate teaching session and/ or who require significant support from the practitioner to understand or produce language targets are more likely to have a language delay (Kapantzoglou, Restrepo, & Thompson, 2012).

Direct observation. A7 recommends "practitioners obtain information about the child's skills in daily activities, routines, and environments such as home, center, and community" (DEC, 2014, p. 8). By observing the child in a typical routine with a familiar communication partner (as determined by information that caregivers share during the ethnographic interview), practitioners can gather information on the child's functional language ability as well as the caregiver-provided supports for child language learning. We advocate that

> Dynamic assessments offer a culturally responsive and unbiased evaluation by informing how well and how quickly the child can acquire a new communicative skill given a supportive learning context.

practitioners prioritize observation as part of the eligibility evaluation and record a child language sample and observation of the child with the primary caregiver(s) simultaneously.

The purpose of caregiver-child observations is to supplement the relative language exposure information gathered in Step 2 and note the quantity and *quality* of communication interactions between the child and their caregiver(s). This information informs the determination of child language ability and eligibility and helps ensure the intervention plan is specific to each family. It is important to gather information about whether the child's present communication difficulties seem to be a result of a true language disorder or perhaps are due to differences in the language environment. Indeed, a strong communicative environment is needed to achieve age-appropriate communication and language skills.

In addition, practitioners should consider cultural, linguistic, and social characteristics of the child and family (A3, that "practitioners use assessment materials and strategies that are appropriate for the child's age and level of development and accommodate the child's sensory, physical, communication, cultural, linguistic, social, and emotional characteristics"; DEC, 2014, p. 8). Ideally, children will have diverse and frequent opportunities to communicate as well as access to strong language models from caregivers (i.e., from native speakers of a language). Specifically, practitioners should observe how the caregiver or caregivers address the child and with what frequency, whether the child initiates communication, and the types of communication opportunities that are available for the child to practice language skills (e.g., asking

questions and using comments that allow the child opportunities to practice responding in any language). Demonstration of communicative delays despite diverse and frequent communicative opportunities with strong native language models provides support for a child's EI eligibility.

Language sampling. One of the most critical and least-biased tools for observing child language ability across cultural and linguistic contexts is language sampling. We recommend using the language environment and child language use information from Step 2 to determine moments in the day that are representative of the child's strongest abilities in *each* language (note that this may mean collecting multiple language samples for a single child if they speak languages in separate contexts with varied caregivers). Although the communication abilities of children from birth to age 3 are still developing, practitioners' transcriptions of language samples can aid in calculating many standard measures of language productivity in a relatively short (i.e., 30 minutes) period of time (Heilmann, Nockerts, & Miller, 2010).

For children from birth to age 3, early markers of communication impairments include delays in several language domains, including semantics (word meanings), grammatical skill, phonology (the sounds of speech), and pragmatics (social language). Thus, measures should include at a minimum those describing sentence organization in each language, such as the child's average length of utterances in words (i.e., Mean Length of Utterance in words), regardless of the language used (Bedore, Peña, Gillam, & Ho, 2010), and lexical diversity (i.e., number of different words). Practitioners who are unfamiliar with the child's speech may also estimate the proportion of intelligible words produced by the child (i.e., intelligibility) to index the child's articulatory and phonological skills or consider using a Likert scale for a parent or teacher report (i.e., Intelligibility in Context Scale for preschoolers; McLeod, Harrison, & McCormack, 2012).

Further, given that social language (i.e., pragmatics) is highly variable depending on culture (relative to the family's beliefs about early communication development as outlined in Step 2), practitioners should carefully denote the function of each child intentional utterance for behavior regulation, joint attention, or social interaction (i.e., measure how the child attracts attention, makes requests, etc.) and measure this against culturally and linguistically matched contexts. Indeed, toddlers with early language delays demonstrate deficits in their ability to play social games and imitate complex play routines (Horwitz et al., 2003). Further, low rates of intentional communication (including nonverbal communication such as the use of gestures) predict current and future deficits in communication.

Practitioners without specific training in dual language development and disorders should work closely with speech-language pathologists (SLPs) to determine whether these measures fall within age expectations for bilingual children. In the context of dual language learners, the presence of a communication disorder is indicated when delays are observed in *both* languages (although the delays may manifest differently in each language).

> Temporary delays in only one language are typical for children in the process of learning two languages and do not indicate disorder.

Temporary delays in only one language are typical for children in the process of learning two languages and do not indicate disorder. Further, it is important that all measures of child language and communication be interpreted against the child's history of language exposure and use. That is, though multilingual exposure does not lead to language disorders, children's rate of development in each language may vary in multilingual contexts as languages interact throughout the process of acquisition (i.e., through acceleration and deceleration; Goldstein, 2012).

Norm- and criterion-referenced tools. Although norm- and criterion-referenced measures can be useful for describing child communication abilities in some cases, a recent research synthesis of assessment measures used in EI stressed that many standardized tests are outdated, based on deficit models of human development, and do not align with the values and purpose of EI eligibility and intervention (Macy et al., 2015). Moreover, practitioners in EI report that existing standardized measures are particularly poor for determining the eligibility of children who speak a language other than English given limitations of the norming samples (de Sam Lazaro, 2017). Clinicians therefore must think critically about norm- and criterion-referenced tools and their applicability to

Figure 1
Decision Matrix for Use of Norm- and Criterion-Referenced Measures

High

Level of validity

Item Development	Norming	Administration
Culturally *and* linguistically* adapted/developed	Child's cultural and linguistic background matches normative sample	Bilingual early interventionist with deep knowledge of Latinx culture
Culturally *or* linguistically adapted/developed	Child's cultural *or* linguistic background matches normative sample	Trained interpreter with monolingual early interventionist
Neither culturally nor linguistically adapted/developed	No match between child's cultural or linguistic background and normative sample	Monolingual early interventionist

Low

* A cultural match should consider the family's country of origin as well as immigration status to the United States, whereas a linguistic match should consider crosslinguistic influence and important dialectal differences in Spanish and English.

individual children and must be sure to prioritize the multiple methods of authentic, unbiased assessment described above.

Figure 1 describes three features to consider when selecting and administering formal language assessment tools. Importantly, measures must be specifically developed and normed for children who have cultural and linguistic characteristics similar to that of the child being evaluated. When the norming sample does not match the target populations, practitioners may consider developing local norms specific to the Latinx populations they evaluate most often (Horton-Ikard, 2010). Measures that allow for administration and scoring in both Spanish and English should be prioritized. (To our knowledge, there are no measures that account for indigenous or third languages.) The development of the test items should also be considered for Latinx children who speak Spanish because items may be biased on specific dialects of Spanish that differ from that of the child (i.e., linguistic bias) or on experiences unfamiliar to the child (i.e., cultural bias). It is possible, however, that scoring may be adapted to take into account some of the limitations of norming samples (Gibson, Jarmulowicz, & Oller, 2018). For example, instructions may be reworded or expanded, response times may be increased, manipulatives might be used instead of pictures, and dialect differences may be given credit rather than marked incorrectly.

Direct translation of English measures is not warranted because doing so reduces the likelihood that the tool will indeed measure what it is intended to assess (Peña, 2007). The background and skills of the person administering the measure can also affect the validity of test results and the use of standard scores. As shown in Figure 1, standard scores should only be reported when the items on a measure were developed to be culturally and linguistically responsive to the diversity within the Latinx community, the norms are linguistically and culturally relevant for the child being evaluated, and the background, skills, and language(s) used by the person administering the measure are specified and followed.

Both families agreed to have Debbie record their typical interactions. Sofia and her mother were observed while playing with a ball in the family's yard, whereas Mateo was observed while his parents read with him and again while his grandmother helped him get dressed. Debbie and the speech-language pathologist also considered the use of norm-referenced tools for each child. Sofia's cultural and linguistic background closely matched that of the Inventarios del Desarrollo de Habilidades Comunicativas (IDHC; Jackson-Maldonado et al., 2003), an adaptation of the MacArthur-Bates Communicative Development Inventory (MCDI; Fenson et al., 2007) that is normed on Spanish-speaking children in Mexico. Mateo's cultural and linguistic characteristics matched the normative sample for the Spanish bilingual editions of the Receptive and Expressive One-Word Picture Vocabulary Tests (e.g., Frauwirth, Michalec, & Henninger, 2018), which allows for administration and scoring in English and Spanish. However, the evaluation team modified administration by using a trained interpreter as the administrator.

Step 4: Determining Eligibility

Practitioners should next integrate evaluation results from multiple sources with informed clinical reasoning to determine whether evaluation results suggest a communication difference or a developmental disorder that supports eligibility for EI services (A8, that "practitioners use clinical reasoning in addition to assessment results to identify the child's current levels of functioning and to determine the child's eligibility and plan for instruction"; DEC, 2014, p. 8). A *communication difference* means that the child shows expected variations in one or both of their languages because of the natural influence of differences in the other language or because of the nature of their language exposure. For example, children who are primarily exposed to Spanish may follow sentence construction rules from Spanish when speaking English, such as placing a descriptive word after a noun (e.g., "car red" rather than "red car"). A *developmental disorder*, on the other hand, means that the child has a true communication delay independent of the influence of learning two languages. As previously noted, disorders will be apparent in all of the child's languages, although specific errors may differ between languages.

Practitioners should consider how each component of the evaluation contributes to eligibility determination and whether an individual source should receive more weight than others (e.g., parent concern and positive family history of language delay; Restrepo, 1998) by triangulating results (de Sam Lazaro, 2017). Ultimately, the more sources that point to the same conclusion, the more confident practitioners can be in their eligibility recommendation. Related to formal and informal measures, practitioners must look at results of testing across languages. To qualify for EI there must be evidence that the child is not meeting age-related communication milestones in both languages.

When interpreting results from language samples and other assessments, contrastive analysis may be used to review structural differences and similarities between two languages (or dialects) to determine which errors might naturally result from differences between the languages and which errors are unexpected (McGregor, Williams, Hearst, & Johnson, 1997; see also www.bilinguistics.com). If the majority of the errors made by the child are not attributable to the differences between the languages or to cross-linguistic influence, a communication disorder is more likely.

A11 recommends that practitioners "report assessment results so that they are understandable and useful to families" (DEC, 2014, p. 8), and we recommend they do so in a culturally and linguistically responsive manner to ensure that families fully understand whether their child is found to be eligible. Eligibility meetings for children from Latinx backgrounds often lack clarity and leave parents feeling excluded from the process (Hardin et al., 2009). To mitigate these concerns, practitioners may provide a written report in the home language ahead of the eligibility meeting; present results in-person, verbally (by a trained interpreter, if needed); and frequently check with family members to ensure comprehension. Information from the ethnographic interview may support how eligibility decisions are explained and inform future caregiver education.

During the parent-child interaction, Sofia primarily demonstrated protesting (by turning away or yelling) and used only one word ("no") while her mother continuously asked yes/no questions. Debbie was unsure whether Sofia's limited communication was due to a reduced variety of opportunities for communication or due to a true language disorder. During a dynamic assessment task examining communicative functions led by the trained interpreter, Debbie noticed that Sofia needed significant support to comment and request when playing with bubbles. Observations of limited word use were corroborated by parent report (IDHC total expressive vocabulary was five words). These results confirmed Sofia's eligibility for EI services.

Although Mateo's parents expressed concerns about his English, the language background questionnaire revealed that his relative exposure to Spanish and English was 68% and 32%, respectively. His language sample showed use of two- to three-word utterances in Spanish but reduced utterance length, and occasional grammatical errors, in English that were expected for his reduced English exposure (i.e., as determined via contrastive analysis). Standardized and dynamic assessments accounting for knowledge in both languages indicated that Mateo had communication skills at a level similar to that of his peers and Mateo was not eligible for EI. However, Debbie made sure to provide Mateo's family with evidence-based information on dual language development.

If the majority of the errors made by the child are not attributable to the differences between the languages or to cross-linguistic influence, a communication disorder is more likely.

Conclusion

Evaluation and assessment of children from Latinx backgrounds requires careful consideration for the members of the evaluation team, respectful information-gathering from a child's family and other caregivers, as well as appropriate use of informal and formal measures to determine child language skill in all languages to which they are exposed. Even if a child is not eligible for services, the steps outlined here allow for an opportunity to provide information and resources to parents and ensure their understanding of the special education process. Although the focus of this article is specific to Latinx children and families, many of the suggestions apply to families from other cultural and linguistic backgrounds, especially those who speak a language other than English. Still, the specific examples in this article are not sufficient to account for the diversity of evaluation situations practitioners will come across, even within Latinx populations. With ongoing professional development and practice, EI providers who implement the Assessment recommended practices can help increase the likelihood that children are appropriately identified for EI services, promote family satisfaction and engagement with the process, and provide tailored interventions with the potential to promote child language outcomes and overall development in linguistically and culturally responsive ways.

Note

1. Throughout the remainder of the article, we will use the more gender inclusive term *Latinx*, except when referring to a person who specifically identifies as Latino/a. There exists diversity within this population, as this label often refers to populations that have ethnic roots in Mexico, Central America, the Caribbean, South America, and Spain.

References

Acar, S., & Blasco, P. M. (2018). Guidelines for collaborating with interpreters in early intervention/early childhood special education. *Young Exceptional Children, 21,* 170–184. doi:10.1177/1096250616674516

Bedore, L. M., Peña, E. D., Gillam, R. B., & Ho, T.-H. (2010). Language sample measures and language ability in Spanish-English bilingual kindergarteners. *Journal of Communication Disorders, 43,* 498–510. doi:10.1016/j.jcomdis.2010.05.002

Cycyk, L. M., & Hammer, C. S. (2018). Beliefs, values, and practices of Mexican immigrant families towards language and learning in toddlerhood: Setting the foundation for early childhood education. *Early Childhood Research Quarterly.* Advance online publication. doi:10.1016/j.ecresq.2018.09.009

De Anda, S., Bosch, L., Poulin-Dubois, D., Zesiger, P., & Friend, M. (2016). The language exposure assessment tool: Quantifying language exposure in infants and children. *Journal of Speech, Language, and Hearing Research, 59,* 1346–1356. doi:10.1044/2016_JSLHR-L-15-0234 de Sam Lazaro, S. L. (2017). The importance of authentic assessments in eligibility determination for infants and toddlers. *Journal of Early Intervention, 39,* 88–105. doi:10.1177/1053815116689061

Division for Early Childhood. (2014). *DEC recommended practices in early intervention/early childhood special education 2014.* Retrieved from https://www.dec-sped.org/dec-recommended-practices

Fenson, L., Marchman, V. A., Thal, D. J., Dale, P. S., Reznick, J. S., & Bates, E. (2007). *The MacArthur-Bates Communicative Development Inventories: User's guide and technical manual* (2nd ed.). San Diego, CA: Singular.

Frauwirth, S., Michalec, D., & Henninger, N. (2018). Expressive one-word picture vocabulary test. In J. Kreutzer, J. DeLuca, & B. Caplan (Eds.), *Encyclopedia of Clinical Neuropsychology.* Cham, Switzerland: Springer. doi:10.1007/978-3-319-56782-2_1544-2

García, S. B., Méndez Pérez, A., & Ortiz, A. A. (2000). Mexican American mothers' beliefs about disabilities: Implications for early childhood intervention. *Remedial and Special Education, 21,* 90–120. doi:10.1177/074193250002100204

Gibson, T. A., Jarmulowicz, L., & Oller, D. K. (2018). Difficulties using standardized tests to identify the receptive expressive gap in bilingual children's vocabularies. *Bilingualism: Language and Cognition, 21,* 328–339. doi:10.1017/S1366728917000074

Goldstein, B. A. (Ed.). (2012). *Bilingual language development and disorders in Spanish-English speakers* (2nd ed.). Baltimore, MD: Paul H. Brookes.

Hammer, C. S. (1998). Toward a 'thick description' of families: Using ethnography to overcome the obstacles to providing family-centered early intervention services. *American Journal of Speech-Language Pathology, 7*(1), 5–22. doi:10.1044/1058-0360.0701.05

Hammer, C. S., Rodriguez, B. L., Lawrence, F. R., & Miccio, A. W. (2007). Puerto Rican mothers' beliefs and home literacy practices. *Language, Speech, and Hearing Services in Schools, 38,* 216–224. doi:10.1044/0161-1461(2007/023)

Hardin, B. J., Mereoiu, M., Hung, H.-F., & Roach-Scott, M. (2009). Investigating parent and professional perspectives concerning special education services for preschool Latino children. *Early Childhood Education Journal, 37,* 93–102. doi:10.1007/s10643-009-0336-x

Hebbeler, K., Spiker, D., Morrison, K., & Mallik, S. (2008). A national look at the characteristics of Part C early intervention services. In C. Peterson, L. Fox, & P. Blasco (Eds.), *Early intervention for infants and toddlers and their families: Practices and outcomes* (Young Exceptional Children Monograph Series No. 10, pp. 1–18). Missoula, MT: The Division for Early Childhood of the Council for Exceptional Children.

Heilmann, J., Nockerts, A., & Miller, J. F. (2010). Language sampling: Does the length of the transcript matter? *Language, Speech, and Hearing Services in Schools, 41,* 393–404. doi:10.1044/0161-1461(2009/09-0023)

Horton-Ikard, R. (2010). Language sample analysis with children who speak non-mainstream dialects of English. *Perspectives on Language Learning and Education, 17*(1), 16–23. doi:10.1044/lle17.1.16

Horwitz, S. M., Irwin, J. R., Briggs-Gowan, M. J., Heenan, J. M. B., Mendoza, J., & Carter, A. S. (2003). Language delay in a community cohort of young children. *Journal of the American Academy of Child & Adolescent Psychiatry, 42,* 932–940. doi:10.1097/01.CHI.0000046889.27264.5E

Hyter, Y. D., & Salas-Provance, M. B. (2018). *Culturally responsive practices in speech, language, and hearing sciences.* San Diego, CA: Plural.

Jackson-Maldonado, D., Thal, D. J., Fenson, L., Marchman, V. A., Newton, T., & Conboy, B. (2003). *MacArthur inventarios del desarrollo de habilidades comunicativas: User's guide and technical manual.* Baltimore, MD: Paul H. Brookes.

Kapantzoglou, M., Restrepo, M. A., & Thompson, M. S. (2012). Dynamic assessment of word learning skills: Identifying language impairment in bilingual children. *Language, Speech, and Hearing Services in Schools, 43,* 81–96. doi:10.1044/0161-1461(2011/10-0095)

Kraemer, R., & Fabiano-Smith, L. (2017). Language assessment of Latino English learning children: A records abstraction study. *Journal of Latinos and Education, 16,* 349–358. doi:10.1080/15348431.2016.1257429

Macy, M., Bagnato, S. J., Macy, R. S., & Salaway, J. (2015). Conventional tests and testing for early intervention eligibility: Is there an evidence base? *Infants & Young Children, 28,* 182–204. doi:10.1097/IYC.0000000000000032

McGregor, K. K., Williams, D., Hearst, S., & Johnson, A. C. (1997). The use of contrastive analysis in distinguishing difference from disorder: A tutorial. *American Journal of Speech-Language Pathology, 6*(3), 45–56. doi:10.1044/1058-0360.0603.45

McLeod, S., Harrison, L. J., & McCormack, J. (2012). The intelligibility in context scale: Validity and reliability of a subjective rating measure. *Journal of Speech, Language, and Hearing Research, 55,* 648–656. doi:10.1044/1092-4388(2011/10-0130)

Orellana, C. I., Wada, R., & Gillam, R. B. (2019). The use of dynamic assessment for the diagnosis of language disorders in bilingual children: A meta-analysis. *American Journal of Speech-Language Pathology, 28,* 1298–1317. doi:10.1044/2019_AJSLP-18-0202

Peña, E. D. (2007). Lost in translation: Methodological considerations in cross-cultural research. *Child Development, 78,* 1255–1264. doi:10.1111/j.1467-8624.2007.01064.x

Peña, E. D., Bedore, L. M., & Kester, E. S. (2016). Assessment of language impairment in bilingual children using semantic tasks: Two languages classify better than one. *International Journal of Language & Communication Disorders, 51,* 192–202. doi:10.1111/1460-6984.12199

Peredo, T. N. (2016). Supporting culturally and linguistically diverse families in early intervention. *Perspectives of the ASHA Special Interest Groups, 1*(1), 154–167. doi:10.1044/persp1.SIG1.154

Restrepo, M. A. (1998). Identifiers of predominantly Spanish-speaking children with language impairment. *Journal of Speech, Language, and Hearing Research, 41,* 1398–1411. doi:10.1044/jslhr.4106.1398

Sarkisian, N., Gerena, M., & Gerstel, N. (2007). Extended family integration among Euro and Mexican Americans: Ethnicity, gender, and class. *Journal of Marriage and Family, 69,* 40–54. doi:10.1111/j.1741-3737.2006.00342.x

U.S. Department of Education. (2018). Part C child count and settings 2017–18. Retrieved from https://www2.ed.gov/programs/osepidea/618-data/state-level-data-files/part-c-data/child-count-and-settings/cchildcountand-settings2017-18.csv

Appendix A
Evaluation Checklist

This checklist is designed to support the evaluation and assessment process of communication abilities in Latinx children from birth to age 3.

Step 1: Developing the assessment team (A1*)
- ☐ Identify relevant caregivers and family (including nonparent caregivers)
- ☐ Recruit interpreters based on language preferences of caregivers and family
- ☐ Discuss purpose and process of evaluation with the family

Step 2: Gathering background information (A2, A6, A7)
- ☐ Interview family about language beliefs, values, and practices (see Table 1)
- ☐ Describe history of language exposure and use

Step 3: Measuring child language ability and experience (A3, A5, A6, A7, A10)
- ☐ Employ parent report to gather child language history and present levels
- ☐ Conduct dynamic assessment
- ☐ Complete direct observation of child-caregiver interactions and language
- ☐ Use norm- and criterion-referenced tools when valid

Step 4: Determining eligibility (A8, A11)
- ☐ Interpret findings, making sure to distinguish language difference from disorder
- ☐ Provide findings to family in a way that is accessible and ensures comprehension

*DEC Recommend Practices aligned with each step are listed in parentheses.

4

Implementing Recommended Assessment Practices in Early Intervention

Corinne F. Hill
Dana C. Childress
Lisa M. Terry
Virginia Commonwealth University

Anne M. Brager
Infant & Toddler Connection of Virginia

U NDER PART C OF THE INDIVIDUALS WITH DISABILITIES EDUCATION Act (2004), assessment is defined as "the ongoing procedures used by qualified personnel to identify the child's unique strengths and needs and the early intervention services appropriate to meet those needs throughout the period of the child's eligibility" (34 CFR §303.321(a)(2)(ii)). As part of that assessment process, caregivers may also voluntarily participate in a "family-directed assessment of the resources, priorities, and concerns of the family and the identification of the supports and services necessary to enhance the family's capacity to meet the developmental needs" of the child (34 CFR §303.321(a)(1)(ii)(B)). Additionally, the Division for Early Childhood Recommended Practices (DEC, 2014) defines assessment as "the process of gathering information to make decisions" (p. 8). These broader definitions provide an overarching framework for assessment in early intervention (EI).

The field of EI, however, calls for a more in-depth process to fully assess a child's functioning across environments, people, and time. How this more in-depth process occurs is reflected in the Latin definition of assessment: to "sit beside and get to know" (Early Intervention-Early Childhood Professional Development Community of Practice - EI Curriculum Workgroup, 2018). This image-inspiring definition aptly describes what should happen throughout EI for practitioners to make informed decisions regarding eligibility and service implementation.

For more than 20 years, researchers (Bagnato, 2005; Bagnato, Goins, Pretti-Frontczak, & Neisworth, 2014; Bagnato & Ho, 2006; Bagnato, McLean, Macy, & Neisworth, 2011; de Sam Lazaro, 2017; Keilty, LaRocco, & Casell, 2009; Macy,

Bagnato, & Gallen, 2016; Macy, Bricker, & Squires, 2005; Neisworth & Bagnato, 2004) have recognized that the types of standardized, conventional testing procedures and tools used in classroom-based programs are not always supported nor are they developmentally appropriate for infants and toddlers in EI. Instead, Macy et al. (2016) reiterated the need for an alternate approach: authentic assessment. Bagnato and Ho (2006) define authentic assessment as "the systematic recording of developmental observations over time about the naturally occurring behaviors and functional competencies of young children in daily routines by familiar and knowledgeable caregivers in the child's life" (p. 29). Early childhood organizations, including the DEC, the National Association for the Education of Young Children (NAEYC), and the National Association of Early Childhood Specialists in State Departments of Education (NAECS/SDE), all support authentic assessment as recommended practice for infants, toddlers, and very young children (Bagnato et al., 2014).

One State's Practical Definition of Assessment

Despite this definition and these endorsements, some EI practitioners still struggle to understand how to successfully implement recommended assessment practices. To address this concern, the state of Virginia convened a workgroup. Members included current practitioners from various disciplines (e.g., physical therapy, speech-language pathology, and education), service coordinators, local-level system managers, and state-level technical assistance, monitoring, and professional development consultants who met regularly to collaborate on this project. All stakeholders identified specific interest in furthering practitioner knowledge and advancing skills related to assessment practices.

The workgroup explored resources to determine effective practices in assessment in EI. Workgroup members agreed that information about authentic and functional assessment from the Birth to Five Evaluation and Assessment Module (Maryland State Department of Education, 2011) matched their understanding of high-quality assessment practices and would guide their work. This module described how, rather than focusing on discrete skills from a test, authentic assessment incorporates observing and gathering information about the infant's or toddler's skills within everyday life contexts (Macy et al., 2016). Functional assessment, as part of authentic assessment, represents how the child is or is not able to fully participate in those routines and activities. Armed with this clarity, workgroup members developed a working definition that conceptualized key components of what EI assessment looks like in practice.

Virginia's definition of functional assessment includes eight components of high-quality assessment practices that represent "a continuous, collaborative process that combines observing, asking meaningful questions, listening to family stories, and analyzing individual child skills and behaviors within naturally occurring everyday routines and activities across multiple situations and settings" (see Figure 1). The definition's components are explained in Figure 1. *Functional assessment* is the descriptor chosen by the state's EI system to refer to EI assessment practices. For the purposes of this article, however, the authors will not label assessment as functional or authentic because of the belief that EI

Figure 1

Virginia's Definition Of Functional Assessment

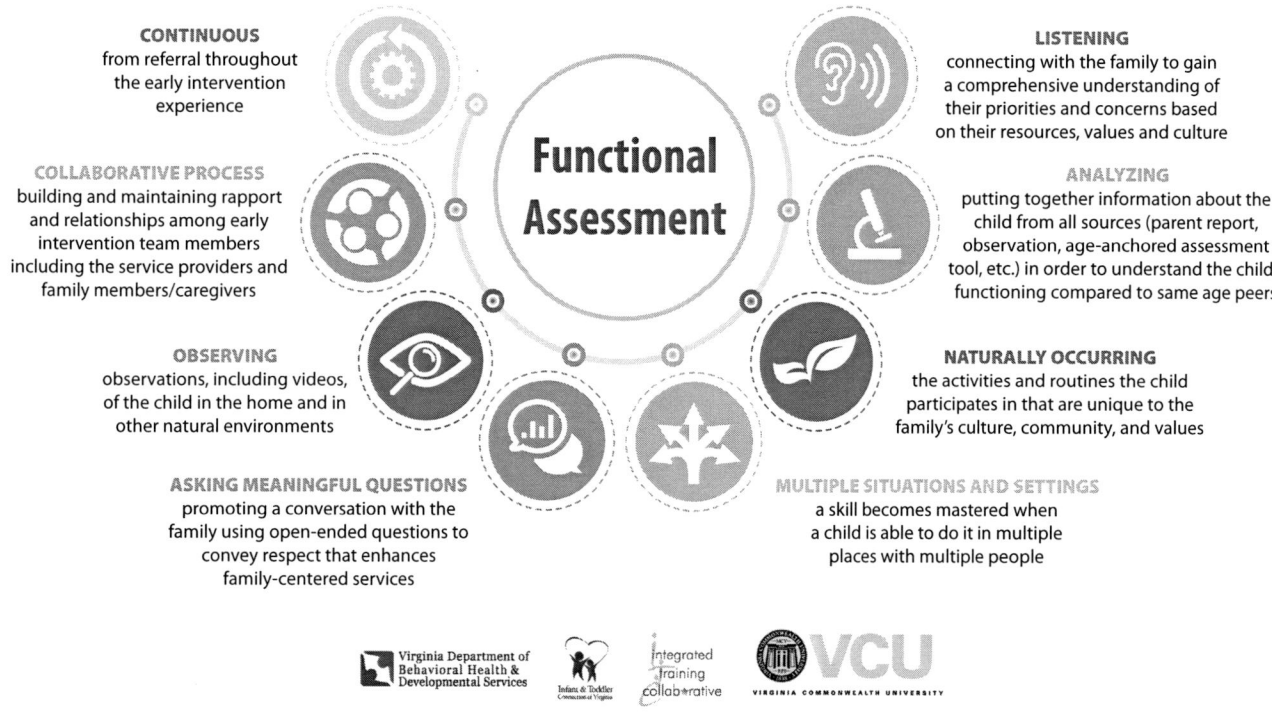

Functional assessment is a continuous <u>collaborative process</u> that combines <u>observing</u>, <u>asking meaningful questions</u>, <u>listening</u> to family stories, and <u>analyzing</u> individual child skills and behaviors within <u>naturally occurring</u> everyday routines and activities across <u>multiple situations and settings</u>.

CONTINUOUS
from referral throughout the early intervention experience

COLLABORATIVE PROCESS
building and maintaining rapport and relationships among early intervention team members including the service providers and family members/caregivers

OBSERVING
observations, including videos, of the child in the home and in other natural environments

ASKING MEANINGFUL QUESTIONS
promoting a conversation with the family using open-ended questions to convey respect that enhances family-centered services

Functional Assessment

LISTENING
connecting with the family to gain a comprehensive understanding of their priorities and concerns based on their resources, values and culture

ANALYZING
putting together information about the child from all sources (parent report, observation, age-anchored assessment tool, etc.) in order to understand the child's functioning compared to same age peers

NATURALLY OCCURRING
the activities and routines the child participates in that are unique to the family's culture, community, and values

MULTIPLE SITUATIONS AND SETTINGS
a skill becomes mastered when a child is able to do it in multiple places with multiple people

Virginia Department of Behavioral Health & Developmental Services · Infant & Toddler Connection of Virginia · Integrated Training Collaborative · VCU VIRGINIA COMMONWEALTH UNIVERSITY

assessment always includes both perspectives. Instead, the authors will use the descriptor *assessment* to describe and illustrate effective practices that are both authentic and functional and reflect the EI field's recommended practices.

Crosswalk of Virginia's Definition With the DEC Recommended Practices

To support early interventionists to use the DEC Recommended Practices more frequently, it may be beneficial to help practitioners understand what these practices look like in their daily work. Components of Virginia's definition of assessment are crosswalked with nine of the Assessment recommended practices to provide this translation for practitioners (see Table 1). Vignettes will highlight implementation of the recommended practices and components of the definition during three important assessment activities: eligibility determination, program planning, and progress monitoring. These activities have also been described as "decision points" (Keilty et al., 2009, p. 244) and "assessment purposes" (Neisworth & Bagnato, 2004) and will provide the context in which the practical implementation of effective EI assessment practices will be illustrated.

Table 1
Crosswalk of Assessment Recommended Practices
With Components of Virginia's Definition of Functional Assessment

Assessment recommended practice	Collaborative process	Naturally occurring everyday routines	Analyzing	Observing	Asking meaningful questions	Listening	Continuous	Multiple situations and settings
A1 Practitioners work with the family to identify family preferences for assessment processes.	X				X	X	X	
A2 Practitioners provide the family with up-to-date, comprehensive, and unbiased information in a way that they can understand and use to make informed choices and decisions.	X	X		X	X	X	X	X	X
A3 Practitioners use assessment materials and strategies that are appropriate for the child's age and level of development and accommodate the child's sensory, physical, communication, cultural, linguistic, social, and emotional characteristics.		X						X
A4 Practitioners conduct assessments that include all areas of development and behavior to learn about the child's strengths, needs, preferences, and interests, analyzing individual child skills and behaviors.		X		X	X			X
A5 Practitioners conduct assessments in the child's dominant language and in additional languages if the child is learning more than one language.	X							X
A6 Practitioners use a variety of methods, including observation and interviews, to gather assessment information from multiple sources, including the child's family and other significant individuals in the child's life.	X	X		X	X	X		X
A7 Practitioners obtain information about the child's skills in daily activities, routines, and environments such as home, center, and community.		X	X	X				
A8 Practitioners use clinical reasoning in addition to assessment results to identify the child's current levels of functioning and to determine the child's eligibility and plan for instruction.	X	X	X	X	X	X		X
A9 Practitioners will implement systematic ongoing assessment to identify learning targets, plan activities, and monitor the child's progress to revise instruction as needed.	X	X	X	X	X	X	X	X

It's Monday morning, and Hazel is reviewing her busy day ahead. She will meet Najari's family for his initial evaluation and assessment. Following that, she will complete an annual IFSP review with Maya's family. Hazel will wrap up her day seeing Kelvin at his child care center for their bimonthly visit. Throughout each of these appointments, Hazel's knowledge of effective assessment practices will guide her EI implementation.

Decision Point: Eligibility Determination (Najari)

Hazel begins her day at Najari's home to complete a multidisciplinary initial evaluation and assessment. She is joined by the service coordinator, occupational therapist, and interpreter. Najari, who was born at 28-weeks gestation, has been referred to the EI program because of prematurity and concerns about feeding and muscle tone. The service coordinator shares referral information with the team, including the Neonatal Intensive Care Unit discharge summary and information gathered from the phone interview with Najari's mother. Since being home, Najari, who is now 5 months old, continues to have difficulty with feeding. Najari's mother reports that he lost weight since his 4-month well-baby checkup.

The Individuals With Disabilities Education Act (IDEA, 2004) requires that evaluation and assessment be used to determine a child's eligibility for EI. Evaluation is the collaborative process that consists of analyzing the information gathered about a child by a multidisciplinary team of qualified personnel (see Table 2 for definition components and the DEC Recommended Practices that correspond to this decision point). Practitioners employ a variety of methods, including observing the child, gathering information from the family, analyzing data collected (comprehensive assessment results, medical records, etc.), and using informed clinical opinion (Keilty et al., 2009). Assessment gathers unique and meaningful information about the child and family and is a way to look at the functional strengths and needs of the child in the naturally occurring activities, routines, and settings that are relevant and important to the family. To the greatest extent possible, linguistically appropriate and culturally sensitive assessment practices are used with children and families (Losardo & Notari Syverson, 2011; McLean, Hemmeter, & Snyder, 2014), including conducting the evaluation and assessment in the child's and family's native language. This process ensures that the necessary information is gathered for the team to make an informed decision for eligibility determination.

Recommended assessment practices that look at the whole child within the context of family and community are essential to identifying children who are eligible for EI and for future program planning. Use of a comprehensive assessment tool is required to ensure providers are analyzing all areas of development. The multidisciplinary team analyzes this information to determine how children integrate skills across developmental domains for successful and active participation in multiple settings and situations. A family-directed assessment allows team members to use active listening while asking meaningful questions to learn families' concerns, priorities, and resources unique to their values and culture. The team also explores which naturally occurring routines and activities are

> A family-directed assessment allows team members to use active listening while asking meaningful questions to learn families' concerns, priorities, and resources unique to their values and culture.

going well for the child and family, which ones are challenging, and any new ones the family might like to explore. Through the collaborative process of involving parents, family members, and practitioners (Bricker, Macy, Squires, & Marks, 2013; Squires, Bricker, & Twombly, 2015), the team uses gathered information to determine eligibility for EI services. Eligibility determination may be the gateway into EI, but assessment is a continuous and collaborative process that happens throughout a child's time in the program.

Hazel and the other team members listen as Najari's parents describe his birth and complications. With the help of the interpreter, Hazel and the team members listen carefully, occasionally asking questions to get a well-rounded picture of Najari's history. Hazel observes how his parents take turns frequently talking softly to him as he sits quietly in his bouncer seat. She notices that they have used small blankets to help him stay upright with his head aligned in midline. Hazel records this information on the assessment tool. Najari's mother shares that in addition to feeding, bath time is challenging because he is unable to hold up his head. She reports having the same difficulty with putting him in the car seat, stating they rarely leave the house anymore, and they really miss going to their mosque. After the evaluation and assessment is complete, findings are reviewed with Najari's parents, with the assistance of the interpreter. Najari is determined eligible based on his feeding difficulties and low muscle tone.

Table 2
Assessment Decision Point: Eligibility Determination (Najari)

Definition components	DEC Recommended Practices
Continuous Collaborative process Observing Analyzing Asking meaningful questions Listening Multiple situations and settings Naturally occurring	A2, A4, A5, A6, A7, A8

Decision Point: Program Planning (Maya)

As Hazel travels to her next appointment, she contemplates her visit, which is an annual IFSP review with Maya's father, the service coordinator, and a physical therapist. As she drives, she reviews Maya's progress over the past year. She thinks about her observations of Maya's development and the intervention strategies she and Maya's father have practiced during visits. She knows that there will be lots of questions about what Maya is doing now and what to include in the annual IFSP. She feels confident that the team will celebrate Maya's progress and collaborate to successfully plan for her next steps in the coming year.

In EI, program planning is also a continuous and collaborative process that begins at, if not before, the development of the initial IFSP (see Table 3 for definition components and the DEC Recommended Practices that correspond to this decision point). During this early phase in the EI process, team members, including the family, determine outcomes that reflect what the family hopes to see as a result of their participation in the program (Neisworth & Bagnato, 2004). These outcomes are based on family preferences, integrate information gathered during the initial assessment, and help the team decide which services are most appropriate (Keilty et al., 2009). This information is gathered through conversations with family members by asking meaningful questions and actively listening to their answers about their daily life (Woods & Lindeman, 2008). The development of IFSP outcomes is an important part of program planning because it guides the initial work to establish individualized, meaningful, and integrated intervention services (Gatmaitan & Brown, 2016; Ridgely, Snyder, McWilliam, & Davis, 2011).

Other EI activities related to program planning include IFSP reviews. These reviews are required at least every six months and annually (within 365 days of the date of the initial IFSP meeting; IDEA, 2004) to ensure that EI services continue to be appropriate and effective in meeting child and family needs. IFSP reviews also occur whenever a change is needed to the plan, such as when a child has met an outcome or service frequency needs to be adjusted. With periodic review, the plan may be adjusted as new outcomes are added, new information is discussed about the child's strengths and needs, or family priorities change.

Service providers and service coordinators are continuously analyzing information they gather about a child (from the family, from observations, from updated medical records, etc.) between IFSP reviews to determine if and when changes are needed. Similarly, when the annual IFSP review is conducted, these considerations are key as the team collaborates to write a completely new plan. This new plan integrates updated information about the child's strengths, needs, preferences, and interests in all areas of development based on ongoing assessment conducted during intervention visits over the past year and any new information from families related to priorities, concerns, resources, daily activities, or routines (Ridgley, Snyder, & McWilliam, 2014). This new information also informs discussions about transition, which occur at all IFSP reviews. As reflected in the DEC Recommended Practices, team members use what they know about the child from observations and talking with the family and others important in the child's life to develop the new plan. At the point of the annual IFSP review, families may be more comfortable and experienced with participating in the process (Ridgley et al., 2014) and the professional team members typically know the family much better. Therefore, the team has more meaningful information on which to base the new or revised IFSP outcomes, service determination, and other important decisions.

Eligibility determination may be the gateway into EI, but assessment is a continuous and collaborative process that happens throughout a child's time in the program.

Hazel has been collaborating with Maya's father for almost a year and has seen Maya develop her abilities to crawl and now take several steps with her hands held. Based on her observations, Hazel knows that Maya is very motivated to walk and her father and siblings practice walking with her often. Hazel also knows that Maya tends to drag her left leg when she tries to walk because of her cerebral palsy. When she arrives at Maya's home, Hazel is prepared to share her observations and ask additional questions as Maya's team develops the new IFSP.

Hazel joins the service coordinator, physical therapist, and Maya's father in the family's playroom. After everyone settles in, team members have a conversation about Maya's progress. They update her assessment information and reconfirm her eligibility for the EI program, then review her IFSP outcomes. Maya's father wants to continue to focus on her mobility, but he is concerned that she continues to drag her leg. Hazel asks several open-ended questions to gather functional information, such as "Where would you like Maya to be able to walk?" and "What do you think Maya needs to help her be able to walk independently?" Maya's father mentions that the neurologist recommended a gait trainer, but he is not familiar with this piece of equipment. The physical therapist provides information about gait trainers and explains how a gait trainer could help Maya develop balance and practice walking safely. Hazel adds her observation that Maya seems to walk better when wearing her sneakers, and Maya's father agrees.

Table 3
Assessment Decision Point: Program Planning (Maya)

Definition components	DEC Recommended Practices
Continuous Collaborative process Analyzing Asking meaningful questions Listening	A1, A2, A4, A6, A9

Based on all of this information, a new outcome is written that describes the family priority that Maya will learn to walk on her own (while using a gait trainer and wearing her sneakers) so she can play in the back yard with her siblings this summer. Current services were reviewed, and the decision was made for Hazel to continue to work with the family. Monthly physical therapy was added to the IFSP to fit Maya for a gait trainer and support Hazel and the family as Maya learns to walk while using it. Maya's father is assured that if the family needs additional support from a physical therapist, these services can be increased at a later time during an IFSP review.

Decision Point: Progress Monitoring (Kelvin)

Next, Hazel will be visiting Kelvin, age 27 months, who has been diagnosed with neonatal abstinence syndrome. His grandparents received full custody six months ago. Hazel sees Kelvin once a month at home and once a month at child care. Kelvin's grandparents report that he frequently seems anxious and overwhelmed. They have identified Kelvin's IFSP outcomes, including using two- to three-word phrases to tell them what he wants or needs, independently exploring near them when they are out in the community, and participating in child care group activities. Kelvin's grandparents' biggest priority is for Kelvin to use words to tell them or his teachers how he is feeling or what he wants. When Kelvin began services, he called for "Gramma" and "Papa" to get their attention and asked for "milk." Now, he uses 10 words consistently. He used to have a hard time during transitions at home, but his grandparents incorporated a predictable schedule and responsive interactions to help him know what to expect throughout the day.

On Hazel's last home visit, Kelvin's grandparents reported that he seems more comfortable at the house, but he becomes very clingy around other people at the grocery store and story time at the library. Kelvin's grandfather shared a video clip he took on his cell phone showing Kelvin at the library crying and clinging to his grandmother's legs. Kelvin's grandfather reflected that he thinks Kelvin avoids situations when he does not know what is going to happen or he is expected to talk and interact with others.

On previous visits at child care, Hazel observed Kelvin during lunch and outside play. His teachers shared that at circle time Kelvin prefers to stand in the corner alone and becomes upset in group activities. It was agreed that Hazel's next visit would be during circle time.

The Individuals With Disabilities Education Act (IDEA, 2004) identifies the ongoing nature of assessment as a continuous process using formal and informal methods to determine the child's progress (see Table 4 for definition components and the DEC Recommended Practices that correspond to this decision point). Progress monitoring in EI uses these methods to capture a child's progress toward IFSP outcomes on an ongoing basis and evaluate the effectiveness of intervention (Gatmaitan & Brown, 2016; Walker, Carta, Greenwood, & Buzhardt, 2008). Through progress monitoring, practitioners and caregivers use a collaborative process, analyzing objective data to make informed decisions about EI implementation to support child development (Gatmaitan & Brown, 2016).

Formal methods of progress monitoring include IFSP reviews every six months or earlier as needed (IDEA, 2004). To prepare for these more formal reviews, practitioners may review assessment tools to measure a child's progress and update developmental scores and the description of a child's skills and abilities on the IFSP. Practitioners also use assessment and progress monitoring to demonstrate a child's improvement on the three global child outcomes identified by the Office of Special Education Programs (OSEP). These functional outcomes include how young children build positive social-emotional skills (including social relationships), acquire and use knowledge and skills (including early language/communication), and use appropriate behavior to meet needs (Early Childhood Technical Assistance Center, n.d.). Practitioners continually monitor outcome progress to ensure the supports and services have a positive benefit for the child and family to promote a child's successful participation in different settings and activities (Early Childhood Technical Assistance Center, n.d.).

Practitioners also informally monitor progress on every visit to inform intervention strategies and consider needed IFSP updates. By listening to the family to keep abreast of current priorities and concerns and observing the child in multiple situations and settings (i.e., child care, home, grocery store, library, meals), practitioners "identify functional capabilities and needs" of the child during naturally occurring activities (Bagnato et al., 2011, p. 246). Informal monitoring methods include gathering data from multiple sources such as observing, asking the parents meaningful questions, videotaping, reviewing assessment portfolios, and using data-based tools, such as the Individual Growth and Development Indicators (IGDIs; Gatmaitan & Brown, 2016; Greenwood, Carta, & McConnell, 2011; Jarrett, Browne, & Wallin, 2006; Thomas & Marvin, 2016). The continuous collection of data seamlessly fits into the practitioner's role in supporting caregivers on every visit.

The continuous collection of data seamlessly fits into the practitioner's role in supporting caregivers on every visit.

Hazel arrives at Kelvin's child care as they begin to transition to circle time. She sees Kelvin standing by a cubby away from the class. When the teachers try to direct him to the carpet, Kelvin begins to cry quietly and tries to move to the corner. Hazel meets with the lead teacher to get an update on Kelvin's progress while the assistant teacher begins story time with the children. The teacher expresses concern that Kelvin continues to "shut down" during group activities, especially circle time. Hazel shares Kelvin's grandparents' concerns that he becomes upset when he does not know what is happening or what he may be asked to do.

Together, Hazel and the teacher strategize ways to help Kelvin stay calmer and engaged by incorporating something he really enjoys during circle time. The teacher states he is planning on reading a book for their dinosaur unit that happens to be Kelvin's favorite because he loves dinosaurs. Kelvin's teacher reflects that Kelvin seems more comfortable when holding little objects and decides to provide small dinosaurs to all of the children to hold during the story.

Hazel and the teacher also decide to have Kelvin sit toward the back of the group beside the assistant teacher. As the teacher hands out the dinosaurs, Kelvin smiles and sits next to the assistant teacher on the rug. Hazel asks the teacher if he could send her a short e-mail or text in a few days to report how things are going. The teacher agrees. Hazel indicates that she will follow up with Kelvin's grandparents about today's visit and the strategies they developed. As Hazel drives home, she reflects on her day, filled with multiple opportunities to use sound assessment strategies to support infants, toddlers, and their families throughout their EI journey.

Table 4
Assessment Decision Point: Progress Monitoring (Kelvin)

Definition components	DEC Recommended Practices
Continuous Collaborative process Observing Analyzing Asking meaningful questions Listening Naturally occurring Multiple situations and settings	A1, A2, A3, A4, A6, A7, A8, A9

Implementing effective assessments requires that early interventionists such as Hazel understand what this looks like in practice. The DEC Recommended Practices provide the framework for best practices used during quality assessment, and Virginia's definition can help practitioners learn to apply those assessment practices in their work.

Using key words and phrases from Virginia's definition, including *continuous, collaborative process, observing, asking meaningful questions, listening, analyzing, naturally occurring,* and *multiple situations and settings* helps paint a picture that strengthens practitioner knowledge and serves as a base from which practitioners can reflect on what they do every day. Just as assessment is a continuous process, so is professional development. Early intervention practitioners must continue to develop their assessment skills to ensure they are successfully sitting beside families, getting to know what is important to them, and providing supports that are meaningful, functional, and authentic throughout the EI process.

References

Bagnato, S. J. (2005). The authentic alternative for assessment in early intervention: An emerging evidence-based practice. *Journal of Early Intervention, 28,* 17–22. doi:10.1177/105381510502800102

Bagnato, S. J., Goins, D. D., Pretti-Frontczak, K., & Neisworth, J. T. (2014). Authentic assessment as "best practice" for early childhood intervention: National consumer social validity research. *Topics in Early Childhood Special Education, 34,* 116–127. doi:10.1177/0271121414523652

Bagnato, S. J., & Ho, H. Y. (2006). High-stakes testing with preschool children: Violation of professional standards for evidence-based practice in early childhood intervention. *KEDI International Journal of Educational Policy, 3*(1), 22–43. Retrieved from http://eng.kedi.re.kr

Bagnato, S. J., McLean, M., Macy, M., & Neisworth, J. T. (2011). Identifying instructional targets for early childhood via authentic assessment: Alignment of professional standards and practice-based evidence. *Journal of Early Intervention, 33,* 243–253. doi:10.1177/1053815111427565

Bricker, D., Macy, M., Squires, J., & Marks, K. (2013). *Developmental screening in your community: An integrated plan for connecting children with services.* Baltimore, MD: Paul H. Brookes.

de Sam Lazaro, S. L. (2017). The importance of authentic assessments in eligibility determination for infants and toddlers. *Journal of Early Intervention, 39,* 88–105. doi:10.1177/1053815116689061

Division for Early Childhood. (2014). *DEC recommended practices in early intervention/early childhood special education 2014.* Retrieved from https://www.dec-sped.org/dec-recommended-practices

Early Childhood Technical Assistance Center. (n.d.). *Outcomes FAQ.* Retrieved from https://ectacenter.org/eco/pages/faqs.asp

Early Intervention-Early Childhood Professional Development Community of Practice - EI Curriculum Workgroup. (2018). *Authentic assessment for early intervention* [Online module]. Retrieved from http://universalonlinepartceicurriculum.pbworks.com/

Gatmaitan, M., & Brown, T. (2016). Quality in individualized family service plans: Guidelines for practitioners, programs, and families. *Young Exceptional Children, 19*(2), 14–32. doi:10.1177/1096250614566540

Greenwood, C. R., Carta, J. J., & McConnell, S. (2011). Advances in measurement for universal screening and individual progress monitoring of young children. *Journal of Early Intervention, 33,* 254–267. doi:10.1177/1053815111428467

Individuals With Disabilities Education Act, 20 U.S.C. § 1400 (2004).

Jarrett, M. H., Browne, B. C., & Wallin, C. M. (2006). Using portfolio assessment to document developmental progress of infants and toddlers. *Young Exceptional Children, 10*(1), 22–32. doi:10.1177/109625060601000103

Keilty, B., LaRocco, D. J., & Casell, F. B. (2009). Early interventionists' reports of authentic assessment methods through focus group research. *Topics in Early Childhood Special Education, 28,* 244–256. doi:10.1177/0271121408327477

Losardo, A., & Notari Syverson, A. (2011). *Alternative approaches to assessing young children* (2nd ed.). Baltimore, MD: Paul H. Brookes.

Macy, M., Bagnato, S. J., & Gallen, R. (2016). Authentic assessment: A venerable idea whose time is now. *Zero to Three, 37*(1), 37–43.

Macy, M. G., Bricker, D. D., & Squires, J. K. (2005). Validity and reliability of a curriculum-based assessment approach to determine eligibility for Part C services. *Journal of Early Intervention, 28,* 1–16. doi:10.1177/105381510502800101

Maryland State Department of Education. (2011). *Authentic and functional* [Online module]. Retrieved from http://olms.cte.jhu.edu/olms2/135091

McLean, M. E., Hemmeter, M. L., & Snyder, P. (2014). *Essential elements for assessing infants and preschoolers with special needs.* Old Tappan, NJ: Pearson.

Neisworth, J. T., & Bagnato, S. J. (2004). The mismeasure of young children: The authentic assessment alternative. *Infants & Young Children, 17,* 198–212.

Ridgley, R., Snyder, P., & McWilliam, R. A. (2014). Exploring type and amount of parent talk during individualized family service plan meetings. *Infants & Young Children, 27,* 345–358. doi:10.1097/IYC.0000000000000021

Ridgley, R., Snyder, P. A., McWilliam, R. A., & Davis, J. E. (2011). Development and initial validation of a professional development intervention to enhance the quality of individualized family service plans. *Infants & Young Children, 24,* 309–328. doi:10.1097/IYC.0b013e318229e54d

Squires, J., Bricker, D., & Twombly, E. (2015). *Ages and stages questionnaires: Social-emotional* (2nd ed.). Baltimore, MD: Paul H. Brookes.

Thomas, A. E., & Marvin, C. A. (2016). Program monitoring practices for teachers of the deaf and hard of hearing in early intervention. *Communication Disorders Quarterly, 37,* 184–193. doi:10.1177/1525740115597862

Walker, D., Carta, J. J., Greenwood, C. R., & Buzhardt, J. F. (2008). The use of individual growth and developmental indicators for progress monitoring and intervention decision making in early intervention. *Exceptionality, 16,* 33–47. doi:10.1080/09362830701796784

Woods, J. J., & Lindeman, D. P. (2008). Gathering and giving information with families. *Infants & Young Children, 21,* 272–284. doi:10.1097/01.IYC.0000336540.60250.f2

5

Beyond Feedback
Communicating Assessment Information With Families

Serra Acar
Stephanie A. Silva
Kelly F. Brown
University of Massachusetts, Boston

George is a 2-year-old boy who was referred to his local early intervention program because of concerns regarding his expressive language development. At the time of the evaluation, George is using five single worlds, including "Mama," "up," "beep" (for all vehicles), "yum" (to indicate any food), and "no." George's mother is worried at the end of the evaluation that most of her son's scores measured by the Battelle Developmental Inventory (BDI-2; Newborg, 2005) are low despite her only concern being his ability to talk. The following dialogue is from the discussion between George's parents and the early interventionist upon completion of the eligibility assessment (see Appendices A and B). This language allows the early interventionists to acknowledge the parents' participation in the evaluation, welcome their input, and provide critical feedback regarding eligibility. The early intervention team consists of a developmental specialist, occupational therapist, and speech-language pathologist; each team member has identification cards with their names and titles on it. The early intervention practitioners work as a team with the family to learn more about George's strengths and needs.

Developmental specialist: "Thank you so much for having us today. We enjoyed meeting with your family. We'd like to talk about what we've noticed during our evaluation. We want this to be a conversation with your full participation. So, please feel free to stop me if you have any questions or concerns. Also, we'd love to hear your experiences. If you have any feedback about the assessment, how we played and asked certain questions of George to have him demonstrate his skills, please feel free to share that with us. You know George the best and your input is invaluable as we continue to get to know him. Would you prefer to go first and share your observations today? Or would you prefer us to go first?"

George's parents prefer the team to share their observations first. The team begins by stating that George is eligible for early intervention services according to the state of Massachusetts guidelines. The developmental specialist pauses and waits for the parents' reaction. After assuring with eye contact that George's mother and father are comfortable with continuing, the team begins sharing their observations by starting with George's strengths in each domain and asks his parents to share. Starting with his strengths and sharing results collaboratively for each domain, the early intervention team helps George's parents to see the similarities and some differences between their observations and the early intervention team's evaluation report.

Note: In Massachusetts the term evaluation *refers to establishing eligibility, and* assessment *is any other type of tool that allows for further information gathering.*

Introduction

Assessment is a multifaceted, complex, and technical procedure. Assessing young children for eligibility to early intervention/early childhood special education (EI/ECSE) services requires training in the selected instrument, experience,

and proficiency in collaborating with other practitioners and families. Part C of the Individuals With Disabilities Education Act (IDEA, 2014) and professional organizations (e.g., Division for Early Childhood [DEC], National Association for the Education of Young Children [NAEYC], and Zero to Three) have recognized families as a valuable resource during the planning and implementation of the Individualized Family Service Plan (IFSP). The substantial documentation of the benefits of empowering families during decision-making and service delivery processes yielded increased parent-child interaction and improved family communication and cohesion (Bruder & Dunst, 2015; Byington & Whitby, 2011; Cheatham & Lim-Mullins, 2018). When family members are supported and equipped, they are more likely to experience a true, equal partnership during the assessment process.

An authentic assessment provides a summary of the child's strengths and needs in the areas assessed (de Sam Lazaro, 2017; Gridley et al., 2019). The results may indicate the child is eligible for services, not eligible for services, or a follow-up assessment is advised within four to six months. The evaluation report may include terminology such as "adaptive, cognition, motor, and score of 77 or below is a qualifying score." It is important for EI/ECSE practitioners to provide a meaningful, functional, and individual evaluation report to primary caregivers. The purpose of this article is to provide guidelines for communicating and presenting assessment findings that support the DEC Recommended Practices (DEC, 2014), specifically addressing A2, that "practitioners work as a team with the family and other professionals to gather assessment information," and A11, that "practitioners report assessment results so that they are understandable and useful to families" (p. 8). The terms *family* and *parent* are used in a broad way and are interchangeable in this article to refer to the most significant group function as a family in a child's life.

Family-Centered Practice in Assessment

A family-centered approach requires including parents in the assessment process in a meaningful and functional way (DEC, 2014; Dunst & Espe-Sherwindt, 2016; Shelden & Rush, 2014). Parents should experience a sense of confidence and feel competent about their child's development and learning (McWilliam, 2016; Trivette, Dunst, Hamby, & Meter, 2012). Following a family-centered approach creates a platform where parents' experiences are welcomed and valued. It guides the EI/ECSE practitioner to meet parents where they are and work together throughout the IFSP process. It can also help the practitioner to communicate accurate and sensitive assessment information. We will discuss two examples to include parents in the assessment process: using an observation form and asking open-ended questions.

Using an observation form. One way to support parent involvement and synchronize with them during the assessment procedure may include requesting specific tasks from parents. For instance, EI/ECSE practitioners can share an observation form with parents to take notes when they observe a strength, excitement, challenging task, or frustration (see Appendix C). Parents can complete the form individually or as a team depending on their comfort level and preferences. However, it is important to take into consideration the parents' reading and writing skills before asking them to observe and document the assessment process. The EI/ECSE team can introduce the observation form, demonstrate how to complete the sections, and provide clarification on the assessment tool.

During the assessment, George's mother fills out the observation form with short sentences. For George's strengths she lists, "George smiled while coloring with crayons. George pointed to our cat, YoYo. George enjoys running and going up and down our stairs." For challenges she shares, "George did not follow directions. George had difficulty sitting and playing with the toys, and George needed a lot of breaks." Filling out the observation form during the assessment encourages George's mother to share further observations of his behaviors. For the last question on the observation form, "Please use the space below to provide any other details (i.e., examples of your child's vocabulary or emotions) that you would like to share with us," his mother shared the following notes:

> George is friendly, has an out-going nature; he has curiosity in his world; and shows his love to his family. George gets frustrated when people cannot understand what he wants; for instance, he will point

> "
>
> When family members are supported and equipped, they are more likely to experience a true, equal partnership during the assessment process.

to the refrigerator, but gets upset if I take out the wrong item. Additional challenges include how busy George can be. At a local library story time, George will not sit for the story, and during the day he doesn't sit and play with one thing for very long.

Asking parents to take observation notes during the assessment can empower and support them to engage in conversations with EI/ECSE practitioners. It can also provide a deeper perspective for EI/ECSE practitioners on how parents perceive and define strengths as well as challenging behaviors in their daily routine. However, it is also important to ensure that this does not become a burden to the parents. In some cases, parents may prefer not to fill out an observation form.

Asking open-ended questions. EI/ECSE practitioners can also encourage parents to share their notes if it is a novice activity or if their child is familiar with that task. For instance, if the item asks the child to throw a ball and the child completes the task successfully, the practitioner can ask, "Do you like to play ball?" This may prompt parents to share their stories that their child loves playing with the ball or show pictures of their child playing with the ball at the park. If the item asks the child to use a pincer grasp to pick up a Cheerio and the child shows no interest, the practitioner can ask, "What is his/her favorite breakfast?" Similarly, the parents may explain that Cheerios are not a preferred snack item in their breakfast/snack routine. Alternatively, some families may not be familiar with or prefer American-style eating.

For instance, a traditional Turkish breakfast may include bread and butter, tomatoes, cucumbers, white cheese, pitted black olives, eggs, and black tea. Another example may include children who drink porridge for breakfast, so they don't necessarily pick up their food. In some cultures, it can be the mother's responsibility to do the major activities for her child, such as getting dressed and feeding, until school age. Therefore, children in these families may show a different pace of developmental growth in the area of self-help skills.

It is important for practitioners to gain an understanding of family cultures and preferences to accurately document a child's strengths and needs. As a result, to observe a child's pincer grasp, practitioners can use other circle-shape cereals, (e.g., puffs or finger foods) or items (e.g., pom-poms or toy buttons) with supervision. Any change during the administration should be documented in the evaluation summary.

Moreover, EI/ECSE practitioners can ask parents "Wh– questions" about their experience and impressions on the assessment procedure. For instance, some questions may include: What do you think about today's meeting? How do you think George is doing? What do you think about the activities we did together? What were some of the activities that George might have enjoyed? What kind of support do you think George might need?

Based on the family's response, practitioners can share feedback with affirming sentences, such as "Your observations and comments agreed with the concerns you've shared with us about George's development." Practitioners can ask one question at a time and pause for a response. They can also ask similar questions to the extended family members (e.g., grandparents and aunts) if

> Communicating assessment information to parents should result in more effective parental involvement in the decision-making process.

Table 1
Two Recommended Practices Used in the Assessment and Related Examples

Assessment recommended practices	Examples
A2. Practitioners work as a team with the family and other professionals to gather assessment information.	1. EI/ECSE practitioners (e.g., developmental specialist, occupational therapist, and speech-language pathologist) work as a team with the family to learn more about George's strengths and needs. 2. EI/ECSE practitioners share an observation form with parents to take notes when they observe a strength, excitement, challenging task, or frustration. 3. EI/ECSE practitioners ask parents "Wh–questions" about their experience and impressions on the assessment procedure.
A11. Practitioners report assessment results so that they are understandable and useful to families.	1. EI/ECSE practitioners use strength-based, jargon-, and acronym-free language. They provide real-life examples to define and explain the technical terms used. 2. EI/ECSE practitioners ask, "If there are any other concerns that I have not addressed, please let me know" or "Do you agree with our evaluations today?"

they are present during the assessment. Table 1 summarizes the two recommended practices used in the assessment and related examples from George's and his parents experience.

Guidelines for Building Collaborative Relationships With Families

EI/ECSE practitioners can take several steps to make communication with parents more meaningful and functional for the team. Communicating assessment information to parents should result in more effective parental involvement in the decision-making process. This section will review a number of strategies that can be used to effectively communicate assessment results to parents following the completion of an evaluation.

Presenting results: Honoring family choice. Before sharing results, EI/ECSE practitioners should first ask the family who they want to be present when the results are shared. EI/ECSE practitioners should also confirm with the family whether they would like their child to be present for the conversation. Not all parents want their child to be present while results are being shared. Therefore the team should try to choose a time and place where they can have a private

Table 2
LAFF don't CRY Strategy in Action

Mnemonic reminder	LAFF steps	Example
L	Listen, empathize, and communicate respect	"I can understand why you are concerned" "I hear what you are saying"
A	Ask questions	"When was the first time you noticed this?" "How long has this been a concern?" "What does your mealtime look like?"
F	Focus on the issues	"I want to make sure I have all of the information"
F	Find a first step	Providing recommendations to families for every child who is assessed, including children who are found to be eligible or ineligible for services at the time of the evaluation.

conversation with the parent while the child is not there or at a time when the child is being supervised by a team member in another room. For instance, the team can share assessment results with the parents in the kitchen as the child continues to play with a team member in the living room. This conversation should be planned for and should not be rushed, allowing time for parents to ask questions and share their child's strengths and concerns.

Active listening: "LAFF don't CRY". Active listening is an important step in establishing two-way communication and collaboration among EI/ECSE practitioners and parents. Through active listening, EI/ECSE practitioners gather information while also showing the parents that they are interested in what the parents have to share about themselves and their child. EI/ECSE practitioners can demonstrate active listening by making empathetic comments, asking related questions by using plain language, and paraphrasing the family's comments to confirm that the family was understood (Cramer, 1997; Gordon, 2003).

One method for active listening includes the "LAFF don't CRY" strategy, which provides a flexible framework that EI/ECSE practitioners can use to demonstrate empathy and respect (McNaughton, Hamlin, McCarthy, Head-Reeves, & Schreiner, 2008). Table 2 illustrates examples from the conversation between George's parents and EI team using the "LAFF don't CRY" strategy. The first step of the strategy reminds EI/ECSE practitioners to listen, empathize, and communicate respect. An example of this includes statements such as "I can understand why you are concerned" and "I hear what you are saying." This also includes making eye contact, nodding when appropriate, and remaining silent while the family is speaking. The second step prompts EI/ECSE practitioners to ask questions to elicit a bigger and deeper picture of the child's strengths and needs. During this time, EI/ECSE practitioners may ask families for more information such as: When was the first time you've noticed this? How long has this been a concern? What does your mealtime look like?

The third step of the strategy, focus on the issues, prompts practitioners to summarize the identified concerns. During this time, the EI/ECSE practitioners check their listening by summarizing the information that the family has shared and asking the family whether there is anything else that they would like to add. By providing a summary, the EI/ECSE team is offering evidence that they have been actively listening and engaging in the conversation. A summary of the family's feedback would also provide an opportunity for the family to add or clarify certain points if needed.

The fourth and final step of the LAFF strategy, find a first step, directs the EI/ECSE practitioners to think about what the next steps are and to make a plan (McNaughton et al., 2008; McNaughton & Vostal, 2010). This step includes providing recommendations to families for their child, including those who are found to be ineligible for services at the time of the evaluation. Recommendations can be developed in collaboration with families based on their concerns, priorities, and resources. It is important to have the family review and finalize the recommendations because some top-down recommendations may not fit with the family due to family commitments and responsibilities.

The second part of the framework, don't CRY, summarizes unintentional behaviors that can impede effective communication, including criticizing people who aren't present, reacting hastily and promising something one cannot deliver, and yakety-yakety-yak or talking to break silence (McNaughton et al., 2008). Implementing LAFF strategies with families can build working relationships that support meaningful parent involvement during the assessment process.

Sharing strengths and concerns: The role of observation. When sharing assessment results with families and talking about developmental concerns, it is important to include specific observations from the assessment, such as "I have noticed that …" Sharing direct observations with families, along with the scores, may help families to reflect on the behaviors that they have noticed and connect them to developmental milestones (Croft, 2010). During George's assessment, he required several opportunities to hear a familiar direction before he was able to respond and follow that direction. The EI/ECSE practitioners would want to link this observation to George's medical history of frequent ear infections and recommend having George's hearing tested because it is harder for children to hear sounds when there is fluid in the middle ear. When sharing observations, EI/ECSE practitioners should highlight and point out the child's strengths and be clear about developmental concerns. During this time, EI/ECSE practitioners should check in with the family to see whether the assessment results and observations that have been shared match the family's perception of their child's potential and the report has captured a good understanding of the child. For instance, they can ask, "If there are any other concerns that I have not addressed, please let me know" or "Do you agree with our evaluations today?"

Communicate using plain language. It is important to pay attention to both verbal and written forms of data that practitioners are communicating to

Through active listening, EI/ECSE practitioners gather information while also showing the parents that they are interested in what the parents have to share about themselves and their child.

parents. When selecting language to communicate assessment results, EI/ECSE practitioners should use strength-based language free of jargon and acronyms. If technical terms are used, it would be better to provide real-life examples to define and explain the terms used. Numerical results can be kept to a minimum with clear descriptions for each developmental domain or assessment area.

EI/ECSE practitioners should be respectful and responsive to families and present information in the family's language, collaborating with interpreters during the assessment as needed (Acar & Blasco, 2018; Gatmaitan & Brown, 2016). Depending on the parents' communication preference, licensed and trained interpreters should be part of the EI/ECSE team. Also, any written communication should be translated into the family's preferred language. EI/ECSE practitioners should share information in a sensitive manner, be supportive, and remain nonjudgmental by confirming the family's observations, such as "I noticed that, too." Finally, EI/ECSE practitioners should be ready to help the family make a plan and take the next steps, such as planning for interventions.

Writing a Collaborative Report

In many cases, the assessment report is written by the EI/ECSE practitioners. The standardized assessment results can be supported with the observations of the EI/ECSE team, parents' comments, and observation notes conducted through-

out the assessment. To continue collaboration with families, the process of writing the assessment report can also be cooperative (A2, A11). Discussion of the assessment report with families is valuable, and it aids in understanding the results for all participants (McLean, Wolery, & Bailey, 2004).

EI/ECSE team members play important roles in promoting child and family outcomes, each bringing unique expertise that can be effective in the EI/ECSE process. In the opening vignette, the team consists of a developmental specialist, occupational therapist, and speech-language pathologist. They have a shared goal, which is to better understand George and his parents' strengths and needs (Salvia, Ysseldyke, & Witmer, 2017). Having a shared goal helps the team members function effectively, articulate their roles as independent assessors as well as team members, and incorporate a unified voice for the evaluation report (A2).

Finally, by sharing a written copy of the evaluation report in the family's preferred language, EI/ECSE practitioners invite families to read and review the information. Appendix A shows a sample follow-up letter that acknowledges the importance of family input and recognizes the purpose of the assessment and limited scope of standardized testing. The letter encourages families to review the report (Appendix B) and continue to make suggestions. The report clearly states the standardized scores from the assessment, but most of the report is a combination of the practitioners' clinical observations and families' observations and input. Also included is any relevant background information related to the child's medical history. The letter includes contact information for all practitioners involved in the assessment so families can communicate any questions or concerns.

Wrap up the meeting. Closing an assessment meeting is as important as the opening. During the final section of the meeting, it is important to share the assessment information in a meaningful and functional way for families so they can have an active role in the decision-making process and feel competent as an equal team member. EI/ECSE practitioners should provide a copy of the written information of the assessment summary along with their contact information and signatures from the family and team members.

They can also provide related resources, such as a list of developmentally, culturally, and socially appropriate activities that families can implement until the next visit; a monthly schedule of inclusive story times at their public library; or free apps that allow family members to track their child's developmental milestones (e.g., Centers for Disease Control and Prevention's [CDC] Milestone Tracker). EI/ECSE practitioners also can introduce professional organizations' websites and social media profiles, such as DEC, NAEYC, and Zero to Three.

Finally, it is important to follow up within a week of the assessment. EI/ECSE practitioners should be aware that some families may need additional time to process the information presented. A follow-up phone call may help families share their concerns, ask additional questions, and feel valued throughout the decision-making process. It can also help practitioners to better understand the family's experiences during the assessment procedure. Even a short phone call can provide additional valuable information to the practitioner, helping them to see the child from the family's perspectives.

When family members and EI/ECSE practitioners establish and maintain an equal partnership, they are more likely to have positive child and family outcomes.

Conclusion

In summary, it is clear that following a family-centered approach while sharing and communicating assessment results with families supports the Assessment recommended practices. When family members and EI/ECSE practitioners establish and maintain an equal partnership, they are more likely to have positive child and family outcomes. EI/ECSE practitioners who use active listening strategies before, during, and after the assessment to recognize and respond to family's concerns, priorities, and resources take the first step in establishing the two-way communication needed for building positive relationships with families. Family members who feel valued and respected throughout the assessment process are more likely to share their observations and concerns for their child, helping the EI/ECSE team to gain a unique perspective of the child and family. Through the establishment of equal partnerships with families throughout the assessment process, the EI/ECSE team communicates to the family that they are prepared and invested in both the child and the family.

References

Acar, S., & Blasco, P. M. (2018). Guidelines for collaborating with interpreters in early intervention/early childhood special education. *Young Exceptional Children, 21,* 170–184. doi:10.1177/1096250616674516

Bruder, M. B., & Dunst, C. J. (2015). Parental judgments of early childhood intervention personnel practices: Applying a consumer science perspective. *Topics in Early Childhood Special Education, 34,* 200–210. doi:10.1177/0271121414522527

Byington, T. A., & Whitby, P. J. S. (2011). Empowering families during the early intervention planning process. *Young Exceptional Children, 14*(4), 44–56. doi:10.1177/1096250611428878

Cheatham, G. A., & Lim-Mullins, S. (2018). Immigrant, bilingual parents of students with disabilities: Positive perceptions and supportive dialogue. *Intervention in School and Clinic, 54*(1), 40–46. doi:10.1177/1053451218762490

Cramer, S. F. (1997). *Collaboration: A success strategy for special educators.* Boston, MA: Allyn & Bacon.

Croft, C. (2010). Talking to families of infants and toddlers about developmental delays. *Young Children, 65*(1), 44–46.

de Sam Lazaro, S. L. (2017). The importance of authentic assessments in eligibility determination for infants and toddlers. *Journal of Early Intervention, 39,* 88–105. doi:10.1177/1053815116689061

Division for Early Childhood. (2014). *DEC recommended practices in early intervention/early childhood special education 2014.* Retrieved from https://www.dec-sped.org/dec-recommended-practices

Dunst, C. J., & Espe-Sherwindt, M. (2016). Family-centered practices in early childhood intervention. In B. Reichow, B. A. Boyd, E. E. Barton, & S. L. Odom (Eds.), *Handbook of early childhood special education* (pp. 37–55). New York, NY: Springer.

Gatmaitan, M., & Brown, T. (2016). Quality in individualized family service plans: Guidelines for practitioners, programs, and families. *Young Exceptional Children, 19*(2), 14–32. doi:10.1177/1096250614566540

Gordon, T. (2003). *Teacher effectiveness training: The program proven to help teachers bring out the best in students of all ages.* New York, NY: Three Rivers Press.

Gridley, N., Blower, S., Dunn, A., Bywater, T., Whittaker, K., & Bryant, M. (2019). Psychometric properties of parent–child (0–5 years) interaction outcome measures as used in randomized controlled trials of parent programs: A systematic review. *Clinical Child and Family Psychology Review, 22,* 253–271. doi:10.1007/s10567-019-00275-3

Individuals With Disabilities Education Act, 20 U.S.C. § 1400 (2004).

McLean, M., Wolery, M., & Bailey, D. Jr. (2004). *Assessing infants and preschoolers with special needs* (3rd ed.). Upper Saddle River, NJ: Pearson.

McNaughton, D., Hamlin, D., McCarthy, J., Head-Reeves, D., & Schreiner, M. (2008). Learning to listen: Teaching an active listening strategy to preservice education professionals. *Topics in Early Childhood Special Education, 27,* 223–231. doi:10.1177/0271121407311241

McNaughton, D., & Vostal, B. R. (2010). Using active listening to improve collaboration with parents: The LAFF don't CRY strategy. *Intervention in School and Clinic, 45,* 251–256. doi:10.1177/1053451209353443

McWilliam, R. A. (2016). Birth to three: Early intervention. In B. Reichow, B. A. Boyd, E. E. Barton, & S. L. Odom (Eds.), *Handbook of early childhood special education* (pp. 75–88). New York, NY: Springer.

Newborg, J. (2005). *Battelle developmental inventory - Second Edition.* Itasca: Riverside Pub.

Salvia, J., Ysseldyke, J. E., & Witmer, S. (2017). *Assessment in special and inclusive education* (13th ed.). Belmont, CA: Wadsworth, Cengage Learning.

Shelden, M. L., & Rush, D. D. (2014). IFSP outcome statements made simple. *Young Exceptional Children, 17*(4), 15–27. doi:10.1177/1096250613499246

Trivette, C. M., Dunst, C. J., Hamby, D. W., & Meter, D. (2012). Relationship between early childhood practitioner beliefs and the adoption of innovative and recommended practices. *Research Brief, 6*(1), 1–12.

Appendix A
Sample Letter and Assessment Report

ABC Early Intervention Program
123 Ocean St.
Saugus, MA 01906
Phone: 123-456-789
e-mail: name.lastname@abceip.com

Dear Mr. & Mrs. Parker,

It was our pleasure to meet your family on Thursday, February 7, 2019, for George's evaluation. We appreciate your thoughtful feedback and participation in the discussion regarding George's eligibility. We recognize that our time with George was limited and the snapshot we got during our time at your home most likely did not capture all the wonderful aspects of your son, and we are looking forward to getting to know him and your family better.

For your reference, we have included a summary of his recent assessment as well as our clinical observations and a copy of his eligibility scores. Please review the assessment summary, and if you have any suggestions, please share them with your early interventionist at the next appointment. Please do not hesitate to contact any member of the evaluation team with questions or concerns.

Family: (Print name[s], signature[s], and date)

Development specialist: (Print name, signature, and date)

Occupational therapist: (Print name, signature, and date)

Speech-language pathologist: (Print name, signature, and date)

Appendix B
Results of the Initial/Reevaluation Assessment

Child's name: George Parker   **Date of birth (DOB):** 10/12/16
Date of assessment: 2/7/2019   **Age:** 2 year(s), 3 month(s), and 25 day(s)
Location of the assessment: Child's home, 123 Winter St., Saugus, MA 01906

Reason for referral: George was referred for an early intervention assessment by his parents, Mr. and Mrs. Parker, because of concerns related to the limited number of words he is using. This document summarizes the results of the initial evaluation for determination of early intervention eligibility.

Health history: George was born full term with no complications, and his parents report he has had no major health problems. George's parents shared that he has been a very healthy little boy, with the exception of several ear infections. George had a hearing screening at birth but has not had a reevaluation since that time. George's father shared that he thinks his son might have some seasonal allergies, but nothing has been diagnosed at this time. George happily engaged with his mother and father throughout the assessment.

Assessment tool: The Battelle Developmental Inventory – 2nd edition (BDI-2) is the test that was used in this evaluation and measures the development of children between the ages of birth and 95 months of age. The BDI-2 is a published, norm-referenced measure that compares George's skills with other children his age. A standard score between 85 and 115, or between the 16th and 84th percentile, is considered within the typical range for children George's age. A percentile rank of 16 indicates that George scored as well or better than 16% of same-age peers on the same tasks. There are five domains that comprise the BDI-2: cognition, personal-social, communication, motor, and adaptive. Each domain is further divided into subdomains. Each domain was adminstered by the team with the communication domain led by the team's speech-language pathologist. Domains were completed using direct testing methods and observation. An interview with George's mother and father provided information necessary to complete items in the personal-social and adaptive domains that related to child's skills in self-help and interacting with adults or other children.

Assessment Results

Per the Massachusetts Department of Public Health, a developmental quotient of 77 or below is a qualifying score for one year of early intervention services. Children can also be eligible for services based on an established condition or child and family risk factors.

According to the BDI-2, developmental quotients are used to compare one child's performance on the assessment with the performance of same-aged peers.

Adaptive: 85   **Communication:** 58   **Motor:** 75   **Personal-social:** 82
Cognitive: 80

Developmental Summary

This summary has been written in collaboration with George's parents and EI team. Clinical observations and information about the child's daily routines, usual behaviors, and typical responses are included to create a complete picture for this report. Relevant medical and social history are included as needed. (Assessment results for each domain can be shared below by using words to describe George's strengths and needs.)

Observations: George was excited to get started and eager to engage with the toys brought by the team. The curiosity George's mother mentioned as a strength was evident from the start of the evaluation as he began jumping up and down, yelling a bit, and saying "beep beep" when he noticed the toy car. He was very motivated by the car throughout the assessment and any time he had a hard time settling down, the car helped him refocus his attention. There were a few times George needed some breaks to jump or run, but overall, he refocused with some support.

George's mother shared that he tends to "run around all the time" and he doesn't really play with any one activity for very long. George was able to sit and look at a book with a lot of exaggerated voices and narration. He was not able to point to any of the animals in the book on demand, but he spontaneously said "moo" and "woof" appropriately for a cow and dog. George's mother and father said that he can point to certain characters from favorite shows, but he is usually not interested in sitting for books, so reading together isn't a familiar activity. The team noted several times when George needed several chances to hear a direction before he was able to carry out the activity—looking for three objects that were hidden, pointing to his parents and pet cat, and identifying body parts.

Because of the standardization of the test, George did not receive credit for following these directions on the test score; however, the team noted that George seemed to understand the language being used, but he had a difficult time calming down his body or attending to the person speaking. This appeared to be typical for George given his mother's reported concern regarding the library story hour and his inability to stay with familiar activities during the day. George did enjoy moving his body and demonstrated good balance skills and the ability to go up and down the stairs.

Again, because of George's inability to sit for long periods of time, it was difficult to assess his ability to use his hands, fingers, and eyes together. While having a snack, George used all of his fingers to pick up Cheerios. George did become upset when the Cheerios came out, and he pointed at the cabinet in his kitchen. His mother recalled her concern regarding George's inability to express what specific snacks he wants during the day. George did eventually settle and ate the Cheerios. George's father reported that his son does use a spoon, but "he usually spills more than he eats." He was observed drinking from an open cup, and his parents shared that they have not tried any version of an open cup because of how busy George can be.

When it was time to color, George was excited to use the crayons and stayed with these activities for longer than most. He was interested in scribbling, holding the crayon with his fingers, but he did not want to copy any shapes or lines. George's mother reported that she and George often color while they are waiting to pick up George's older brother from preschool. It seems to be an activity that he is comfortable with and enjoys. George asked for "more" when it was time to put the crayons away and said "yeah" when asked if he wanted to color more. George also said "Mama," "Dada," and "YoYo" (their cat's name). In total, George used fewer than 10 words and/or approximations throughout the assessments. There were no other words that his parents could recall George using on a regular basis.

Summary and recommendations: Because of George's scores in the communication and motor domain, he was determined eligible for early intervention services. George's mother and father felt the assessment team saw an accurate picture of George. He was at his typical energy level and acted how he usually does with familiar people. They did share that George had a rough night's sleep, but they didn't think it impacted the assessment. It is recommended that the information from this assessment be considered when discussing next steps for George. A list of activities on supporting George's communication skills and CDC's Milestone Tracker App were shared with the parents.

Family: (Print name[s], signature[s], and date)
Development specialist: (Print name, signature, and date)
Occupational therapist: (Print name, signature, and date)
Speech-language pathologist: (Print name, signature, and date)

Contact Information of the EI/ECSE Team
Development specialist: (Print name, e-mail, and day phone)
Occupational therapist: (Print name, e-mail, and day phone)
Speech-language pathologist: (Print name, e-mail, and day phone)

Appendix C
Sample Observation Form for the Family

Instructions: Dear family, please use this form to take notes during the assessment. Please carefully observe your child's behaviors and actions. Please write down any strengths and challenges that you observe today. Also, please write down any unfamiliar activity. Feel free to write in short phrases/sentences or bullet form. Thank you.

Strengths that I observe are ...

Challenges that I observe are ...

Unfamiliar, novice activities are ...

Please use the space below to provide any other details (e.g., examples of your child's vocabulary or emotions) that you would like to share with us. Thank you.

Note: The observation form is modified to fit into one-page because of page limitations.

6

Family-Centered Assessment of Young Children Who Are Refugees

SHERESA B. BLANCHARD
East Carolina University

SERRA ACAR
University of Massachusetts Boston

JENNIFER HURLEY
University of Vermont

KATRINA P. CUMMINGS
Simpson College

LILLIAN DURÁN
University of Oregon

Binod is a 4-year-old Bhutanese refugee whose family resettled in the United States three years ago from Eastern Nepal. Binod's mother, Asmita, and father, Chandra, spent 20 years in a refugee camp where they met, got married, and had three children: Binod, Asmita, and Chandra. They mainly speak Nepali, but they also speak Dzongkha and some English. Binod attends a Head Start preschool program five days per week.

According to the United Nations High Commission for Refugees (UNHCR, 2019), a refugee is someone who has been forced to flee their country because of persecution, war, or violence. Our world is experiencing the highest number of forcibly displaced people in history, with 25.4 million people—more than half children—fleeing persecution or conflict. If refugees are not allowed to resettle in other countries, they will experience violence, extreme hardship, and even death (UNHCR, 2019). Although some of the experiences and challenges faced by refugees are similar to those faced by immigrants, for the purpose of this article, we highlight issues that are particularly salient for the refugee population, which may be different due to being forced to flee, enduring extended stays in refugee camps and sometimes harsh treatment in the United States, and the likelihood of speaking a rare or low-incidence language. Despite a Presidential Executive Order (Executive Order No. 13,769, 2017) restricting the resettlement of refugees in the United States, refugee children and families from a variety of countries, including but not limited to Afghanistan, Bhutan, Burma, the Democratic Republic of Congo, Iraq, and Somalia, continue to live and work in the United States, contributing capabilities and strengths to U.S. communities and schools (Office of Refugee Resettlement, 2018).

Refugee families who resettle in the United States often have limited resources and are often provided with insufficient support for their transition. Forced to flee their homelands, frequently in the midst of toxic stress, trauma, and malnutrition, many refugee families with young children may spend years in refugee camps under difficult conditions, with poor nutrition and health care and little access to early childhood education and/or family support. Furthermore, many adults who are refugees or asylum seekers have a high percentage of emotional and social challenges resulting from exposure to traumatic events leading to probable posttraumatic stress disorder and other disorders that likely impact children under the same circumstances in similar and different ways as adults (Spiller et al., 2019).

Research indicates that quality early childhood education can support development and learning of children who are refugees (Golden & Fortuny, 2010). Furthermore, comprehensive services for family members can support the family functioning and capacity (Matthews & Ewen, 2010). We outline assessment considerations for refugee families that take into account sociohistorical factors as well as best practices (i.e., family-centered and culturally and linguistically responsive practices such as those in the Division for Early Childhood Recommended Practices [DEC, 2014]).

Refugee families who resettle in the United States often have limited resources and are often provided with insufficient support for their transition.

Understanding the Context

Crystal is an early childhood special educator working in a community rich with resettled refugees. She recently received a referral from Binod's Head Start program. They are concerned because even though Binod has been in class for a few months, he is not talking and seems behind on self-help skills such as feeding himself and putting on his coat. Crystal wonders how she can assess Binod in his native language when she does not speak Nepali or Dzongkha. She considers eliciting the help of a cultural liaison but knows that a cultural liaison alone will not lead to a quality assessment. What assessment tool has evidence of reliability and validity for Bhutanese children? What if the developmental milestones assessed and the toys used as part of the assessment are unfamiliar to Binod and his family?

Early intervention/early childhood special education (EI/ECSE) practitioners increasingly find themselves assessing children who are culturally and linguistically diverse. For most practitioners, assessing and documenting the strengths and needs of children who are dual language learners (DLLs) and/or multilanguage learners such as Binod, who speaks three languages at home, presents a significant challenge. In addition to language barriers, the lasting impact of the conditions that surround resettlement, such as toxic stress levels, malnutrition, living in poverty once in the United States, and the families' potential isolation from the community and support, can all negatively influence well-being and development (Cervantes, Ullrich, & Matthews, 2018; Schmidt, 2019). The purpose of this article is to provide assessment guidelines for practitioners who support the use of the DEC Recommended Practices while working with children who are refugees.

Diverse Refugee Backgrounds

The refugee population in the United States is becoming increasingly diverse. One of the assets that refugees bring to their new communities is the ability to speak, and perhaps read, more than one language with some of the most common being Arabic, Nepali, Somali, Sgaw Karen, Spanish, Kiswahili, Chaldean, Burmese, Armenian, and Kinyarwanda (Refugee Processing Center, 2019). In total more than 350 languages and dialects are spoken in the United States (United States Census Bureau, 2015). In addition to speaking a variety of languages, refugees speak regional variations of dominant languages, called dialects, that have distinct vocabulary and grammar. Importantly, refugees from the same country of origin do not necessarily speak the same language. Dual language or multilanguage learners might speak a rare language, referred to here as a low-incidence language (e.g., Oromo, Anuak, or Nuer), and this could be an additional challenge for children who are refugees because it may add additional complications to their parents' interactions with EI/ECSE practitioners in the resettlement countries (United States Census Bureau, 2015).

Families new to the United States may be unfamiliar with the EI/ECSE system and dealing with the effects of trauma from the immigration journey; in addition, there may not be an EI/ECSE system in their home country (Cummings & Hardin, 2016). Furthermore, effects of trauma can also linger and impact developmental outcomes (Schmidt, 2019). Additionally, EI/ECSE professionals could have difficulty securing adequate interpretation services in communities with small pockets of certain language groups. All of these challenges should be considered in the assessment process.

Assessment Considerations

There has been little systematic research on children who are refugees with disabilities in the United States (Graham, Minhas, & Paxton, 2016; Szente, Hoot, & Taylor, 2006). ECSE providers have shared that the assessment process for children who are refugees is challenging, and there is concern about eligibility determination because of language and cultural differences and a lack of assessment tools normed for children who are refugees (Hurley, Warren, Habalow, Weber, & Tousignant, 2014). Understanding the development of children who are refugees may require additional time and effort, especially because of trauma the child and family may have experienced. It often takes more time to build systematic collaborations with important stakeholders, such as cultural liaisons, interpreters, and extended family members.

The DEC Recommended Practices provide guidance and support for effective assessment practices with children who have diverse backgrounds. However, many practitioners will also need practical information about the unique circumstances of assessment with young children whose families are refugees and/or who speak low-incidence languages. Furthermore, additional difficulties exist, such as how to assess children in their home languages when technically adequate diagnostic assessments do not exist in languages other than Spanish, English, and simplified Chinese and how to thoughtfully consider how cultural differences in experience and child rearing might also influence a child's performance on standardized test measures. Importantly, most of the "toys" or "items" in an assessment kit may not be familiar to the child.

Currently, available assessment tools are not validated for use with children from many refugee backgrounds (Gadeberg, Montgomery, Frederiksen, & Norredam, 2017). This makes examining child development and learning a challenging process in families marginalized by culture, education level, language, and familiarity with the EI/ECSE system. Parents' education/literacy level in their native language and/or in English may also be a challenge during the assessment process. These issues may create difficulties in locating trained interpreters or translators and using tools that require parents to complete them.

> It is critically important that families are actively involved in providing information about their child's development and that they are given ample opportunities to describe their child's strengths and needs.

Guiding Policies

According to the Individuals with Disabilities Education Act (IDEA, 2004), assessments

> are provided and administered in the child's native language or other mode of communication and in the form most likely to yield accurate information on what the child knows and can do academically, developmentally, and functionally, unless it is clearly not feasible to so provide or administer. (§300.304)

The spirit of the law is to collect assessment data in the form most likely to yield accurate information. The DEC Recommended Practices translate law and research into practice by providing evidence-based recommendations relevant for children who are dual language learners.

Practitioners can conduct assessments, such as the Battelle Developmental Inventory-Second Edition (Bliss, 2007) or Bayley Scales of Infant and Toddler Development, Third Edition (BSID-III; Bayley, 2005), in more than 300 languages spoken in the United States, but they often must hire interpreters to assist with the process. Regularly, language items are not functionally equivalent across languages (Peña & Halle, 2011). For example, practitioners could consider how English items on an expressive language section of a test may be probing whether a child is using the present progressive "ing," the past tense "ed," or irregular past tense "come, came; run, ran." Obviously not all languages have an "ing" and "ed" or a different structure across tenses. Also, languages develop differently, and in assessment one would be looking for different markers for impairment based on the specific features of that language and the typical developmental sequence of specific morphosyntactic features in that language.

These important differences are not taken into consideration when practitioners translate a test verbatim. Without normative data in other languages to compare development, scores then become meaningless. Although practitioner translation of an existing measure is one solution, practitioners should not have confidence in the results. When a standardized instrument is administered in a nonstandardized manner, the standard scores are no longer valid (Stone-MacDonald, Pizzo, & Feldman, 2018). This is why it is critically important that families are actively involved in providing information about their child's development and that they are given ample opportunities to describe their child's strengths and needs from their perspective. EI/ECSE practitioners also need to conduct observations in natural settings and work with an interpreter to better understand that child's functioning.

For families to be more actively involved in the assessment process, it is critically important to update families about their rights and EI/ECSE laws and regulations in the United States. Procedural Safeguards is a section of IDEA that outlines rights and the protections parents have. These assure that parents have an important role in planning and decision-making for their child. Providing handbooks, recorded webinars, question-and-answer sessions, and parent-to-parent support groups, all in families' native language, can be helpful to inform parents about the EI/ECSE services in their resettled states. The provision of such EI/ECSE services to families and children who are refugees is complicated, with challenging factors such as the shortage of bilingual, trained staff and licensed EI/ECSE practitioners; a lack of confidence in working with children who are refugees; and the use of assessment tools with limited validity with refugee populations (Banerjee & Luckner, 2014; Lee, Ostrosky, Bennett, & Fowler, 2003).

Given the unique sociohistorical experiences and linguistic differences of refugee families, practitioners need authentic assessment and alternative approaches for gathering critical data to make an informed decision about a child's need for special education services. The following section will outline an information-gathering process that can be used to evaluate children who are refugees broadly because there is no one-size-fits-all approach to the evaluation of the diverse range of young children in the United States. Table 1 summarizes four

Table 1
Connections: DEC Recommended Practices and Binod's Story

Relevant DEC Recommended Practices	Examples of practices from Binod's story
A3. Practitioners use assessment materials and strategies that are appropriate for the child's age and level of development and accommodate the child's sensory, physical, communication, cultural, linguistic, social, and emotional characteristics. **A5.** Practitioners conduct assessments in the child's dominant language and in additional languages if the child is learning more than one language. **A6.** Practitioners use a variety of methods, including observation and interviews, to gather assessment information from multiple sources, including the child's family and other significant individuals in the child's life. **A8.** Practitioners use clinical reasoning in addition to assessment results to identify the child's current levels of functioning and to determine the child's eligibility and plan for instruction.	• Programwide information gathering for all children (screening). • Information-gathering survey in primary language. • Record review of Binod's hearing, vision, and medical records. • Observations of Binod across time, settings, peers, and adults. • A cultural liaison is part of the team and serves as a resource. This person may be able to participate in several ways, including language interpretation in conversations, translation of documents from English to family's preferred language, and provision of cultural information and interaction recommendations. • Team members do research to learn more about the family's culture before home visits. • Home visits with the cultural liaison along with a member of the assessment team. • Interpretation of developmental milestones in tandem with consideration of cultural norms.

Assessment recommended practices and examples from how they apply to learning more about Binod's life.

1. Gather referral information. Practitioners should have medical records, hearing and eye exams, information from the child's current preschool or child care provider, and a thorough explanation of the reason for referral (A3, A6, A8).

Binod's Head Start program conducts hearing and vision screenings and maintains a copy of Binod's medical records. This information, in addition to ongoing observations from Binod's Head Start teacher, is shared with Crystal at the time of referral. Observations occurred across time, settings, peers, and adults to develop a deeper and broader repertoire regarding Binod's strengths and needs.

2. Interpreter. The team also will need to locate and train interpreters (Acar & Blasco, 2018). The interpreter should receive training in the assessments that will be administered to improve accuracy for delivery of the assessment protocol and the scoring. Binod's program follows a culturally and linguistically responsive approach to support child and family outcomes. For instance, they ask family members if there is a need for an interpreter/translator to facilitate verbal and written communication with the family and to complete the family survey. This simple question also provides some background information on the language dominance and proficiency of the main caregivers (A5).

Even though Binod's parents speak some English, his mother and father feel more comfortable with an interpreter. Crystal's ECSE program works with a variety of cultural liaisons who are members of various refugee communities from the area and typically serve as a bridge between cultures through functioning effectively cross-culturally in communication, social norms, and cultural knowledge. When there is a rarely spoken language, it may be difficult to find a licensed, trained interpreter, so in these cases a cultural liaison can serve as an interpreter and a person who connects both cultures. Crystal is referred to Phul, a cultural liaison, who is also a Bhutanese refugee and a respected member of the community able to provide interpretation and translation services.

3. Initial meeting in natural environment such as home. EI/ECSE practitioners must work harder to develop practices that not only foster strong relationships with, and participation from, families who are refugees but also honor and draw from the cultural and linguistic capital that they possess. One way to make this shift is by engaging with refugee families on their territory where their cultural and linguistic capital are likely to be accessible (A6; Hurley et al., 2014).

Crystal and Phul work together to call Binod's family to arrange for a home visit. Binod and his family have visited Binod's Head Start classroom, but this will be their first meeting with Crystal, who is conducting the assessment for ECSE services. Crystal hopes that scheduling a home visit will provide an opportunity to observe Binod in a context where his family is comfortable and able to discuss and share Binod's strengths. Crystal has learned that during the first visit, the family may not feel comfortable enough to share everything. She realizes additional visits may be necessary to more fully understand Binod's development in context and the family's perspective.

4. Culture-specific practices. While engaging with families, EI/ECSE practitioners should observe for and research deep cultural practices (e.g., patterns of interaction, child guidance strategies, or learning modalities [Chan, 2011; Hedegaard, 2009]). Practitioners can increase their knowledge regarding a specific culture by observing parents' explicit and implicit feedback patterns and daily routines. Culture is fluid (Chan, 2011); therefore, it will be important to observe family-specific patterns of behavior during home visits. Careful attention to family-specific behaviors will help alleviate the potential for stereotypes. EI/ECSE practitioners can increase their knowledge by reading about the family's country of origin and culture (Acar & Blasco, 2018). For instance, they can become more familiar with the history of a family and what their exodus may have been like from their country of origin. In addition, providers can learn about daily routines unique to a family's culture, such as taking off your shoes before entering the house, waiting to be seated, or learning how to refuse food in a home visit without offending the family.

> "
>
> Practitioners can increase their knowledge regarding a specific culture by observing parents' explicit and implicit feedback patterns and daily routines.

Crystal prepares for meeting Binod's family by doing some online research about the history of Bhutanese refugees. She also learns from Phul about etiquette when visiting the home of a family from Nepal, such as the importance of removing shoes at the door and that while in America it might be acceptable to pat children on the head, it is considered rude in Bhutanese culture. Crystal reminds herself that she wants to avoid stereotypes and that all families are unique. She wants to visit Binod's family with an understanding of their etiquette and history.

5. Family interview. Practitioners should contact the child's family, with the assistance of an interpreter, and conduct a thorough family interview to more fully understand whether they have any concerns regarding their child's development. Practitioners should learn more about the child's functioning during daily routines and communication patterns in their home language (A5, A6). When possible and as appropriate, information about the family's resettlement can be gathered during the family interview. It is important to probe, when possible, to gather details that will help build a picture of the child's developmental course, with the sociohistorical journey of the family in mind. For example, how might the social norms, sleeping quarters, or understanding of their new status in the United States intersect with the child's language and motor skills?

> It is important to probe, when possible, to gather details that will help build a picture of the child's developmental course, with the sociohistorical journey of the family in mind.

Binod's Head Start program collects information on child and family background for each child enrolled in the program. The program director collaborates with local cultural organizations for interpretation and translation purposes. Family members are asked to fill out a short survey that includes items such as "Tell us about your child's likes, interests, strengths, and dislikes" and "What are your concerns, priorities, and resources regarding your child's development and learning?" Binod's Head Start teacher reviews this information carefully to make better instructional decisions in her classroom and shares the information with Crystal when making her referral (A3, A6, A8).

6. Language exposure. Practitioners need to determine how much both the home language and English are used throughout daily routines (e.g., through a home language survey; A3, A6, A8). The items on the survey can be administered by written format or verbally, with assistance from interpreters or cultural liaisons. Like cultural capital, the linguistic capital of families is often overlooked, even though language is the foundation of learning and development (Vygotsky, 1978). Foremost, EI/ECSE practitioners must work to alleviate challenges or misunderstandings during assessment that could be linked to language differences between them and families.

Based on results of the home language survey, Crystal knows that Binod's family speaks Nepali, Dzongkha, and English, but they mostly speak Nepali or Dzongkha at home. She plans to observe language use and communication patterns during routines in forthcoming home visits.

7. Assessment plan and administration. Practitioners should develop an evaluation plan that includes an emphasis on measurement in the child's language (all languages if possible) and multiple sources of data such as observations in natural settings, parent and teacher reports, medical reports, and descriptive performances on standardized assessments translated and adapted into their home language, when available (A6, A8).

When Crystal and Phul arrive, they see Binod kicking a ball around with some other children in the park next to the home. Binod runs from the park and proudly shows Crystal a kite he built, and Crystal notes the detailed fine-motor work. Crystal begins to ask Asmita about the routines of Binod's day and learns that a satisfying part of Asmita's day is when she dresses Binod and feeds him by hand. Noting the concerned expression on Crystal's face, Phul explains that many Bhutanese families feed their children by hand until they are 4 and make a practice of assisting with dressing. Asmita shares her worry that it is hard to understand what Binod is trying to say, and she can only understand a few of the words he uses in Nepali. Asmita shares that Binod's siblings learned to speak Nepali, Dzongkha, and English with ease. After interviewing Binod's family about his routines and considering his development in relation to what Asmita shared about his siblings, Crystal realizes that the concerns about Binod's self-help skills may not be warranted. After seeing Binod in his home with a cultural liaison and Binod's mother, Crystal has a better understanding of his strengths and needs and realizes that Binod's expressive language is a concern that may warrant an evaluation as well as the inclusion of a speech-language pathologist on the team.

Next Steps

Once the assessment process is complete, the team should meet to review all data from multiple sources to make an informed decision about the child's eligibility. The team needs to ensure the child's family is fully informed of the results and has the opportunity to comment. If not reporting standard scores as part of the rationale for their decision on eligibility, practitioners can use a statement such as:

> The standard assessment tools used with the majority of children were not used with this child because the instrument was not normed on bilingual children who speak languages other than English. Such norm-referenced scores are not considered valid for this child. The objective data used to conclude that this child has a disability and is

in need of special education included parent comments, Head Start teacher comments, developmental data, medical records, observation of the child in the home/school setting, the child's responses to items from standardized instruments used with young children, and comparison of his/her skill development with that of peers from the same culture.

Conclusion

This article extends our understanding of culturally responsive assessment practices (Banerjee & Guiberson, 2012) to include considerations for families of young children who are refugees and also extends our understandings for this population through a vignette following Binod, his family, and the early childhood team. The lens through which we work with children and families who are refugees has great bearing on assessment practices (Friesen, Hanson, & Martin, 2015). For some time, we have advocated for building family partnerships (Ramirez, 2001) and family-centered practices (Dunst, 2002). Such approaches embody relational and participatory principles that lay the foundation for working with families. However, they do not explicitly address distal forces that shape the outcomes of parent-teacher relationships and participation, which often disenfranchise children and families who are refugees. This article attempts to highlight some of the critical forces that impact refugee families within the EI/ECSE assessment process and propose ways that practitioners might engage in more equitable assessment practices.

To gain more pertinent information about Binod's development and take his family's culture and language into account, Crystal used several strategies, including:

- *Gathering care provider perspectives on strengths and needs to undergird decisions and observations of the child before making decisions about the child's developmental priorities.*
- *Taking the time to research the child's country of origin and the refugee experience for families from specific countries.*
- *Working with an interpreter or cultural liaison to learn more about etiquette and culturally relevant developmental milestones throughout the assessment process.*
- *Choosing the best available assessment tool and supporting it with non-standardized methods that allow for parent-provider input reflecting the development of the child within their culture.*
- *Visiting the child in their natural environment, such as their home, and in the context of care providers to get the most accurate picture of the child's strengths and needs.*
- *Collaborating with multiple team members who are knowledgeable about the child, such as the classroom teacher and caregivers.*
- *Sharing results with the parents and seeking parental input regarding the accuracy of her preliminary findings.*

Crystal reflects that as the cultural and linguistic diversity in her community continues to increase, being able to provide culturally appropriate assessments will become a more pertinent practice.

References

Acar, S., & Blasco, P. (2018). Guidelines for collaborating with interpreters in early intervention/ early childhood special education. *Young Exceptional Children, 21*, 170–184. doi:10.1177/1096250616674516

Banerjee, R., & Guiberson, M. (2012). Evaluating young children from culturally and linguistically diverse backgrounds for special education services. *Young Exceptional Children, 15*, 33–45. doi:10.1177/1096250611435368

Banerjee, R., & Luckner, J. (2014). Training needs of early childhood professionals who work with children and families who are culturally and linguistically diverse. *Infants & Young Children, 27*, 43–59. doi:10.1097/IYC.0000000000000000

Bayley, N. (2005). *Bayley scales of infant and toddler development* (3rd ed.). San Antonio: TX: Psychological.

Bliss, S. L. (2007). Test reviews: Newborg, J. (2005). Battelle Developmental Inventory–Second Edition. Itasca, IL: Riverside. *Journal of Psychoeducational Assessment, 25*, 409–415. doi:10.1177/0734282907300382

Cervantes, W., Ullrich, R., & Matthews, H. (2018). *Our children's fear: Immigration policy's effects on young children*. Washington, DC: Center for Law and Social Policy.

Chan, A. (2011). Critical multiculturalism: Supporting early childhood teachers to work with diverse immigrant families. *International Research in Early Childhood Education, 2*, 63–74.

Cummings, K. P., & Hardin, B. J. (2016). Navigating disability and related services: Stories of immigrant families. *Early Child Development and Care, 187*, 115–127. doi:10.1080/03004430.2016.1152962

Division for Early Childhood. (2014). *DEC recommended practices in early intervention/early childhood special education 2014*. Retrieved from https://www.dec-sped.org/dec-recommended-practices

Dunst, C. J. (2002). Family-centered practices: Birth through high school. *The Journal of Special Education, 36*, 141–149. doi:10.1177/00224669020360030401

Exec. Order No. 13,769, 3 C.F.R. 8,977 (2017).

Friesen, A., Hanson, M., & Martin, K. (2015). In the eyes of the beholder: Cultural considerations in interpreting children's behaviors. *Young Exceptional Children, 18*, 19–30. doi:10.1177/1096250614535222

Gadeberg, A. K., Montgomery, E., Frederiksen, H. W., & Norredam, M. (2017). Assessing trauma and mental health in refugee children and youth: A systematic review of validated screening and measurement tools. *European Journal of Public Health, 27*, 439–446. doi:10.1093/eurpub/ckx034

Golden, O., & Fortuny, K. (2010). *Young children of immigrants and the path to educational success: Key themes from an Urban Institute roundtable*. Washington, DC: Urban Institute.

Graham, H. R., Minhas, R. S., & Paxton, G. (2016). Learning problems in children of refugee background: A systematic review. *Pediatrics, 137*(6), e20153994. doi:10.1542/peds.2015-3994.

Hedegaard, M. (2009). Children's development from a cultural-historical approach: Children's activity in everyday local settings as foundation for their development. *Mind, Culture, and Activity, 16,* 64–82. doi:10.1080/10749030802477374

Hurley, J. J., Warren, R. A., Habalow, R. D., Weber, L. E. & Tousignant, S. R. (2014). Early childhood special education in a refugee resettlement community: Challenges and innovative practices. *Early Child Development and Care, 184,* 50–62. doi:10.1080/03004430.2013.769214

Individuals With Disabilities Education Act, 20 U.S.C. § 1400 (2004).

Lee, H., Ostrosky, M. M., Bennett, T., & Fowler, S. A. (2003). Perspectives of early intervention professionals about culturally-appropriate practices. *Journal of Early Intervention, 25,* 281–295. doi:10.1177/105381510302500404

Matthews, H., & Ewen, D. (2010). *Early education programs and children of immigrants: Learning each other's language.* Washington, DC: Urban Institute.

Office of Refugee Resettlement. (2018, June 14). Office of Refugee Resettlement annual report to Congress 2016. Retrieved from https://www.acf.hhs.gov/orr/resource/office-of-refugee-resettlement-annual-report-to-congress-2016

Peña, E. D., & Halle, T. G. (2011). Assessing preschool dual language learners: Traveling a multiforked road. *Child Development Perspectives, 5,* 28–32. doi:10.1111/j.1750-8606.2010.00143.x

Refugee Processing Center. (2019, September 30). Top 10 languages spoken by arrived refugees. Retrieved from http://www.wrapsnet.org/admissions-and-arrivals

Ramirez, A. Y. (2001). Parents as our allies: Creating parent partnerships. *The Journal of Adventist Education, 63*(4), 23–29.

Schmidt, L. M. (2019). Trauma in English learners: Examining the influence of previous trauma and PTSD on English learners and within the classroom. *TESOL Journal, 10,* e00412. doi:10.1002/tesj.412

Spiller, R. R., Liddell, B. J., Schick, M., Morina, N., Schnyder, U., Pfaltz, M., . . . Nickerson, A. (2019). Emotional reactivity, emotion regulation capacity, and posttraumatic stress disorder in traumatized refugees: An experimental investigation. *Journal of Traumatic Stress, 32,* 32–41. doi:10.1002/jts.22371

Stone-MacDonald, A., Pizzo, L., & Feldman, N. (2018). *Fidelity of implementation in assessment of infants and toddlers: Evaluating developmental milestones and outcomes.* Cham, Switzerland: Springer International.

Szente, J., Hoot, J., & Taylor, D. (2006). Responding to the special needs of refugee children: Practical ideas for teachers. *Early Childhood Education Journal, 34,* 15–20. doi:10.1007/s10643-006-0082-2

United Nations High Commission for Refugees. (2019). Refugees. Retrieved March 7, 2019, from https://www.unhcr.org/pages/49c3646c125.html

United States Census Bureau. (2015, November 3). Census Bureau reports at least 350 languages spoken in U.S. homes. Retrieved from https://www.census.gov/newsroom/press-releases/2015/cb15-185.html

Vygotsky, L. S. (1978). *Mind in society: The development of higher psychological processes.* Cambridge, MA: Harvard University Press.

7

The Roadmap for Assessing Meaningful Participation
Gathering Information, Participation-Based Assessment, and IFSP Development

DATHAN RUSH
KRIS EVERHART
SARAH SEXTON
Family, Infant and Preschool Program

M'LISA SHELDEN
Wichita State University

Ethan is a 19-month-old boy who enjoys spinning the wheels on his Tonka trucks and holding spatulas, one in each hand, as he runs around his house. Ethan's parents, Simon and Ericka, used to wonder if the day would ever come when Ethan would finally walk. They were overjoyed two months ago when Ethan let go of the couch and took his first steps. Now, just eight weeks later, he runs, climbs, and moves around his home all the time. His father says only two things make Ethan stop moving. One is when Ethan's favorite show comes on the television, and the other is when someone sings a song. Given Ethan's interest in moving, it wasn't long before Ethan discovered the kitchen cabinets and subsequently uncovered his love for spatulas. Ericka says, "It is just his thing. He likes to hold them and carry them everywhere." Ethan also loves his bath time. In fact, Ethan loves his bath so much that when it is time to get out he shares his displeasure with such intensity that Simon and Ericka are sure their neighbors two doors down can hear Ethan's protests. Ethan also shares his displeasure with diaper changes and getting dressed. Simon and Ericka jokingly try to pass the responsibility for bath, dressing, and diaper duty between themselves. They worry that Ethan's reactions are more intense than most toddlers.

At Ethan's 18-month checkup, his pediatrician completed a screening and expressed concerns regarding Ethan's development. The pediatrician asked Ethan's parents about his communication and interaction at home. Simon and Ericka shared with the pediatrician that Ethan sometimes acts as if he cannot hear them when they call his name and that even though he makes lots of sounds, he isn't yet using any words. A referral was made to the local early intervention program while Ethan's parents anxiously awaited support.

Introduction

Gathering information in real-life contexts (i.e., bath time, diaper changes, getting dressed) to support a child's interest-based participation across everyday activities with responsive caregivers is critical to providing early intervention services in accordance with the DEC Recommended Practices (Division for Early Childhood [DEC], 2014). Many programs and practitioners recognize the importance of this information, and several different tools and methods for gathering essential information from families have been developed (Fettig, Barton, Carter, & Eisenhower, 2016; McWilliam, Casey, & Sims, 2009; Woods & Lindeman, 2008). The information-gathering process, however, should also include a participation-based assessment (PBA). Participation-based assessment occurs after a child has been determined eligible for the early intervention program but prior to development of the Individualized Family Service Plan (IFSP). The PBA helps to inform the development of meaningful, participation-based IFSP outcomes (Shelden & Rush, 2014) because the practitioner can see the caregiver and child engaged in a typical activity (e.g., mealtime, toothbrushing) that illustrates the need for change or improvement. In some situations, the practitioner and caregiver even try specific intervention strategies to inform them about what might work best for intervention.

The research and recommendations for use of everyday activities and child interests (i.e., people, objects, and happenings that hold the child's attention) as the context for intervention, promotion of caregiver responsiveness, and implementation of a coaching interaction style are plentiful (Akamoglu & Dinnebeil, 2017; American Occupational Therapy Association, 2013; American Physical Therapy Association, 2008; American Speech-Language-Hearing Association, 2008; DEC, 2014; Dunn, Cox, Foster, Mische-Lawson, & Tanquary, 2012; Dunst, Bruder, & Espe-Sherwindt, 2014; Dunst, Bruder, Trivette, & Hamby, 2006; Friedman, Woods, & Salisbury, 2012; Rush & Shelden, 2011; Salisbury et al, 2018; Swanson, Raab, & Dunst, 2011; Workgroup on Principles and Practices in Natural Environments, 2008).

Many early intervention practitioners, however, struggle in their attempts to systematically use these practices in their daily work (Campbell & Sawyer, 2007). The difficulty of translating research findings to the everyday practice of early intervention providers negatively impacts practitioner competence and child and family outcomes.

The Roadmap for Assessing Meaningful Participation provides a culturally sensitive, unbiased process for information-gathering, participation-based assessment, and IFSP development.

Implementation Science

The field of implementation science (Fixsen, Naoom, Blase, Friedman, & Wallace, 2005) has helped administrators and teams understand the conditions under which practices and innovations are most likely to be adopted with fidelity. Innovations based on research take time and energy to be implemented reliably enough to result in the intended outcomes. Some estimates calculate that it can take up to 17 years for practices to be implemented with even a marginal degree of reliability (Balas & Boren, 2000, Fixsen, Blase, Metz, & van Dyke, 2013). Several possible reasons for the disparity exist at both the systems level (e.g., lack of acceptance or involvement by management and insufficient organizational resources, infrastructure, and supports) and the practitioner level (e.g., lack of practitioner buy-in, practitioner inertia). One possible reason for practitioner inertia (overcoming the tendency to continue a current set of practices) is that it takes practitioners too long to move from awareness to implementation after having participated in a training. Even conscientious, dedicated providers are not immune to the research-to-practice gap. Fixsen et al. (2013) estimate that it can take up to three years for a team of practitioners focused on an initiative to develop competence and confidence with using the innovation. During that time, many practitioners can become disheartened with the struggle to be more competent and supplant or abandon innovations with old practices, diluting the potential positive effects.

Operationalization is the critical link between research and practice. Attending to how practitioners move from knowledge to practice may narrow the gap. Fixsen et al. (2013) note that in the absence of effective implementation, even the most effective intervention will not result in intended outcomes. This article presents a framework that operationalizes a process practitioners can use to collect information about child interests, family routines, and family priorities to inform the development of authentic child and family outcomes that set the stage for natural learning environment practices (i.e., everyday activities, child interests, and caregiver responsiveness).

The Roadmap for Assessing Meaningful Participation (RAMP; Family, Infant and Preschool Program [FIPP], 2014a) bridges the research-to-practice gap by providing a culturally sensitive, unbiased process for information-gathering, participation-based assessment, and IFSP development as described in the DEC Recommended Practices.

Overview of the RAMP

The RAMP assists in operationalizing the requirements of Individuals With Disabilities Education Act (IDEA), Part C, which differentiates evaluation and assessment (IDEA, 2004). The RAMP also addresses the literature supporting the use of authentic assessment techniques rather than solely relying on conventional testing as part of the evaluation or diagnostic procedures, which has dominated the "mismeasurement" (Neisworth & Bagnato, 2004, p. 198) of young children and failed to meet the intended purposes of early intervention and the needs of the child (Bagnato, 2005; Bagnato, Goins, Pretti-Frontczak, & Neisworth, 2014; Neisworth & Bagnato, 2004). Early intervention calls for assessment processes

Selected Assessment Recommended Practices

A1. Practitioners work with the family to identify family preferences for assessment processes.

A2. Practitioners work as a team with the family and other professionals to gather assessment information.

A4. Practitioners conduct assessments that include all areas of development and behavior to learn about the child's strengths, needs, preferences, and interests.

A6. Practitioners use a variety of methods, including observation and interviews, to gather assessment information from multiple sources, including the child's family and other significant individuals in the child's life.

A7. Practitioners obtain information about the child's skills in daily activities, routines, and environments such as home, center, and community.

that gather real-life competencies in everyday settings (e.g., snack time, putting toys away, going to the mailbox). Bagnato (2005) emphasizes that assessments for young children should focus on capturing the authenticity of children's functional capabilities within the contexts they occur, enable practitioners to plan and evaluate the effectiveness of individualized goals (utility), and incorporate a process that can be universally applied for all children regardless of their abilities.

The RAMP is a step-by-step process for assisting early intervention team members in gathering critical information about the child's interests and the family's everyday activities and priorities, conducting a PBA within at least one of the family's real-life contexts, and developing participation-based IFSP outcomes and strategies that match the family's natural contexts. The RAMP can be used with all children regardless of functional capabilities and limitations and is naturally individualized to each family's routines and priorities regardless of culture.

The RAMP is unique for a number of reasons. The RAMP collects information about all three characteristics of natural learning environment practices necessary for effective intervention (Campbell & Sawyer, 2007; Davis, 2014; Dunst et al., 2014; Dunst, Raab, & Hamby, 2016). The RAMP includes roadmaps (FIPP, 2014a, pp. 5–7) for coaching conversations used by an early intervention team member to obtain and share information (Akamoglu & Dinnebeil, 2017; Dunn, Little, Pope, & Wallisch, 2018; Graham, Rodger, & Ziviani, 2013; Rush & Shelden, 2011). The roadmaps are not scripts but rather serve as a diagram, outline, or flow chart for the coaching conversation the provider has with the family.

The roadmaps include the five research-based characteristics of a coaching interaction style (Rush & Shelden, 2011) embedded to systematically gather information across all areas of development and focus on the child's and family's strengths, priorities, interests, and preferences (A4). Roadmaps are color-coded based on the purpose of each step in the coaching conversation (e.g., green boxes represent reflective questions, yellow boxes indicate use of informative feedback or joint brainstorming, blue boxes are actions to be taken, and pink circles are for planning next steps). The roadmaps operationalize the use of a jargon-free, collaborative, family-friendly, culturally sensitive conversation format and rely on a combination of contextualized observations and information provided by informed and familiar caregivers in the child's life (A6, A7; Bagnato, 2005; Bagnato et al., 2014).

Also unique to the RAMP is that it provides an opportunity for a practitioner to observe the family, other caregivers, and the child within a real-life activity/ routine in which the family or child care provider needs support. The RAMP enables practitioners to immediately identify strategies that might successfully promote the child's participation in an activity and inform IFSP development. Using the RAMP assists in the development of participation-based IFSP outcomes resulting from the information gathered to date from the family and participation-based assessment. Finally, use of the RAMP allows for immediate parent-implemented interventions as well as a plan for the first service visit following development of the IFSP.

Use of the RAMP

Part I: Gathering Information

Part I is the initial conversation to identify family priorities for child learning and activity/routines in which opportunities for the priorities occur. This part of the process also helps determine successful responsive strategies (i.e., offering choices, getting on the child's level, talking in a pleasant voice) used by the family in existing activities and analyze what works or does not work and why. This conversation may also reveal additional information about child interests, other activities, and caregiver responsiveness. The first interaction is intended to gather information about the family's priorities related to the child's participation in a family or community activity and challenges or barriers the family is experiencing because of the child's present level of development. The conversation typically begins when a family member expresses what he/she wants for the child (e.g., "I want my child to walk," "I want my child to talk," "I want my child be able to sleep through the night").

The team member gathering the information then asks what the family has already tried that has worked or not. This may be followed by a brief explanation about how young children learn needed skills. The team member also asks about child interests and daily activities and routines that would likely provide opportunities for the child to participate (i.e., engage meaningfully) in ways that address the family's priority. If the family is unsure, then the team member can divert from the roadmap to the Interest Assessment (see sidebar) and Activity Setting Assessment (FIPP, 2014b, p. 3), which provide a more systematic exploration of typical family routines and associated child.

In accordance with Assessment recommended practice A2 and professional standards for authentic assessment (Bagnato et al., 2014), the RAMP is to be used by an early intervention team that includes the family, a team member functioning as service coordinator, and potential service provider(s) who would participate alongside the family in the participation-based assessment. The RAMP Part I conversation ends with a plan to identify a member or members of the early intervention team to conduct the PBA by observing the child and family or other caregiver during an everyday activity or routine the family has prioritized as a challenge or potential opportunity for the child to learn the desired skills. Ideally, the team members conducting the eligibility evaluation and participation-based assessment would be the same and one could potentially serve as the primary service provider if this model of teaming interaction is used by the program. If not, then these individuals could likely be service providers, but no decision is made about service delivery until the IFSP service delivery portion of the RAMP.

If the child has a delay or diagnosis that automatically qualifies him/her for the early intervention program, then the team should be able to proceed directly to Part II of the RAMP and any needed information at that point can be collected during the participation-based assessment. Children who are not automatically eligible will require an evaluation to determine whether the child meets the program eligibility criteria. The information gained from RAMP Part I can still be beneficial even if a child is determined ineligible because it may be used during

Interest Assessment

To gather more information about child interest, consider asking the following prompts to help the parent think more broadly:

- What makes him/her smile?

- What excites him/her?

- What makes him/her laugh?

- Where does he/she choose to spend his/her time?

- What keeps him/her interested?

- What keeps his/her attention?

the ineligibility conversation to support the family in determining how to further promote the child's development using interest-based everyday routines and activities outside the early intervention system.

Three days after their trip to the pediatrician, Simon and Ericka received a phone call from Thomas. Thomas introduced himself as an early intervention service coordinator and indicated the program had received a referral for Ethan. After talking about the program and gathering some initial identifying information, Thomas explained that he would like to meet with the family to gather more information about their priorities for Ethan's participation in family life and everyday activities. Thomas welcomed Simon and Ericka to consider and be prepared to share their successes as well as any challenges or barriers they faced because of Ethan's present level of development. Thomas, Simon, and Ericka scheduled a visit at the family's home the following week.

When Thomas arrived for the first visit, he reviewed the necessary early intervention program enrollment documentation and then began gathering information using Part 1 of the RAMP (A2; FIPP, 2014a, p. 5). Simon and Ericka said they wanted Ethan to "talk." Thomas, using a coaching interaction style and the RAMP Part I roadmap, discovered Simon and Ericka had already been doing many things to support Ethan's communication, including talking to him more slowly, repeating words, and praising Ethan when he followed simple directions such as putting garbage in the trash bin. Thomas also learned more about Ethan. Simon and Ericka listed Ethan's interests, including music, singing, water, climbing, helping, his favorite television show, and, of course, his spatulas. Thomas shared information with Ethan's parents about the importance of using Ethan's interests paired with their responsive parenting strategies during the family's typical routines and interactions in supporting Ethan's communication.

As he continued to organize information and coordinate the events for an effective participation-based assessment, Thomas learned that Ericka and Simon were most interested in supporting Ethan's communication and participation during diaper changes, getting dressed, and bath time because these activities were the most challenging for them. Thomas then explained that the next step would be to document Ethan's eligibility and then to arrange an observation of Ethan, Simon, and Ericka engaged in one of the activities they had just identified as a priority (A4, A6). Simon and Ericka chose dressing as the activity to be observed and scheduled the participation-based assessment at the time Ethan typically finishes his breakfast and gets dressed for the day (A1). Thomas used the information from RAMP Part I to thoroughly prepare the rest of the team for the upcoming participation-based assessment.

Part II: Observing and Assessing Meaningful Participation

The intent of RAMP Part II (FIPP, 2014a, p. 6), the participation-based assessment, is to observe the family or other caregivers and child within the context of a typical activity related to one of the family priorities (A6, A7). This process supports analyzing what works or does not work and why, developing alternative activities and responsive strategies that support child interest and learning and/or modifying existing activities and strategies. This part of the RAMP also involves observing the family and child trying the alternatives as part of the immediate activity and then evaluating the new strategies.

Based on the evaluation results, Ethan was determined eligible for Part C services. Ethan, his parents, Thomas, and the rest of the team proceeded with RAMP Part II, which would begin with an observation of the dressing routine previously identified by Ethan's family as a priority. The participation-based assessment is facilitated by a team member who could be selected as the best person (long-term view) to provide ongoing supports. Shanice, the speech-language pathologist that served on Ethan's evaluation team, joined Thomas, Ethan, and his parents during Ethan's typical dressing time to complete the participation-based assessment.

Shanice observed Ethan's dressing routine, used the roadmap in RAMP Part II to guide her conversation with Ethan's parents, and made notes about her observations and their discussion in the RAMP workbook (A4, A6, A7; FIPP, 2014b).

Ericka pulled off Ethan's pajama top and bottoms and then laid him down on a blanket to change his diaper before attempting to get him dressed in his shirt and pants. Ethan protested very strongly during his diaper change. Ericka tried to calm him by talking to him using a soft voice. Once the new diaper was on, Ethan rolled to his belly still clutching his spatulas, jumped up, and ran out of the room and down the hall.

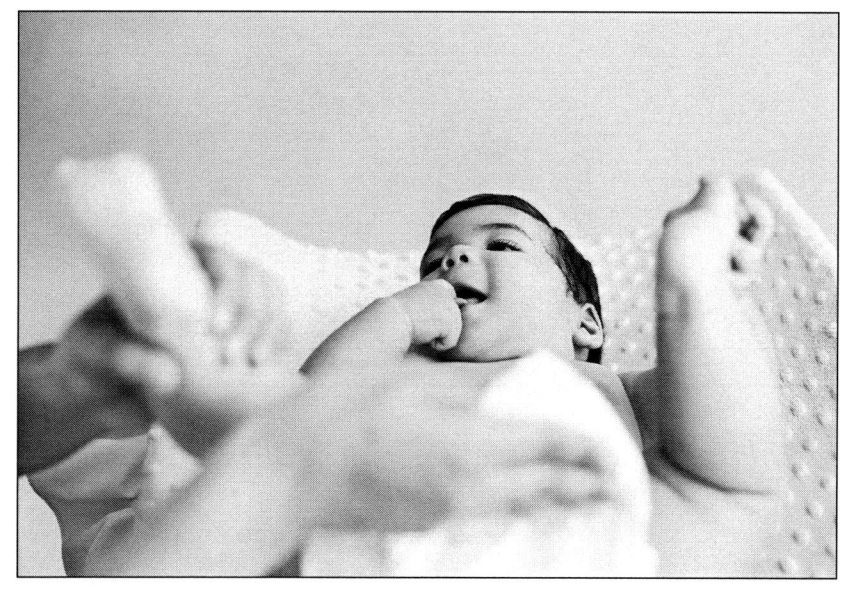

As Ericka got up to follow, Shanice asked how what she had just observed matched what typically happens during this activity (see Box A in FIPP, 2014a, p. 6). Ericka indicated Ethan's response was "always like this" during diaper changes and when she is trying to get him dressed. Ericka picked Ethan up and brought him back to the room so she could finish getting him dressed. Ericka asked Ethan to let go of his spatulas so she could get his shirt on. She was face to face with Ethan as he stood in front of her, and she pulled the shirt over his head. Ethan assisted by putting his arms through the sleeves, and Ericka gave him his spatulas back as he completed the task. She looked at Shanice, mouthing the words "here it comes…" as she laid him down to slide his pants on. Ethan again became very upset, and once his pants were on, he rolled to his belly and once more took off running and crying out of the room with spatulas in hand.

Shanice continued to use the RAMP Part II to guide the assessment and her use of a coaching interaction style. Shanice asked Ericka to reflect on what she thought worked during the activity to support Ethan's participation and communication (see Box B in FIPP, 2014a, p. 6). Ericka indicated she thought Ethan liked handing her his spatulas and then getting them right back after his arms were through his shirtsleeves. She added that she knows Ethan likes to be a helper and that maybe he could help more during dressing by picking out his clothes for the day or his pajamas at bedtime. Shanice asked Ericka to consider what Ethan might have an opportunity to say during this routine. Ericka thought for a moment and said, "maybe he could tell me what shirt he wants, say 'here you go' when he hands me his spatulas, or say 'all done' when we are finished." Shanice then asked Ericka to reflect on what she thought did not work (see Box B in FIPP, 2014a, p. 6). Ericka said she thought what upsets Ethan is having to lie down on his back. She went on to say she could try letting Ethan stand and even pull up his pants independently. Shanice shared the responsive strategies she noticed Ericka already using (speaking with a calm voice, being face to face) and suggested some additional strategies Ericka might consider (modeling words for Ethan, using wait time when expecting Ethan to respond or imitate her) and asked her what she thought she might do differently during the activity (see Box C in FIPP, 2014a, p. 6).

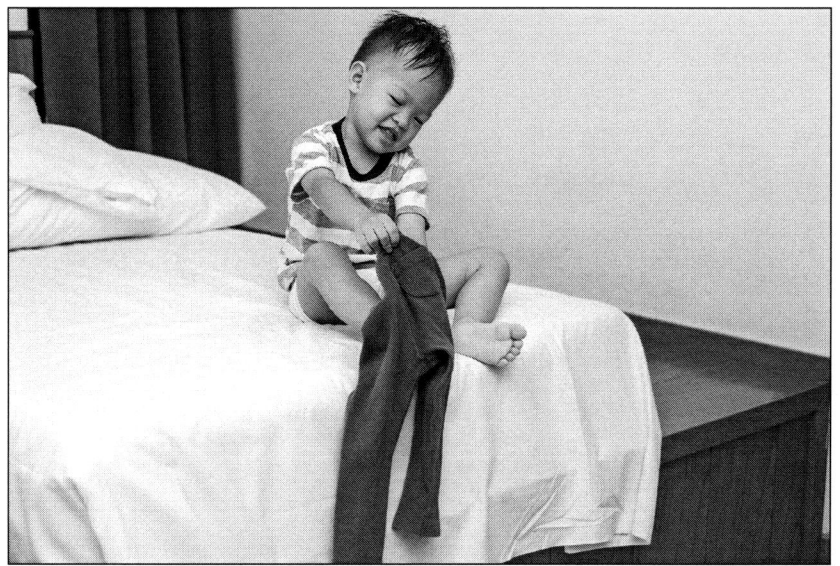

During the participation-based assessment (RAMP Part II), Ericka reflected on how typical the activity appeared and assisted in generating ideas for what to do differently to improve Ethan's participation. She then immediately had the opportunity to analyze the new ideas with Shanice. RAMP Part II may also include opportunities for the practitioner to model strategies for the caregivers if needed. After each demonstration and/or observation, the practitioner prompts the caregivers to reflect on and evaluate the strategies using the reflective questions provided on the roadmap. This process allows the practitioner to observe and gather further information about the child's development and participation in addition to the caregiver's degree of responsiveness to the child in ways that encourage learning. Part II of the RAMP should provide information necessary for writing functional, meaningful, participation-based IFSP outcomes and flows directly into the IFSP conversation (RAMP Part III; FIPP, 2014a, p. 7), which is the next part of this scheduled visit.

Part III: Planning

The focus of Part III is to develop the IFSP outcomes and summary of service delivery, explain the next steps in the early intervention process, and plan the first intervention visit. RAMP Part III provides the family's service coordinator and/or the person completing the participation-based assessment, who may likely be the ongoing service provider, with guidance for helping families identify IFSP outcomes and intervention strategies. RAMP Part III helps the service coordinator/

practitioner and family use the information gained through the first two parts to develop meaningful participation-based outcome statements for the child. This conversation builds on previous discussions targeting family priorities and connects the priorities to the everyday activities in which the skill would be learned and used.

As indicated on the roadmap for RAMP Part III, the service coordinator (Thomas) begins the conversation by asking, "Based on what we just learned during the assessment, between now and Ethan's birthday (approximately six months) what would you like dressing to be like for your family and child?" (FIPP, 2014a, p. 7). The family member is then prompted to reflect on what he or she tried during the assessment that worked as well as other ideas that could be used and documented as strategies.

Ericka said she would like Ethan to help more when he is getting dressed and maybe start talking. Thomas and Shanice agreed that this would be important. Thomas then asked Ericka what Ethan would get to do during dressing time if he was talking (FIPP, 2014a, p. 7). Ericka said she thought Ethan would be able to choose his shirt. Thomas indicated it sounded like a possible outcome might be: "Ethan will get to help during dressing by pulling up his pants and choosing his shirt." This process is repeated until all the family priorities are included as part of the child's outcomes.

Once the outcomes are developed, the roadmap provides wording for identifying the team member (i.e., primary service provider) or team members who will provide ongoing support. This includes how much support the family thinks they will need to achieve the outcomes.

Once the outcomes are developed, the roadmap provides wording for identifying the team member (i.e., primary service provider) or team members who will provide ongoing support.

Thomas and Shanice's team uses a primary service provider approach to teaming, so Thomas shared that Shanice is being recommended as their primary service provider, which was why she participated in the evaluation, assessment, and IFSP outcome development process. Ericka and Simon indicated they liked working with Shanice, and she had already been very helpful to them, so they would prefer for her to continue to support them.

The caregivers and service provider then develop a plan for what the caregivers will do based on what was learned during the assessment until the first visit with the service provider.

Ultimately, Ericka decided to try modeling the words "here you go" when Ethan handed her his spatulas and again when she handed them back to him. She also made a plan to offer Ethan a choice between two shirts during dressing time, wait to see which one he picked, and then model the words he would say to make his selection.

Finally, the participation-based assessment and planning process assist the family and practitioners to develop the frequency and intensity of services uniquely suited to the child's and family's needs and priorities. The activity/routine for the first visit (e.g., getting dressed, leaving the park, snack time, walking to the mailbox, feeding the new puppies), if not the same as the context for the participation-based assessment, is determined and the visit is scheduled based on the usual time the planned activity occurs. Documentation of RAMP Part III may occur directly on the program's IFSP form during this conversation, or the RAMP workbook (FIPP, 2014b) can be used to draft information to be transferred to the IFSP during the meeting.

Thomas asked Ericka and Simon to consider how often they thought it would be helpful for Shanice to come visit and provide support. Ericka and Simon shared that they wanted support perhaps weekly or as often as Shanice thought would be effective. Shanice agreed that at least weekly visits made sense to begin with and that perhaps in a few months the family may need less intensive supports.

The team agreed to 12 visits over the next three months. Shanice then made a between-visit plan with Ericka and Simon. She asked Ericka what she planned to do to support Ethan during dressing between now and their first visit. Ericka indicated she would try singing with Ethan during the activity and let Ethan choose his shirt and stand up to get his pants on. Simon added that he planned to sing with Ethan during Ethan's bath time and to keep singing with him when he is getting Ethan out of the tub. Shanice asked Ericka and Simon during which activity they would like for her to return. Ericka and Simon both answered they wanted Shanice to come back during Ethan's dressing time again so they could review his progress or any problems they had encountered. Shanice verified the typical time of day when that activity happens and scheduled her return.

Conclusion

Operationalization of the evidence-based characteristics of a practice is critical to achieving the intended outcomes of the practice. The RAMP is a process for the effective implementation of the early intervention participation-based assessment. The RAMP is consistent with the Assessment recommended practices and supports early intervention practitioners' gathering of the type of information needed to provide support through conversation with the family and observation of an actual routine or activity during the participation-based assessment. This information assists with the use of the Environment, Family, Instruction, Interaction, and Teaming and Collaboration recommended practices as part of the intervention process. The RAMP process establishes how individuals from the early intervention program can use a coaching interaction style to identify and build on what families already know and do, as well as support families by building their capacity to further support their child's learning and development while participating in the activities of daily life.

References

Akamoglu, Y., & Dinnebeil, L. (2017). Coaching parents to use naturalistic language and communication strategies. *Young Exceptional Children, 20,* 41–50. doi:10.1177/1096250615598815

American Occupational Therapy Association. (2013). *Occupational therapy practice guidelines for early childhood: Birth through 5 years.* Bethesda, MD: AOTA Press.

American Physical Therapy Association. (2008). *Natural environments in early intervention services* [Fact sheet]. Alexandria, VA: Author. Retrieved from: https://pediatricapta.org/includes/fact-sheets/pdfs/Natural%20Env%20 Fact%20Sheet.pdf

American Speech-Language-Hearing Association. (2008). *Roles and responsibilities of speech-language pathologists in early intervention: Guidelines* [Technical report]. Rockville, MD: Author. Retrieved from https://www.asha. org/policy/GL2008-00293/

Bagnato, S. J. (2005). The authentic alternative for assessment in early intervention: An emerging evidence-based practice. *Journal of Early Intervention, 28,* 17–22. doi:10.1177/105381510502800102

Bagnato, S. J., Goins, D. D., Pretti-Frontczak, K., & Neisworth, J. T. (2014). Authentic assessment as "best practice" for early childhood intervention: National consumer social validity research. *Topics in Early Childhood Special Education, 34,* 116–127. doi:10.1177/0271121414523652

Balas, E. A., & Boren, S. A. (2000). Managing clinical knowledge for healthcare improvement. In J. Bemmel & A. T. McCray (Eds.), *Yearbook of medical informatics* (pp. 65–70). Stuttgart, Germany: Schattauer Verlagsgesellschaft.

Campbell P. H., & Sawyer L. B. (2007). Supporting learning opportunities in natural settings through participation-based services. *Journal of Early Intervention, 29,* 287–305. doi:10.1177/105381510702900402

Davis, F. A. (2014). Promoting responsive parent/caregiver-child interactions during natural learning activities. *CASEinPoint, 6*(1). Retrieved from https:// fipp.org/static/media/uploads/caseinpoint/caseinpoint_6-1.pdf

Division for Early Childhood. (2014). *DEC recommended practices in early intervention/early childhood special education 2014.* Retrieved from https://www. dec-sped.org/dec-recommended-practices

Dunn, W., Cox, J., Foster, L., Mische-Lawson, L., & Tanquary, J. (2012). Impact of a contextual intervention on child participation and parent competence among children with autism spectrum disorders: A pretest–posttest repeated-measures design. *American Journal of Occupational Therapy, 66,* 520–528. doi:10.5014/ajot.2012.004119

Dunn, W., Little, L. M., Pope, E., & Wallisch, A. (2018). Establishing fidelity of occupational performance coaching. *The Occupational Therapy*

Journal of Research: Occupation, Participation, and Health, 38, 96–104. doi:10.1177/1539449217724755

Dunst, C. J., Bruder, M. B., & Espe-Sherwindt, M. (2014). Family capacity-building in early childhood intervention: Do context and setting matter? *School Community Journal, 24*(1), 37–48.

Dunst, C. J., Bruder, M. B., Trivette, C. M., & Hamby, D. W. (2006). Everyday activity settings, natural learning environments, and early intervention practices. *Journal of Policy and Practice in Intellectual Disabilities, 3*, 3–10. doi:10.1111/j.1741-1130.2006.00047.x

Dunst, C. J., Raab, M., & Hamby, D. W. (2016). Interest-based everyday child language learning. *Revista de Logopedia, Foniatría y Audiología, 36*, 153–161. doi:10.1016/j.rlfa.2016.07.003

Family, Infant and Preschool Program. (2014a). *Roadmap for assessing meaningful participation* [Manual]. Morganton, NC: Author. Retrieved from https://www.assurethefuture.org/roadmap-to-assess-meaningful-participation.html

Family, Infant and Preschool Program. (2014b). *Roadmap for assessing meaningful participation* [Workbook]. Morganton, NC: Author. Retrieved from https://www.assurethefuture.org/roadmap-to-assess-meaningful-participation.html

Fettig, A., Barton, E. E., Carter, A. S., & Eisenhower, A. S. (2016). Using e-coaching to support an early intervention provider's implementation of a participation-based assessment-based intervention. *Infants & Young Children, 29*, 130–147. doi:10.1097/IYC.0000000000000058

Fixsen, D., Blase, K., Metz, A., & van Dyke, M. (2013). Statewide implementation of evidence-based programs. *Exceptional Children, 79*, 213–230. doi:10.1177/001440291307900206

Fixsen, D. L., Naoom, S. F., Blase, K. A., Friedman, R. M., & Wallace, F. (2005). *Implementation research: A synthesis of the literature* (FMHI Publication No. 231). Tampa: University of South Florida, Louis de la Parte Florida Mental Health Institute, The National Implementation Research Network.

Friedman, M., Woods, J., & Salisbury, C. (2012). Caregiver coaching strategies for early intervention providers: Moving toward operational definitions. *Infants & Young Children, 25*, 62–82. doi:10.1097/IYC.0b013e31823d8f12

Graham, F., Rodger, S., & Ziviani, J. (2013). Effectiveness of occupational performance coaching in improving children's and mothers' performance and mothers' self-competence. *American Journal of Occupational Therapy, 67*, 10–18. doi:10.5014/ajot.2013.004648

Individuals With Disabilities Education Act, 20 U.S.C. § 1400 (2004).

McWilliam, R. A., Casey, A. M., & Sims, J. (2009). The routines-based interview: A method for gathering information and assessing needs. *Infants & Young Children, 22*, 224–233. doi:10.1097/IYC.0b013e3181abe1dd

Neisworth, J. T., & Bagnato, S. J. (2004). The mismeasure of young children: The authentic assessment alternative. *Infants & Young Children, 17*, 198–212.

Rush, D. D., & Shelden, M. L. (2011). *The early childhood coaching handbook.* Baltimore, MD: Paul H. Brookes.

Salisbury, C., Woods, J., Snyder, P., Moddelmog, K., Mawdsley, H., Romano, M., & Windsor, K. (2018). Caregiver and provider experiences with coaching and embedded intervention. *Topics in Early Childhood Special Education, 38*, 17–29. doi:10.1177/0271121417708036

Shelden, M. L., & Rush, D. D. (2014). IFSP outcome statements made simple. *Young Exceptional Children, 17*, 15–27. doi:10.1177/1096250613499246

Swanson, J., Raab, M., & Dunst, C. J. (2011). Strengthening family capacity to provide young children everyday natural learning opportunities. *Journal of Early Childhood Research, 9*, 66–80. doi:10.1177/1476718X10368588

Woods, J. J., & Lindeman, D. P. (2008). Gathering and giving information with families. *Infants & Young Children, 21*, 272–284. doi:10.1097/01.IYC.0000336540.60250.f2

Workgroup on Principles and Practices in Natural Environments, OSEP TA Community of Practice: Part C Settings. (2008, March). *Agreed upon mission and key principles for providing early intervention services in natural environments.* Retrieved from http://ectacenter.org/~pdfs/topics/families/Finalmissionandprinciples3_11_08.pdf

8

Assessment of Executive Function in Everyday Environments

PATRICIA M. BLASCO
Oregon Health & Science University

SERRA ACAR
University of Massachusetts, Boston

Andie, who graduated from an early childhood education teacher preparation program with a focus on inclusion, recently attended a workshop on executive function (EF) at a local Head Start conference. She is very excited about implementing some of the ideas she learned with all the children in her 3- to 5-year-old class, including children who are dual language learners and children with disabilities. She discussed assessment of EF in her program with the early intervention/early childhood special education (EI/ECSE) consultant. Many of the daily routine observations and anecdotal notes that she has been collecting are related to EF components, but she realized that she was not looking at each child's development through an EF lens. During the conference, she learned about standardized EF tools that she might use in her classroom. The workshop helped her learn about ways to evaluate a child's cognitive and social processes and to learn strategies to strengthen working memory, inhibition, emotional control, and the ability to shift between attributes and concepts. She is excited about adding EF assessment to ongoing assessment for children in her classroom, which will also affect her data-driven instructional approach.

To help children develop executive function skills, early childhood educators and EI/ECSE practitioners should observe and document EF components in a systematic way. How can practitioners assess EF skills, particularly for children who are at risk for EF deficits and for children who are dual language learners (DLLs)? The purpose of this article is twofold: to address assessment for the purpose of individualized planning for EF skills and to address progress monitoring of EF skills for young children in inclusive settings.

This article will address three Assessment recommended practices (Division for Early Childhood [DEC], 2014) that are particularly relevant to practitioner Andie's daily classroom routine: A2, that "practitioners work as a team with the family and other professionals to gather assessment information"; A6, that "practitioners use a variety of methods, including observation and interviews, to gather assessment information from multiple sources, including the child's family and other significant individuals in the child's life"; and A9, that "practitioners implement systematic ongoing assessment to identify learning targets, plan activities, and monitor the child's progress to revise instruction as needed" (p. 8).

As a general statement, assessment procedures should be developmentally, age, culturally, and linguistically appropriate. These procedures should address all domains of early development, including EF as aspects of cognition. Information for assessment purposes should be gathered from multiple sources, incorporating information from family members and practitioners who work with the child.

> Executive function deficits may be the silent disability, often not identified until school age, when the child is then placed in special education for learning disabilities and/or attention deficit hyperactivity disorders.

The Definition of EF

Executive function refers to a wide range of central control processes in the brain that link and categorize information and are discernible in the cognitive, motor, and behavioral responses of young children (Zelazo, Blair, & Willoughby, 2016). The beginnings of EF skills are evident within the first year of life (Diamond, 2006). Early childhood years are transformative years in the development of EF. There are periods of rapid development from ages 1 to 6 (Diamond, 2006). According to Zelazo et al. (2016), the early childhood years provide a "window of opportunity" for the nurturing of these skills with targeted intervention and scaffolding supports (p. 16). Longitudinal studies have also provided evidence that preacademic learning opportunities improve EF when provided in the early childhood years (Fuhs, Nesbitt, Farran, & Dong, 2014).

Researchers who have studied EF intervention in early childhood have found many essential outcomes that last a lifetime. These include early kindergarten success (Blair & Razza, 2007; McClelland et al., 2007), social competence in adolescence (Devine, White, Ensor, & Hughes, 2016), improved physical health, higher socioeconomic status, and fewer drug and criminal convictions in adulthood (McKewen et al., 2019; Moffitt et al., 2011). For example, McClelland et al. (2007) found that complex memory performance at age 5 was a significant predictor of performance on measures of language, mathematics, and literacy at age 8.

Executive function is often considered an umbrella term that encompasses multiple components (Keilty, Blasco, & Acar, 2015). EF components are manifested in numerous behaviors as children play or carry out daily routines and activities. These behaviors may also include or contribute to self-regulation, inhibitory control, working memory, and goal-directed persistence.

Planning/organization and cognitive flexibility (shifting) are EF component skills that are considered more observable in older children. However, recent studies have demonstrated that children at earlier ages also engage in planning/organization (Keilty et al., 2015) and shifting (Lind, Raby, Caron, Roben, & Dozier, 2017).

Theoretical and Empirical Rationale for Assessing EF

EF has been associated with important functional outcomes, including social competence and academic achievement in both typically developing children and children with developmental delays (Zelazo et al., 2016). Studies that have examined white matter injury in preschoolers born low birth weight (LBW) and preterm, a population at high risk for development delays, have found deficits in EF via structural magnetic resonance imagings (MRIs; Woodward, Clark, Pritchard, Anderson, & Inder, 2011). Although early intervention practitioners and early childhood educators are aware of developmental milestones across domains, EF deficits may be the silent disability, often not identified until school age, when the child is then placed in special education for learning disabilities and/or attention deficit hyperactivity disorders.

While there is research on young children and EF assessment for the at-risk population (Bierman, Nix, Greenberg, Blair, & Domitrovich, 2008; White, Alexander, & Greenfield, 2017; White & Greenfield, 2017), further research is needed on the effects of EF assessment and intervention for young children with disabilities (Kuhn, Willoughby, Blair, & McKinnon, 2017; Maiman et al., 2018). There is a growing concern that we often wait until children fail before addressing EF skills and deficits.

As stated by Diamond (2016), "EFs can be improved. This is true throughout life from infancy through old age" (p. 20). To develop EF potential, the early childhood education field needs sensitive and specific measures that can, first, identify the child's EF strengths and concerns, and, second, develop effective interventions to improve child outcomes. This need for assessment is critical, especially for children with or at high risk for developmental delays who are more vulnerable for learning difficulties at school age (Blasco, Guy, Saxton, & Duvall, 2017).

It is known that children who begin school with challenging behaviors, such as uncontrollable feelings, inability to stay seated, and lack of attention to tasks, may be negatively viewed by their teachers, resulting in low expectations that, in turn, lead to poor performance by the child (Diamond, 2016). Kindergarten teachers rated difficulties with following directions and controlling attention as the main cause of children's lack of ability to succeed in school (Blair & Razza, 2007). As a result, deficits in EF can be a silent disability that leads to later diagnoses at school age (e.g., ADHD, learning disabilities). It is important to observe, assess, and implement successful strategies to improve EF skills prior to school age. Diamond (2016) could not have stated it better:

One of the most critical societal needs is to develop effective, scalable, sustainable, and affordable strategies for supporting children from the youngest age possible, their parents, and their early child care providers to get children started with good EF skills when they first enter school, thereby launching them on a promising, positive trajectory, improving their life prospects and preventing problems, rather than trying to treat problems after they have been allowed to develop. To be able to determine whether a strategy is successful or not, sensitive and valid measures of EF that can be administered longitudinally are absolutely essential. (p. 26)

Children at Risk or With Developmental Delays and Disabilities

There is research evidence that the development of EF activities protects against risks associated with low birth weight (LBW), poverty, and adversity, including the risk of school-age difficulties in academic tasks such as reading and mathematics (Masten et al., 2012). A meta-analysis of neurodevelopmental and behavioral outcomes of children who are very low birth weight (VLBW, less than 1,500 grams) and very preterm (less than 33 weeks gestation) showed that they were more likely to have moderate to severe performance difficulties on measures of academic achievement and to exhibit both challenging behaviors and EF skill deficits (Aarnoudse-Moens, Weisglas-Kuperus, van Goudoever, & Oosterlaan, 2009). EF deficits include difficulties with behavioral regulation, working memory, cognitive flexibility, and verbal fluency.

DEC (2018) has developed a position statement related to LBW, prematurity, and early intervention. DEC supports the premise that children born early are at high risk for cognitive difficulties, including EF, and that practitioners should be aware of the need to assess EF and implement appropriate services.

The magnitude of the effect of socioeconomic status is substantial. The effects of low socioeconomic status have been found in all medical risk categories after premature delivery (Landry, Smith, & Swank, 2006). Children with autism have been shown to have difficulty with EF and self-regulation (Jahromi, Bryce, & Swanson, 2013; Schneider, Schumann-Hengsteler, & Sodian, 2014). Other researchers have found a relationship between working memory and specific language impairments (Vugs, Hendriks, Cuperus, & Verhoeven, 2014).

Difficulties with EF, including cognitive flexibility, planning/organization, and working memory, have been associated with autism spectrum disorder (ASD) and ADHD (Barkley, 2014; Bryson et al., 2018; O'Hearn, Asato, Ordaz, & Luna, 2008). In a recent review of EF in autism, Craig et al. (2016) indicated that children diagnosed with ASD and ADHD have difficulties in both cognitive flexibility and planning/organization, whereas children diagnosed with ADHD have inhibition deficits, although other literature shows multiple deficits in EF skills in ADHD (Barkley, 2014). Literature reviews on ASD, ADHD, and EF deficits reveal that EF deficits reflect an additive comorbidity, rather than a separate condition from developmental delays or disabilities. Pellicano et al. (2017) studied 30 preschool-age children with autism and 30 children who were typically developing on several EF tasks and school preparation tests. The children with autism scored significantly lower than their peers. Individual differences found in EF skills of inhibitory control and working memory were related to school preparedness across both groups. This study provides evidence for the importance of strengthening EF skills to improve functional outcomes for children with autism.

Children with ADHD or ASD may not receive official diagnoses prior to age 3 but may be in early intervention because of developmental delays. Impairments in EF skills often are not identified but can be common across groups of children with developmental delays, regardless of their ultimate diagnoses.

Children Who Are DLLs

The lack of EF skills can be a deficit for children who are developmentally delayed; however, the presence of EF skills conversely has been shown to give young children who are DLLs a slight advantage. Carlson and Meltzoff (2008) found that native bilingual children performed significantly better on EF assessment tasks than their English-speaking and second-language immersion peers. DLLs, defined as children ages 8 and under with at least one parent who speaks a language other than English at home, now make up 32% of the nation's young population (Park, O'Toole, & Katsiaficas, 2017). A similar increase has been observed in the preschool population, with approximately 30% of Head Start children learning two languages (Hammer, Lawrence, & Miccio, 2007). In this population, the effect of a second language on cognitive development, including EF, can be a strength for the children (Bialystok, 2015). For example, working memory and inhibitory control have been identified as potential contributors to language aptitude (DeKeyser & Koeth, 2011).

The acquisition of vocabulary is one of the critical components of early childhood development. In early stages of language acquisition, language enrichment during early periods of life may promote the development of new neural connections, furthering the development of neural networks (Baum & Titone, 2014; Werker & Hensch, 2015). At the classroom level, an enriched bilingual environment may result in an increased production of EF skills because of cognitive demands that are placed on the child. Early childhood educators need to be equipped with information on supporting children who speak a language other than English at home.

Assessment for Individualized Planning

To plan for successful implementation of EF strategies, practitioners must first identify areas of strength and concern in terms of EF skills. The

Executive function deficits include difficulties with behavioral regulation, working memory, cognitive flexibility, and verbal fluency.

Table 1
Executive Function Skills Observation Form

Child's name and date of observation	Assessment tool	EF component(s)	Daily routine	Demonstrated skill (Yes/No)	Anecdotal notes
Jack (4/12/19)	BRIEF-P	I	AT	No	He joined the activity table to make a flower. He became distracted and did not finish the task that required cut, paste, and color.
Amy (4/12/19)	DMQ18 EF Touch	I & EC	T	Yes	She used self-talk to remind herself "your turn" then "my turn."
Peter (4/12/19)	BRIEF-P, DMQ18, EF Touch	WM & P/O	A & D	Yes No	He greeted teachers and friends when he arrived at preschool but was reminded by the teacher using visual cues to say goodbye at the end of the day.
Carol (4/12/19)	BRIEF-P, MEFS	CF	AT	Yes	She identified two attributes: first stars by color and then by shape when the rule was changed.

Note. EF components include CF = cognitive flexibility; EC = emotional control; I = inhibit; PO = plan/organize; WM = working memory. Daily routines include A = arrival; T = transition; M = meal; AT = activity time; D = departure.

following instruments are designed to identify EF to individually plan intervention targets with young children. The first two instruments rely on partnering with families and other professionals to gather the information through observation in natural environments. Table 1 provides a template of an observation form to document children's EF skills during daily practices. This observation form does not diagnose or pinpoint a specific problem, but it can be helpful as a way to document practitioners', like Andie's, observations and concerns and can be used to start a conversation with a specific child's family and/or other practitioners.

Parent report assessment tools. The *Behavior Rating Inventory of Executive Function-Preschool Version* (BRIEF-P; Gioia, Espy, & Isquith, 2003) can be administered to parents and caregivers by professionals who have completed coursework in test interpretation, psychometrics, and measurement theory and have backgrounds in psychology or related fields. The BRIEF-P is the first standardized rating scale designed to specifically measure the range of behavioral manifestations of EF in preschool-aged children (ages 2 to 5.11) within the context of everyday environments. The parent-rating form consists of 63 items that measure various aspects of EF: inhibit, shift, emotional control, working memory, and plan/organize. This measure also is available in Spanish.

The *Dimensions of Mastery Questionnaire – Infant and Preschool Version* (DMQ 18; Morgan et al., 2017) is designed to assess children's mastery motivation–related behaviors. Mastery motivation (engaging in goal-directed tasks) is a key developmental construct related to EF. The DMQ 18 measures persistence in child mastery tasks across the dimensions of both cognitive (complex tasks such as puzzles, cause and effect) and social tasks (self-regulation and persistence at social play with adults and other children). The infant version (38 items) is for children of developmental ages approximately 6–23 months, and the preschool version (39 items) is for children of developmental ages approximately 2–6 years. The DMQ 18 has seven scales, uses Likert-type items rated 1–5 (from [1] not at all like this child to [5] exactly like this child). Both the practitioner and parent can complete this assessment to compare findings across perspectives and environments. It is available in several languages, including Spanish and Russian. It is available from the author's website at https://sites.google.com/a/rams.colostate.edu/georgemorgan/mastery-motivation.

Performance-based assessment tools. *EF Touch* (Willoughby, Kuhn, Blair, Samek, & List, 2016) was developed to provide a psychometrically sound, highly portable, and developmentally scalable battery of EF tasks for use with preschool-aged children (ages 3–6; Willoughby, Blair, Wirth, & Greenberg, 2012; Willoughby et al., 2016). According to the technical manual, the computerized battery is composed of seven EF and two non-EF tasks. The non-EF tasks are administered first to support the child in how to respond to questions using the touch screen. Each EF task takes three to seven minutes to complete and has been deemed age appropriate for children starting at age 3. Although computerized, the activities were originally developed using flip pages and hands-on materials. EF touch has been used with children born LBW and children with disabilities. This assessment has multiple language versions, including Spanish. The product has gone through extensive reliability and validity testing, including with children who are developmentally delayed and/or born preterm. Information on testing of the product is available at https://eftouch.fpg.unc.edu/.

The *Minnesota Executive Function Scale* (MEFS; Carlson & Zelazo, 2014) is "a subscription service for assessing EF skills using a brief, standardized instrument administered on an iPad" that takes three to six minutes to administer (MN Executive Function Scale, (n.d.). According to the online description, the MEFS is a virtual card-sorting task that is an age-appropriate, brief, reliable, and valid measure of EF abilities for children ages 2–7. The assessment begins automatically at age-appropriate starting points according to task instructions. Once a basal is established, testing continues until the child fails a level. The results provide early detection of potential EF difficulties. This assessment provides one global

EF score and does not provide results across EF components. It is available in English, Spanish, Dutch, German (Swiss), Swedish, Mandarin, Somali, Hmong, French, and Arabic. Children must have good auditory, visual, and motor skills to use the tablet and respond correctly to directions. The measure, which has national norms developed in the United States, is available from https://reflectionsciences.com/mefs-app/.

Assessment for Monitoring Child Progress Through Ongoing Assessment

Based on identified EF skills and deficits, practitioners can implement planned intervention and monitor the child's progress to ensure positive outcomes for the child and family. EI/ECSE practitioners and families would benefit from an understanding of EF components for young children with or without disabilities and assessment/intervention strategies that facilitate effective intervention.

Retrospective research studies have shown that a young child's developmental trajectory is influenced adversely when EF skills are not strengthened and deficits are not addressed. Targeting EF skills in young children has the potential to buffer EF deficits, build on strengths, and improve outcomes before school age (Diamond, 2016). Table 2 provides a summary of EF components.

Emotional control refers to when the child learns to control their emotions and impulses. Emotional control is related to self-regulation, which starts early in life and develops throughout an individual's lifetime. For example, a newborn baby must regulate breathing effort, heart rate, reflexes, and state (crying vs. calming). Some of these attributes are measured by the Apgar score immediately after birth to gage the baby's tolerance of the birthing process (American Academy of Pediatrics, 2015). For older children, an example of self-regulation is emotional control. When children have emotional control, they can regulate their feelings. Practitioners and parents can help by talking about feelings and showing empathy when a child is struggling. Self-regulation in the preschool years has been predictive of early academic achievement (Becker, Miao, Duncan, & McClelland, 2014). Self-regulation overlaps with inhibitory control but also addresses the importance of motivation and individual interest (self-determination) as emotional responses that can be critical to persistence and achievement of outcomes (Diamond, 2016).

Inhibitory control refers to stopping a behavior that can be either an automatic or reflexive response to comply with a request. For example, a toddler may try to place a crayon in his or her mouth. When the adult says, "No, crayons go on paper," the child may stop this response. For older preschoolers, the skill to pause and think before acting can be suggested in classroom visuals or by an adult's request. Andie supports this skill by using visuals to remind children that running is for outside and gym play.

Some children stop and use walking steps when they see Andie is showing the visual cue for walking feet. However, some children still keep running. To support children to develop inhibitory control, Andie asks questions such as "Do you remember this one? What does it tell you? Why?" rather than immediately saying,

Retrospective research studies have shown that a young child's developmental trajectory is influenced adversely when EF skills are not strengthened and deficits are not addressed.

Table 2
Executive Function (EF) Components

EF component	Definition
Emotional control	Related to self-regulation. Children learn to control their emotions and impulses early in life, and this continues to adulthood.
Inhibit	Refers to stopping a behavior that can be either an automatic or reflexive response to comply with a request.
Working memory	Refers to the ability to remember and hold information in mind.
Cognitive flexibility	Refers to the ability to switch between tasks or activities or to adjust to changed requests or demands.
Plan/organize	This includes planning and sequencing to achieve a goal-directed task.

"Walking steps only." By asking Wh– questions, Andie is supporting children to pause and think. She believes in the long run these opportunities will allow them to develop inhibitory control skills. She uses a similar strategy to support cleanup time, such as "Where do we put our markers after the activity? Where do we keep our glue and scissors?" She observes their responses and takes daily notes to measure progress toward individual learning targets.

Working memory refers to the ability to remember and hold information in mind, despite competing information or distractions. When an infant searches for her parent's face in a crowd, she is responding to visual, auditory, and/or olfactory recall of the parent. For an older child, remembering concepts and learning to recall the sequence in a story are examples of working memory.

Andie uses every single teachable moment to support working memory of young children. For instance, when she is reading a familiar book, she starts with asking questions such as "Do you remember what this book is about? Who were the main characters?" or "What happens to the dinosaur?" (implying a dinosaur is the main character printed on the cover page). These questions prompt children to think and remember from their previous experiences. Andie uses these daily conversations to collect language samples for assessment purposes, such as correct use of simple past tense. She wears an apron with pockets where she keeps a pencil and notebook. She documents child responses with each child's initials and date using sticky notes on an observation grid. At the end of the day, she quickly enters her notes into her computer for each child.

For Nicky, a child with a communication board, Andie and the speech-language pathologist have devised a picture dictionary on his board so he can answer *questions about the daily schedule. For example, Andie will ask him to recall a character from a book he is reading. The physical therapist reviews the activities for the week, including the books used in class and has preprogrammed the scanner to identify characters and sequences in the story to help him develop his working memory and complete ongoing alternative assessment of his EF skills.*

Cognitive flexibility refers to the ability to switch between tasks or activities or to adjust to changed requests or demands. Children who are DLLs switch back and forth between two languages. Being exposed to two languages leads to early benefits in cognitive flexibility before language production even begins (Bialystok, 2015). It is important to provide explicit conceptual links between language(s) used and daily activities. Andie uses labels in both English and Spanish and other visual cues (i.e., activity schedules, choice boards, first/then boards) to support cognitive flexibility.

During daily routines, Andie provides opportunities for children to use their home language. For instance, she plays a familiar children's song in the child's home language and then plays the same song in English. In doing this, she is also supporting the cognitive flexibility of all children in her classroom. Moreover, she asks simple questions, such as "How do you say, 'Can I have more crackers please?' in your language?" during a snack time, while children are eating cheese and crackers.

After attending the state Head Start conference, Andie created an activity to support children's cognitive flexibility. She cut and laminated several shapes (e.g., circle, triangle, and square) in three colors: blue, green, and red. She arranges the colors in a pattern on a Velcro board and says, "Let's look at the colors and shapes. Tell me what you see." She asks children to name the colors and shapes. Finally, she asks the same questions in Spanish (e.g., How do you say blue/green/red in Spanish?), so children switch to a different language. She observes and collects anecdotal notes on the children's responses (A9).

Planning/organization, which includes skills such as planning and sequencing, is needed to stay on task and direct goal-oriented behavior when multiple steps are required to reach the goal. Children often have difficulty staying focused and organizing their behavior during play, routine daily activities such as dressing or getting ready to go out, and household routines such as bedtime. Setting expectations and discussing the sequence of routines will help young children learn to plan and organize.

Andie has a child diagnosed with autism, Tim, who has challenging behaviors, especially during transitions. One goal on his Individualized Education Program (IEP) states: "Tim will independently prepare to go outside at home and while at school, including having his shoes and coat on for two consecutive days during a five-day week." One short-term goal is that he will be given verbal prompts and visual support to put on his shoes and coat. Andie is preparing all the children to go outside. She asks the children to look outside and tell her what they will need to wear for the weather. As children answer that they will need a coat, another child says hats, and a third one says gloves. As the children move toward their cubbies to

Table 3
Tim's Assessment and Functional Plan

Assessment	Comments
Assessment tool(s), administrator, and administration date	BRIEF-P on MM/DD/YY Tim's mother administered the protocol. There are no missing responses in the protocol, providing a complete data set for interpretation.
Strengths	Enjoys music, outdoor play, joint attention ability
Areas of concerns	Mother reported "transitions are difficult for him, especially from home to outside."
Long-term goal	Tim will independently prepare to go outside at home and while at school, including having his shoes and coat on over two consecutive days during a five-day week.
Short-term objectives	1. Tim will be given verbal prompts and visual support to put on his shoes and coat. 2. Tim will be given visual support to put on his shoes and coat. 3. At the end of group time, Tim will independently put on his shoes and coat.
Criteria	Weekly logs, for tracking progress
Evaluation	Parents will use a log to track progress at home, and practitioners will use an observation grid to track progress in his daily routine.

gather these items, Andie holds up a picture of a coat for Tim and prompts him to the cubby area to put on his coat.

If he does this with a single prompt, she praises him by saying, "I like the way you put on your coat." She asks Tim's friend, Brian, to help him with the zipper. She uses the same procedure for hat and gloves. Andie creates a checklist to record each time Tim responds accurately to a visual prompt for progress monitoring. The checklist has "Yes, No, and Other (please, specify)" options to record observations. Andie shares the information with her team members, including her assistant teacher, practicum student, and Tim's parents so each member of the EI/ECSE team can collect similar data, including his parents in the home. Tim's parents report that they feel empowered when they actively contribute to Tim's assessment process and IEP goals (A2).

In the example above, Andie uses the EF component of "plan and organize" with all the children as they prepare for a transition outdoors. The children need to plan what they need to wear and then organize their coats, hats, and gloves for a successful transition outside. She provides assistance to the children who might

Table 4
Reflection Questions for Practitioners

Area	Question
Observation and documentation	• Did I complete daily observations on child's EF skills? • Did I include at least three to five data points for each child on each EF component? (A9)
Assessment and implementation	• Did I take into consideration the child's linguistic and cultural background in choosing the appropriate assessment tool? • Did I incorporate EF skill development into the IFSP/IEP goals? • Did the observation and instruction lead to improved assessment outcomes? (A6)
Family involvement	• Have I informed families about my observations focused on EF? • Did I use parent-reported EF assessments? • Have I involved the team, including the family, in decision-making about the use of these measures? (A2)

need it and also encourages children to help their peers. In Table 3, Andie individualized the process for Tim because he has difficulty with transitions and would benefit from strategies to improve his cognitive flexibility (shift).

All of her daily classroom activities are based on data-driven decisions. For instance, using a checklist to enhance effectiveness and generalizability guides Andie's next step in the classroom. Based on the data, she can discuss with the EI/ECSE team when to gradually decrease use of the visuals of clothes as Tim begins to follow the daily schedule more independently.

Andie uses a systematic observation, documentation, and data collection approach in her classroom. She uses this information to record strengths and needs of children in all EF components. Practitioners and parents can assess the EF skills of each child through a variety of observational, parent report, and performance-based measurements. This assessment can easily be incorporated in the program's evaluation expectations for practitioners in any early childhood program. For programs that do not include formal assessment measures, observation and recording of behavior can be done informally along with parent-completed rating forms.

Conclusion

Andie is very pleased to see how easy it is to incorporate EF skills for all children using recommended practices on assessment. After consulting with the team, including family members (A6), they have decided to use a combination of observation and parent report forms as the assessment tools. The team agrees this would be a good start by gathering information during daily routines and across environments, including the home, community-based classroom, and the community. She would love to add a performance-based measure but would need to have more training, which requires time and funding. She has spoken with her administrator about investigating some of the available measures in terms of training for herself and colleagues as a group.

Andie uses self-reflection to improve her observation and documentation of EF components. Table 4 provides a list of self-reflection questions. Answering these questions can address the best way to facilitate the assessment and development of EF skills that will support young children and their families. Responsive, meaningful, and linguistically and culturally sensitive assessments that target EF as well as overall development will lead to establishing the foundation for child development, leading to positive outcomes in early childhood, school, and throughout life.

Observing and documenting children's development and learning in their natural environment on a regular basis through an EF lens provides invaluable information for practitioners such as Andie. It is important to collect and use observational and performance-based ongoing assessment to improve child and family outcomes. By providing this type of assessment and intervention, we can support children and their families on a promising, positive trajectory toward learning and development during the early childhood years.

References

Aarnoudse-Moens, C. S. H., Weisglas-Kuperus, N., van Goudoever, J. B., & Oosterlaan, J. (2009). Meta-analysis of neurobehavioral outcomes in very preterm and/or very low birth weight children. *Pediatrics, 124,* 717–728. doi:10.1542/peds.2008-2816

American Academy of Pediatrics. (2015). The Apgar score. *Pediatrics, 136,* 819–822. doi:10.1542/peds.2015-2651

Barkley, R. A. (Ed.). (2014). *Attention-deficit hyperactivity disorder: A handbook for diagnosis and treatment* (4th ed.). New York, NY: The Guilford Press.

Baum, S., & Titone, D. (2014). Moving toward a neuroplasticity view of bilingualism, executive control, and aging. *Applied Psycholinguistics, 35,* 857–894. doi:10.1017/S0142716414000174

Becker, D. R., Miao, A., Duncan, R., & McClelland, M. M. (2014). Behavioral self-regulation and executive function both predict visuomotor skills and early academic achievement. *Early Childhood Research Quarterly, 29,* 411–424. doi:10.1016/j.ecresq.2014.04.014

Bialystok, E. (2015). Bilingualism and the development of executive function: The role of attention. *Child Development Perspectives, 9,* 117–121. doi:10.1111/cdep.12116

Bierman, K. L., Nix, R. L., Greenberg, M. T., Blair, C., & Domitrovich, C. E. (2008). Executive functions and school readiness intervention: Impact, moderation, and mediation in the Head Start REDI program. *Development and Psychopathology, 20,* 821–843. doi:10.1017/s0954579408000394

Blair, C., & Razza, R. P. (2007). Relating effortful control, executive function, and false belief understanding to emerging math and literacy ability in kindergarten. *Child Development, 78,* 647–663. doi:10.1111/j.1467-8624.2007.01019.x

Blasco, P. M., Guy, S., Saxton, S. N., & Duvall, S. W. (2017). Are we missing a vulnerable population in early intervention? *Infants & Young Children, 30,* 190–203. doi:10.1097/IYC.0000000000000097

Bryson, S., Garon, N., McMullen, T., Brian, J., Zwaigenbaum, L., Armstrong, V., . . . Szatmari, P. (2018). Impaired disengagement of attention and its relationship to emotional distress in infants at high-risk for autism spectrum disorder. *Journal of Clinical and Experimental Neuropsychology, 40,* 487–501. doi:10.1080/13803395.2017.1372368

Carlson, S. M., & Meltzoff, A. N. (2008). Bilingual experience and executive functioning in young children. *Developmental Science, 11,* 282–298. doi:10.1111/j.1467-7687.2008.00675.x

Carlson, S. M., & Zelazo, P. D. (2014). *Minnesota executive function scale: Test manual.* St. Paul, MN: Reflection Sciences.

Craig, F., Margari, F., Legrottaglie, A. R., Palumbi, R., de Giambattista, C., & Margari, L. (2016). A review of executive function deficits in autism spectrum disorder and attention-deficit/hyperactivity disorder. *Neuropsychiatric Disease and Treatment, 12,* 1191–1202. doi:10.2147/NDT.S104620

DeKeyser, R. M., & Koeth, J. (2011). Cognitive aptitudes for second language learning. In E. Hinkel (Ed.), *Handbook of research in second language teaching and learning* (Vol. 2, pp. 395–406). New York, NY: Routledge.

Devine, R. T., White, N., Ensor, R., & Hughes, C. (2016). Theory of mind in middle childhood: Longitudinal associations with executive function and social competence. *Developmental Psychology, 52,* 758–771. doi:10.1037/dev0000105

Diamond, A. (2006). The early development of executive functions. In E. Bialystok & F. I. M. Craik (Eds.), *Lifespan cognition: Mechanisms of change* (pp. 70–95). New York, NY: Oxford University Press.

Diamond, A. (2016). Why improving and assessing executive functions early in life is critical. In J. A. Griffin, P. McCardle, & L. S. Freund (Eds.), *Executive function in preschool-age children: Integrating measurement, neurodevelopment, and translational research* (pp. 11–43). Washington, DC: American Psychological Association.

Division for Early Childhood. (2014). *DEC recommended practices in early intervention/early childhood special education 2014.* Retrieved from https://www.dec-sped.org/dec-recommended-practices

Division for Early Childhood. (2018, September). *Low birth weight, prematurity, & early intervention* [Position statement]. Retrieved from https://www.dec-docs.org/position-statement-low-birth-weight

Fuhs, M. W., Nesbitt, K. T., Farran, D. C., & Dong, N. (2014). Longitudinal associations between executive functioning and academic skills across content areas. *Developmental Psychology, 50,* 1698–1709. doi:10.1037/a0036633

Gioia, G. A., Espy K. A., & Isquith, P. K. (2003). *Behavior rating inventory of executive function, preschool version (BRIEF-P).* Odessa, FL: Psychological Assessment Resources.

Hammer, C. S., Lawrence, F. R., & Miccio, A. W. (2007). Bilingual children's language abilities and early reading outcomes in Head Start and kindergarten. *Language, Speech, and Hearing Services in Schools, 38*, 237–248. doi:10.1044/0161-1461(2007/025)

Jahromi, L. B., Bryce, C. I., & Swanson, J. (2013). The importance of self-regulation for the school and peer engagement of children with high-functioning autism. *Research in Autism Spectrum Disorders, 7*, 235–246. doi:10.1016/j.rasd.2012.08.012

Keilty, B., Blasco, P. M., & Acar, S. (2015). Re-conceptualizing developmental areas of assessment for screening, eligibility determination and program planning in early intervention. *Journal of Intellectual Disability-Diagnosis and Treatment, 3*, 218–229. doi:10.6000/2292-2598.2015.03.04.8

Kuhn, L. J., Willoughby, M. T., Blair, C. B., & McKinnon, R. (2017). Examining an executive function battery for use with preschool children with disabilities. *Journal of Autism and Developmental Disorders, 47*, 2586–2594. doi:10.1007/s10803-017-3177-2

Landry, S. H., Smith, K. E., & Swank, P. R. (2006). Responsive parenting: Establishing early foundations for social, communication, and independent problem-solving skills. *Developmental Psychology, 42*, 627–642. doi:10.1037/0012-1649.42.4.627

Lind, T., Raby, K. L., Caron, E. B., Roben, C. K. P., & Dozier, M. (2017). Enhancing executive functioning among toddlers in foster care with an attachment-based intervention. *Development and Psychopathology, 29*, 575–586. doi:10.1017/S0954579417000190

Maiman, M., Salinas, C. M., Gindlesperger, M. F., Westerveld, M., Vasserman, M., & MacAllister, W. S. (2018). Utility of the Behavior Rating Inventory of Executive Function–Preschool version (BRIEF-P) in young children with epilepsy. *Child Neuropsychology, 24*, 975–985. doi:10.1080/09297049.2017.1365829

Masten, A. S., Herbers, J. E., Desjardins, C. D., Cutuli, J. J., McCormick, C. M., Sapienza, J. K., . . . Zelazo, P. D. (2012). Executive function skills and school success in young children experiencing homelessness. *Educational Researcher, 41*, 375–384. doi:10.3102/0013189X12459883

McClelland, M. M., Cameron, C. E., Connor, C. M., Farris, C. L., Jewkes, A. M., & Morrison, F. J. (2007). Links between behavioral regulation and preschoolers' literacy, vocabulary, and math skills. *Developmental Psychology, 43*, 947–959. doi:10.1037/0012-1649.43.4.947

McKewen, M., Skippen, P., Cooper, P. S., Wong, A. S., Michie, P. T., Lenroot, R., & Karayanidis, F. (2019). Does cognitive control ability mediate the relationship between reward-related mechanisms, impulsivity, and maladaptive outcomes in adolescence and young adulthood? *Cognitive, Affective, & Behavioral Neuroscience, 19*, 653–676. doi:10.3758/s13415-019-00722-2

MN Executive Function Scale. (n.d.). Retrieved from https://apps.apple.com/us/app/mn-executive-function-scale/id967184252

Moffitt, T. E., Arseneault, L., Belsky, D., Dickson, N., Hancox, R. J., Harrington, H., . . . Caspi, A. (2011). A gradient of childhood self-control predicts health, wealth, and public safety. *Proceedings of the National Academy of Sciences, 108*, 2693–2698. doi:10.1073/pnas.1010076108

Morgan, G. A., Liao, H.-F., Nyitrai, Á., Huang, S. Y., Wang, P.-J., Blasco, P. M., . . . Józsa, K. (2017). The revised Dimensions of Mastery Questionnaire (DMQ 18) for infants and preschool children with and without risks or delays in Hungary, Taiwan, and the US. *Hungarian Educational Research Journal, 7*(2), 48–67.

O'Hearn, K., Asato, M., Ordaz, S., & Luna, B. (2008). Neurodevelopment and executive function in autism. *Development and Psychopathology, 20,* 1103–1132. doi:10.1017/S0954579408000527

Park, M., O'Toole, A., & Katsiaficas, C. (2017, October). *Dual language learners: A national demographic and policy profile.* Washington, DC: Migration Policy Institute.

Pellicano, E., Kenny, L., Brede, J., Klaric, E., Lichwa, H., & McMillin, R. (2017). Executive function predicts school readiness in autistic and typical preschool children. *Cognitive Development, 43,* 1–13. doi:10.1016/j.cogdev.2017.02.003

Schneider, W., Schumann-Hengsteler, R., & Sodian, B. (Eds.). (2014). *Young children's cognitive development: Interrelationships among executive functioning, working memory, verbal ability, and theory of mind.* New York, NY: Psychology Press.

Vugs, B., Hendriks, M., Cuperus, J., & Verhoeven, L. (2014). Working memory performance and executive function behaviors in young children with SLI. *Research in Developmental Disabilities, 35,* 62–74. doi:10.1016/j.ridd.2013.10.022

Werker, J. F., & Hensch, T. K. (2015). Critical periods in speech perception: New directions. *Annual Review of Psychology, 66,* 173–196. doi:10.1146/annurev-psych-010814-015104

White, L. J., Alexander, A., & Greenfield, D. B. (2017). The relationship between executive functioning and language: Examining vocabulary, syntax, and language learning in preschoolers attending Head Start. *Journal of Experimental Child Psychology, 164,* 16–31. doi:10.1016/j.jecp.2017.06.010

White, L. J., & Greenfield, D. B. (2017). Executive functioning in Spanish- and English-speaking Head Start preschoolers. *Developmental Science, 20*(1), e12502. doi:10.1111/desc.12502

Willoughby, M. T., Blair, C. B., Wirth, R. J., & Greenberg, M. (2012). The measurement of executive function at age 5: Psychometric properties and relationship to academic achievement. *Psychological Assessment, 24,* 226–239. doi:10.1037/a0025361

Willoughby, M. T., Kuhn, L. J., Blair, C. B., Samek, A., & List, J. A. (2016). The test–retest reliability of the latent construct of executive function depends on whether tasks are represented as formative or reflective indicators. *Child Neuropsychology, 23,* 822–837. doi:10.1080/09297049.2016.1205009

Woodward, L. J., Clark, C. A., Pritchard, V. E., Anderson, P. J., & Inder, T. E. (2011). Neonatal white matter abnormalities predict global executive function impairment in children born very preterm. *Developmental Neuropsychology, 36,* 22–41. doi:10.1080/87565641.2011.540530

Zelazo, P. D., Blair, C. B., & Willoughby, M. T. (2016). *Executive function: Implications for education* (NCER 2017-2000). Washington, DC: National Center for Education Research, U. S. Department of Education.

9

Needs Assessment Through the Routines-Based Interview

R. A. McWilliam
The University of Alabama

Cami M. Stevenson
Multnomah Early Childhood Program

I F WE KNOW HOW TO ASK CAREGIVERS ABOUT CHILD, FAMILY, AND classroom functioning, we learn what children, parents, and teachers need. Early intervention/early childhood special education (EI/ECSE) professionals are then poised to provide targeted, meaningful support to children's caregivers. It all begins with a functional needs assessment. The Routines-Based Interview (RBI; McWilliam, Casey, & Sims, 2009) is a semistructured interview conducted with one or more parent. The early intervention professional conducting the interview asks detailed questions about the child's engagement, independence, and social relationships in the family's everyday routines. At the end of the interview, the family reflects on this in-depth report they provided and decides on 10–12 goals. Most goals are usually targeted on skills the parent wants the child to acquire, but some are for the parents and siblings of the child in EI. The RBI, therefore, is used for programmatic assessment—for determining what the child and family need and what should consequently go on the intervention plan.

Here, we discuss the value of needs assessment, an interview, an ecomap, and participation-based outcomes/goals. We tie the RBI (Boavida, Aguiar, McWilliam, & Correia, 2016; McWilliam, 1992) to the Assessment recommended practices. A brief explanation about how to conduct an RBI with fidelity is presented, along with the impact on support provision. Finally, we talk about what you can do until you are trained on the RBI with fidelity.

Previous writings about the RBI have focused on what the interview consists of (McWilliam, 2010a; McWilliam et al., 2011; McWilliam et al., 2009), the effects of training professionals to conduct RBIs (Boavida, Aguiar, & McWilliam, 2014; Boavida et al., 2016), the psychometric properties of the RBI Checklist (Boavida, Akers, McWilliam, & Jung, 2015), and the types of family concerns elicited

Figure 1
Routines-Based Model of Early Intervention (Birth to Age 5)

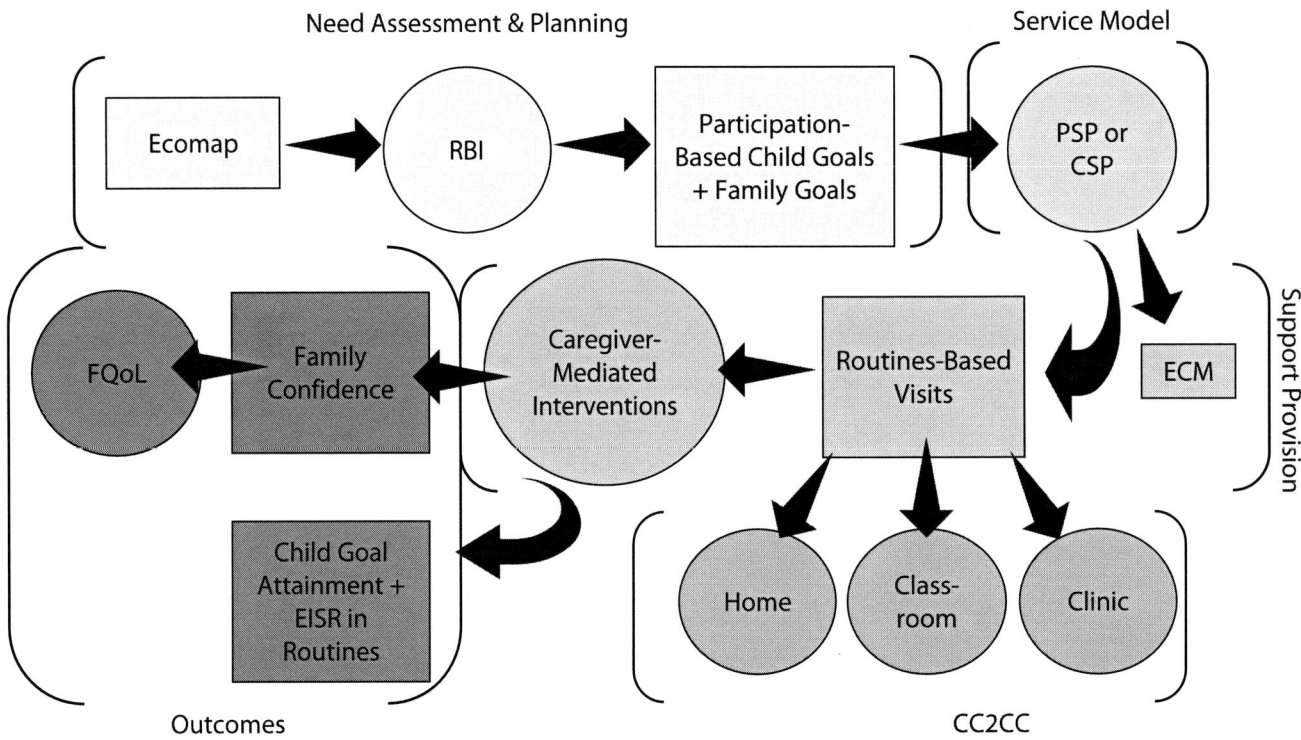

Note. RBI = Routines-Based Interview; PSP = primary service provider; CSP = comprehensive service provider; ECM = Engagement Classroom Model; CC2CC = collaborative consultation to children's classrooms; FQoL = family quality of life; EISR = engagement, independence, and social relationships.

through the RBI (Hughes-Scholes, Gavidia-Payne, Davis, & Mahar, 2019). This article is the first to focus on the importance of fidelity to the model and on how to take a routines-based approach to assessment if you are not trained to fidelity.

Value of Needs Assessment

EI/ECSE professionals often focus assessment on a child's status relative to other children; much of assessment is about whether the child can do this skill or that skill. Assessment of needs, however, is based more on determining how a child functions, rather than his or her status relative to other children (i.e., standardized-test score). Furthermore, even lists of skills typically expected at different ages might not necessarily be functional for the child in question (Macy, Bagnato, Macy, & Salaway, 2015).

In the development of the initial individualized family service plan (IFSP) or individual education program (IEP), the RBI is typically conducted after eligibility has been determined. This ensures we do not conduct an RBI, which is labor intensive, about a child who is then found ineligible for services. As states have raised the bar of eligibility on the basis of developmental delay (Rosenberg, Robinson, Shaw, & Ellison, 2013), it's become important to evaluate for eligibility first.

The RBI is part of the needs assessment and planning process in the Routines-Based Model of Early Intervention (Birth–5), a set of practices emphasizing child functioning in everyday routines and emphasizing the building of families' confidence in meeting their child's and family's needs (McWilliam, 2010b). Figure 1 shows the important elements of the model.

On the second and subsequent updates of IFSPs and IEPs, unless continued eligibility is in question, the "review RBI" is conducted soon before the review or annual update. If the child and family received ongoing support in the home, the subsequent RBI process might be truncated because the primary or comprehensive service provider has been talking to the family about child functioning in routines and about family needs at every visit. Therefore, the provider has much of the pertinent information for this RBI. A full RBI has to be conducted, however, at subsequent IFSP/IEP meetings if a dedicated service coordinator (i.e., nonprovider) is conducting the meeting and RBI or the provider visited the classroom, predominantly, not the home.

Assessing what the child and family actually need is related to the concept of goodness of fit (Simeonsson, Bailey, Huntington, & Comfort, 1986). The RBI, as mentioned, is a core component of the Routines-Based Model (RBM; McWilliam, 2016). In this model, it is essential to understand goodness of fit, defined as the match between (a) the abilities and interests of the child and (b) the demands of the routine. If the child can do what is expected for that routine and is interested in being thus engaged, we have functioning. If the child cannot perform the skills needed to match what is expected in that routine or is not interested in performing those skills, we have poor functioning. When assessing needs, then, we need to determine this goodness of fit or ecological congruence (Wolery, Brashers, & Neitzel, 2002).

If the fit is good and the child is therefore functioning well, we interpret that as the child's participating meaningfully in the routine. In turn, meaningful participation means the child is engaged during the routine. In addition to the idea of overall engagement, we are interested in the child's independence and social relationships. These "foundations of learning" (McWilliam, 2006) are similar to the federal outcomes of acquiring knowledge and skills, taking actions to meet needs, and having social relationships. Engagement is the overarching concept of meaningful participation, defined as the amount of time a child spends interacting with adults, peers, or materials in a developmentally and contextually appropriate manner, at different levels of competence (McWilliam & Casey, 2008). Important aspects of engagement—and therefore considered as two more dimensions of functioning—are the extent to which children can do things on their own as well as an assessment of their social relationships, which are composed of communication and getting along with others.

When assessing a child's functioning, either for developing a plan or in the course of ongoing supports (i.e., service delivery), we ask caregivers about the child's usual engagement, independence, and social relationships (EISR) in the context of typical routines. This focus on EISR allows us to gather relevant information without the artificially and professionally constructed developmental domains (e.g., cognitive, communication, motor) or professional disciplines (e.g., speech-language pathology, occupational therapy, physical therapy). By law in

> Assessment of needs is based more on determining how a child functions, rather than his or her status relative to other children.

the United States, infants and toddlers receiving early intervention must have present levels of development reported by developmental domain. We recommend using conventional normative test scores to document delay, as needed, but using information about EISR, rather than information about test performance, in the description of present levels of functioning in the five domains. Similarly, in assessment reports and discussions with families and teachers, focusing on EISR makes the information more function-based than would a focus on domains or discipline areas. In sum, assessing needs, not only status, is vital to effective EI/ECSE.

Value of Interview

An interview provides a rich and thick description of child and family functioning as it happens when early interventionists are not present—in real life.

What is the value of an interview, compared with observing the child and administering standardized items? First, the child's caregivers can consider multiple exemplars rather than the single exemplar of a child's skill when observed or when an item is administered (Weisner, 2002). When you ask the caregiver, "What is he like to hold, when you lift him out of his crib?" you get an answer that talks about the child's muscle tone, affect, and communication (if you follow up with questions about these topics), as happens morning after morning, rather than a therapist's assessment through a one-time picking up of a child during a clinic or even home visit.

A problem with direct administration or even observation is the Heisenberg uncertainty principle, in which Heisenberg posited that the instrument used for measurement changed the very nature of the property you were trying to measure (McKerrow & McKerrow, 1991). For example, if you want to measure the exact temperature in a glass, the thermometer you use for measurement has inherent heat, so it changes the temperature of the water. Similarly, when EI/ECSE professionals are present during regular caregiving routines, we change the environment and might not have a realistic picture of child and family functioning in that routine. This phenomenon is also known as the examiner effect.

As valued as an objective picture of a child's functioning might be, actually, the subjective picture from the child's caregiver and therefore intervener is probably more valuable (Hughes-Scholes, Gatt, Davis, Mahar, & Gavidia-Payne, 2016). A skilled interviewer can elicit descriptions of children's functioning from almost any caregiver but can also ask that caregiver *why* the child does what he or she does. The caregiver's answer can say much about the child (after all, who knows the child better than the parents?) or the caregiver.

For example, if a child is restless at mealtimes, and you ask the caregiver why, the caregiver might say, "I just do not think he cares about eating." That would lead to a series of questions, which, in the RBI is called "digging deeper." Or the caregiver might have said, "He's just trying to provoke me." Or "He's lazy." Or "He wants to play on his tablet." These answers to "why" questions lead to a number of important questions that tell us more about the child's functioning at mealtimes and about the caregiver than would a simple description of the child being restless. An interview therefore provides a rich and thick description of child and family functioning as it happens when early interventionists are not present—in real life.

Value of Ecomap

At the beginning of an RBI, the interviewer draws a picture of the family's supports by asking questions about who the family deals with (Jung, 2010). First, the people living with the child are drawn in the middle of the ecomap. Second, the interviewer asks the family about extended family, neighbors, and friends, including how often they talk to or see these informal supports. The answer to frequency of contact guides the interviewer about how thick the connecting line is between the family and the support. Third, the interviewer asks about work and recreation, again getting an indication of how supportive they are. Fourth, the interviewer asks about professionals, agencies, child care or preschool, and financial supports. The question guiding the thickness of the connecting line is how much the parent likes these people. We explain to families that the ecomap is to help us identify who might be able to help, when we're working with the family, especially to meet family needs, such as information, transportation, and child care.

Some ecomaps in early intervention (birth to 5) have many people in the informal support network, some with thick lines (strong support), some moderate lines, and some thin lines (present but not particularly supportive). Occasionally, we see dashed lines, indicating a source of stress. The ecomap can also show when early intervention has gone awry. One family had few people in the informal network and eight professionals seeing the child regularly, often weekly, all at separate times. On looking at her completed ecomap, the mother said she wished she had more friends, but she had no time to cultivate friendships because she spent all her time taking her child to services or being at home for those that were home based.

Knowing about the family's informal support network is important, because informal supports are what families rely on first, before formal supports (Whittaker & Garbarino, 1983). The whole EI/ECSE approach of the RBM is based on an understanding of the socioecological influence or environmental press of a child's and family's interactions with the environment, such as the social networks, the settings where family members find themselves, and the routines of the day (Bronfenbrenner, 1979; Lewin, 1939).

Value of Participation-Based Outcomes/Goals

To promote children's functioning effectively in the different kinds of routines or activities of their day, we frame child goals (i.e., goals for the child to learn to do

Table 1
Informal Goals With Priority Order and Type of Goal

Priority order	Informal goal	Type of goal
1	Ride in car without tantrums (outings)	Child
6	Eat without shoveling (meals)	Child
4	Play with toys independently (dinner prep, when mother is caring for younger sibling, when mother is on the phone)	Child
5	Use soft voice (hanging out, meals)	Child
2	Family night (family does something together) every two weeks	Family-level
7	Run without falling (child care, outside time)	Child
8	Eat in regular chair (meals)	Child
9	Drink from open cup without playing in the liquid (meals)	Child
10	Play in a variety of ways, without fixating on one thing (hanging out, bedtime)	Child
11	Use clear words to be understood by people other than parents (child care, outings, church)	Child
3	Get an appointment with a developmental-behavioral pediatrician	Child-related family

something) with participation as the purpose of the goal (Fleming, Sawyer, & Campbell, 2011). Therefore, if a family wanted a child to use three-word sentences, in the RBI this would have come up when talking about certain routines, perhaps meals, hanging-out time, and outings. The goal statement would therefore be "Carlos will participate in meals, hanging-out time, and outings by using three-word sentences."

The emphasis on participation is consistent with the World Health Organization's concept of disability, as seen in the International Classification of Functioning (ICF), Disability, and Health (World Health Organization, 2007). The extent to which a person is disabled is not just a matter of the severity of the impairment but rather the person's participation in activities, and that participation is affected by the supports and hindrances in those activities. Again, the issue is that functioning is the goodness of fit between the child's characteristics and the routine. Therefore, this routines-based assessment—the RBI—leads to the family's deciding on goals that promote functioning. Table 1 shows an example of a list of informal goals a family decided upon at the end of an RBI. We have identified the goals as child or family goals.

From the list of informal goals (e.g., use three-word sentences [meals, hanging-out, outings]), we first state them as participation-based goals and then make them measurable (Bateman & Herr, 2010). We write, "We will know he can do this when . . ." and we consider an acquisition criterion for six months hence. In this case, as with most language goals, we would aim for a number of three-word sentences—in other words, a frequency criterion. The goal could be, therefore, three 3-word sentences. We then consider a generalization criterion. In this example we have three or more routines in the day because multiple mealtimes, hanging-out times, and even outings could occur in one day.

If the family and we thought that using three 3-word sentences would be difficult for Carlos to master in six months, the generalization criterion might be "in one mealtime, one hanging-out time, and one outing in 1 day." If we thought Carlos might easily master the skill, the generalization criterion might be "in all mealtimes, all hanging-out times, and all outings in 1 day." Finally, because performance in one day could be a fluke, we write a maintenance criterion such as "in 5 consecutive days." This criterion can also go up or down, depending on our estimate of how much is reasonable for Carlos to achieve in six months. Therefore, from the informal goal of "Use 3-word sentences (meals, hanging-out, outings)," we might end up with "Carlos will participate in meals, hanging-out time, and outings by using three-word sentences. We will know he can do this when he uses three 3-word sentences in all mealtimes, all hanging-out times, and all outings in 1 day for five consecutive days." Not only do we have three criteria, but they are meaningful, not "in 8 out of 10 opportunities" or "75% of the time." The problem with these criteria is that no one is counting the denominator, making the measurement system invalid.

Consistency With Assessment Recommended Practices

The RBI is consistent with 5 of the 11 Assessment recommended practices as shown in Table 2 (Division for Early Childhood, 2014). Again, the RBI is for selecting meaningful goals, not for securing a developmental score or determining eligibility.

How to Conduct a Routines-Based Interview With Fidelity

Over the years, the RBI has been refined to the point that the RBI checklist, including ecomap development and selecting criteria for goals with the family, has 95 items. Selecting individualized-goal criteria with the family is optional. This can be done in the office and then discussed at a future meeting with the family. The checklist has been shown, with Rasch analysis, to produce reliable scores (Boavida et al., 2015).

The interview has the following general stages:
1. Greeting and reassurance that family members do not have to answer any question they do not want to.
2. Ecomap development.

The extent to which a person is disabled is not just a matter of the severity of the impairment but rather the person's participation in activities.

Table 2
Recommended Practices and Routines-Based Interview (RBI) Elements

Assessment recommended practices	RBI elements
A2. Practitioners work as a team with the family and other professionals to gather assessment information.	Practitioners ask families about details of child functioning and family needs in everyday routines.
A4. Practitioners conduct assessments that include all areas of development and behavior to learn about the child's strengths, needs, preferences, and interests.	Practitioners find out about child engagement, independence, and social relationships, covering all developmental domains and what children can and cannot do.
A6. Practitioners use a variety of methods, including observation and interviews, to gather assessment information from multiple sources, including the child's family and other significant individuals in the child's life.	The RBI captures information from multiple quotidian observations by the child's caregivers. It is complemented by the Measure of Engagement, Independence, and Social Relationships.
A7. Practitioners obtain information about the child's skills in daily activities, routines, and environments such as home, center, and community.	The RBI captures information about child functioning in everyday routines and places.
A9. Practitioners implement systematic ongoing assessment to identify learning targets, plan activities, and monitor the child's progress to revise instruction as needed.	Once RBI-generated outcomes/goals have been written with acquisition, generalization, and maintenance criteria, progress is monitored through goal attainment scaling or the Therapy Goals Information Form.

3. Family's main concerns.
4. In-depth discussion of EISR in routines.
5. Time, worry, and change questions.
6. Recap (5–7 minutes).
7. Goal decision-making.

The criteria for approval as competent in conducting an RBI we recommend are that the person must receive a score of (a) 80% of all scored items correct, (b) 80% of the bold items, and (c) at least 6 of the engagement, independence, and social relationships items. We also recommend these scores be observed on two consecutive live observations or one submitted video recording of an RBI. Different entities are free to establish different criteria.

How does one receive training to fidelity? One option, which has led to the certification of 120 trainers around the world, is the annual RBI Certification Institute, run by Robin McWilliam. Another is at state RBI bootcamps, which have the RBI Certification Institute as the model. Institutes and bootcamps last one week, and then participants go back to work, practice, and send in a video recording of their conducting an RBI. Coaches view the videos and approve them. A third option is to have job-embedded coaching on the RBI, where an approved trainer observes with a checklist and provides performance-based feedback. A fourth option, studied in Portugal, is five face-to-face sessions and a follow up three months later (Boavida et al., 2014). With this course, quality ratings of goals and objectives increased by more than three standard deviations (Boavida et al., 2016).

In a small randomized control trial, the RBI produced better outcomes than IFSPs developed without the RBI (McWilliam et al., 2009). In a randomized control trial, comparing routines-based early intervention (RBEI, now called RBM) with traditional home visits in Taiwan, in the former group, interventionists supported families in identifying functional goals, whereas in the latter group, interventionists instructed parents to identify developmental goals (Hwang, Chao, & Liu, 2013).

In this study, "RBEI was more effective than THV [traditional home visiting] in promoting functional outcomes and reaching family-selected goals, while both interventions allowed equal improvement in developmental domains" (Hwang et al., 2013, p. 3112). In an Australian qualitative study, professionals were positive about implementation of the RBM, but the quality of RBIs and resulting participation-based goals was variable (Hughes-Scholes et al., 2016).

What to Do Until You Can Be Trained

To help early interventionists who are not yet trained to conduct RBIs with fidelity, we have developed the Routines-Based Conversation (McWilliam & Stevenson, 2019). This conversation is like the RBI but produces fewer goals and has the danger of missing important child and family needs. On the other hand, it gives practitioners a way to focus their needs assessment on routines. It is not, however, an RBI and shouldn't be called one because that practice has fidelity criteria that the conversation does not meet.

Impact on Support Provision

Once an individualized plan is developed with the RBI, the early interventionist has a list of meaningful goals to work on with the family or the classroom teacher. Because the goals are meaningful to the family, they are interested in collaborating with the early interventionist. (Again, we use "early interventionist" to mean professionals working with children birth to age 5 and their families.) Collaborations with families involve interventionists' using family consultation, which consists of their asking families many questions (McWilliam, 2010b).

Family consultation is a specific practice including different questions depending on the family's report of the child's progress and whether the caregiver and professional had previously discussed intervention strategies. It uses collaborative consultation to determine the problem, arrive at strategies, and evaluate the efficacy of the strategies. The term *family consultation* is derived from "behavioral" or "collaborative" consultation. We consider such home or classroom visits mini-RBIs.

> Once an individualized plan is developed with the RBI, the early interventionist has a list of meaningful goals to work on with the family or the classroom teacher.

Conclusion

Because of the value of the RBI as a framework for assessing child and family needs, systems should develop implementation plans to adopt the RBI. Individuals, in the meantime, should use Routines-Based Conversations to shift to functional, routines-based outcomes/goals and make plans to be trained to conduct RBIs with fidelity. This article has added to writings on the RBI by showing the alignment with the DEC Recommended Practices, by focusing on the functionality of child goals produced by the RBI, and by introducing the Routines-Based Conversation.

References

Bateman, B. D., & Herr, C. M. (2010). *Writing measurable IEP goals and objectives.* Verona, WI: Attainment.

Boavida, T., Aguiar, C., & McWilliam, R. A. (2014). A training program to improve IFSP/IEP goals and objectives through the routines-based interview. *Topics in Early Childhood Special Education, 33,* 200–211. doi:10.1177/0271121413494416

Boavida, T., Aguiar, C., McWilliam, R. A., & Correia, N. (2016). Effects of an in-service training program using the routines-based interview. *Topics in Early Childhood Special Education, 36,* 67–77. doi:10.1177/0271121415604327

Boavida, T., Akers, K., McWilliam, R. A., & Jung, L. A. (2015). Rasch analysis of the Routines-Based Interview Implementation Checklist. *Infants & Young Children, 28,* 237–247. doi:10.1097/IYC.0000000000000041

Bronfenbrenner, U. (1979). Contexts of child rearing: Problems and prospects. *American Psychologist, 34,* 844–850. doi:10.1037/0003-066X.34.10.844

Division for Early Childhood. (2014). *DEC recommended practices in early intervention/early childhood special education 2014.* Retrieved from https://www.dec-sped.org/dec-recommended-practices

Fleming, J. L., Sawyer, L. B., & Campbell, P. H. (2011). Early intervention providers' perspectives about implementing participation-based practices. *Topics in Early Childhood Special Education, 30,* 233–244. doi:10.1177/0271121410371986

Hughes-Scholes, C. H., Gatt, S. L., Davis, K., Mahar, N., & Gavidia-Payne, S. (2016). Preliminary evaluation of the implementation of a routines-based early childhood intervention model in Australia: Practitioners' perspectives. *Topics in Early Childhood Special Education, 36,* 30–42. doi:10.1177/0271121415589546

Hughes-Scholes, C. H., Gavidia-Payne, S., Davis, K., & Mahar, N. (2019). Eliciting family concerns and priorities through the routines-based interview. *Journal of Intellectual & Developmental Disability, 44,* 190–201. doi:10.3109/13668250.2017.1326591

Hwang, A.-W., Chao, M.-Y., & Liu, S.-W. (2013). A randomized controlled trial of routines-based early intervention for children with or at risk for developmental delay. *Research in Developmental Disabilities, 34,* 3112–3123. doi:10.1016/j.ridd.2013.06.037

Jung, L. A. (2010). Identifying families' supports and other resources. In R. A. McWilliam (Ed.), *Working with families of young children with special needs* (pp. 9–26). New York, NY: The Guilford Press.

Lewin, K. (1939). Field theory and experiment in social psychology: Concepts and methods. *American Journal of Sociology, 44*, 868–896. doi:10.1086/218177

Macy, M., Bagnato, S. J., Macy, R. S., & Salaway, J. (2015). Conventional tests and testing for early intervention eligibility: Is there an evidence base? *Infants & Young Children, 28*, 182–204. doi:10.1097/IYC.0000000000000032

McKerrow, K. K., & McKerrow, J. E. (1991). Naturalistic misunderstanding of the Heisenberg uncertainty principle. *Educational Researcher, 20*, 17–20. doi:10.2307/1176157

McWilliam, R. A. (1992). *Family-centered intervention planning: A routines-based approach.* Tucson, AZ: Communication Skill Builders.

McWilliam, R. A. (2006). *The three foundations for learning for children birth to 6 years of age.* Paper presented at the Associação Nacional de Intervenção Precoce, V Congreso Nacional de Intervención Precoce, Aveiro, Portugal.

McWilliam, R. A. (2010a). Assessing families' needs with the routines-based interview. In R. A. McWilliam (Ed.), *Working with families of young children with special needs* (pp. 27–59). New York, NY: The Guilford Press.

McWilliam, R. A. (2010b). *Routines-based early intervention: Supporting young children and their families.* Baltimore, MD: Paul H. Brookes.

McWilliam, R. A. (2016). Metanoia in early intervention: Transformation to a family-centered approach. *Revista Latinoamericana de Educación Inclusiva, 10*, 133–153. doi:10.4067/S0718-73782016000100008

McWilliam, R. A., & Casey, A. M. (2008). *Engagement of every child in the preschool classroom.* Baltimore, MD: Paul H. Brookes.

McWilliam, R. A., Casey, A. M., Ashley, D., Fielder, J., Rowley, P., DeJong, K., . . . Votava, K. (2011). Assessment of family-identified needs through the routines-based interview. In M. E. McLean & P. Snyder (Eds.), *Gathering information to make informed decisions: Contemporary perspectives about assessment in early intervention and early childhood special education* (Young Exceptional Children Monograph Series No. 13, pp. 64–78). Missoula, MT: The Division for Early Childhood of the Council for Exceptional Children.

McWilliam, R. A., Casey, A. M., & Sims, J. L. (2009). The routines-based interview: A method for gathering information and assessing needs. *Infants & Young Children, 22*, 224–233. doi:10.1097/IYC.0b013e3181abe1dd

McWilliam, R. A., & Stevenson, C. M. (2019, January 10). *Assessing the needs of families of children with special needs or vulnerabilities* [Webinar]. Laramie: University of Wyoming Early Care and Education Center.

Rosenberg, S. A., Robinson, C. C., Shaw, E. F., & Ellison, M. C. (2013). Part C early intervention for infants and toddlers: Percentage eligible versus served. *Pediatrics, 131*, 38–46. doi:10.1542/peds.2012-1662

Simeonsson, R. J., Bailey, D. B., Jr., Huntington, G. S., & Comfort, M. (1986). Testing the concept of goodness of fit in early intervention. *Infant Mental Health Journal, 7*, 81–94. doi:10.1002/1097-0355(198621)7:1<81::AID-IMHJ2280070109>3.0.CO;2-3

Weisner, T. S. (2002). Ecocultural understanding of children's developmental pathways. *Human Development, 45,* 275–281. doi:10.1159/000064989

Whittaker, J. K., & Garbarino, J. (1983). *Social support networks: Informal helping in the human services.* Piscataway, NJ: Transaction.

Wolery, M., Brashers, M. S., & Neitzel, J. C. (2002). Ecological congruence assessment for classroom activities and routines: Identifying goals and intervention practices in childcare. *Topics in Early Childhood Special Education, 22,* 131–142. doi:10.1177/02711214020220030101

World Health Organization. (2007). *International classification of functioning, disability, and health: Children & youth version: ICF-CY.* Geneva, Switzerland: Author.

10

Assessment and Assistive Technology
Providing Support
for Early Childhood Teams

NANCY FARSTAD PECK
LANCE S. NEEPER
Keene State College

ASSESSMENT PRACTICES ARE AN ESSENTIAL PART OF THE WORK THAT early interventionists and early childhood special educators do with children and families. Assessment enables access to the supports and services that help facilitate growth and learning for children with developmental delays and/or disabilities and informs ongoing interventions (Individuals With Disabilities Education Act [IDEA], 2004). It may also be a factor to help in decision-making related to assistive technology (AT) for a child and their family (Parette & Brotherson, 2004).

Empowering a child and supporting their development using AT requires an open-minded team with knowledge of AT and the use of quality assessment practices and resources. Not all teams have ready access to an AT specialist, so building a team's capacity by increasing access to quality AT assessment resources may support children and families' opportunities for early adoption of AT. The term *team(s)* will be used throughout this article to be inclusive of family members and practitioners.

The purpose of this article is to provide teams with an overview of an assessment process applied to AT that incorporates the Division for Early Childhood (DEC) Recommended Practices (2014). Free online resources that have been developed by experts in the AT field have been compiled and are aligned with each stage of the process to support team implementation. Common barriers to implementation are shared throughout the article to guide teams through the process. A vignette is included to reinforce the concepts and cyclical nature of the AT assessment process.

Assessment as a Cyclical Process

Assessment practices are critical to the work early childhood practitioners do. IDEA (2004), the DEC Code of Ethics (DEC, 2009), and the DEC Recommended Practices (DEC, 2014) all highlight the importance not only of assessments (i.e., the tools used) but also assessment practices (i.e., how the assessment process is implemented). Assessment is "the process of gathering information to make decisions" (DEC, 2014, p. 8). This ongoing process can be thought of as cyclical and consists of four basic steps: asking questions, collecting data, interpreting data, and taking action (Dichtelmiller, 2011). This cyclical process can be used by teams as a critical component for ensuring children and families have the supports and services in place to meet their strengths, needs, and preferences across contexts. Information garnered from the assessment process is used to guide decisions with a big impact, such as eligibility for services, but it is also used to guide more nuanced decisions such as choosing AT devices and monitoring progress of interventions (Sadao & Robinson, 2010). Practitioners may already be familiar with the basic assessment cycle as it applies to classroom practices such as planning curriculum and assessing learning, but applying it to the context of AT may be a new concept for teams.

Assistive technology examples run the gamut from pencil grips (low-tech), to talking calculators (mid-tech), to head-switch controlled communication devices (high-tech).

Assistive Technology: A Brief Primer

IDEA (2004) requires teams to consider assistive technology devices and services to "maximize the accessibility of the child." The term *device* refers to the equipment or product being used. AT devices fall into a variety of categories (e.g., communication, mobility, reading, recreation) and can provide greater access to play, self-help, learning, and social tasks for children with a range of strengths and support needs (Dugan, Campbell, & Wilcox, 2006; Parette & Brotherson, 2004; Sadao & Robinson, 2010).

AT can be purchased or created, and devices vary in their complexity (i.e., no-tech/low-tech, light-tech/mid-tech, high-tech; Sadao & Robinson, 2010). Differences among the devices typically range on an increasing level of cost, training, and electronic components. Examples in the continuum run the gamut from pencil grips (low-tech), to talking calculators (mid-tech), to head-switch controlled communication devices (high-tech).

A broad definition of AT is presented in IDEA (2004); however, the law clarifies that AT is not a medical device that has been surgically implanted, such as a cochlear implant. In addition, AT differs from instructional technology in that it is used to meet the specific needs of a child rather than deliver instruction or educational content to all (Shepley, Lane, Ayres, & Douglas, 2017). As technology has evolved, these concepts have become increasingly intertwined, and it may be difficult to distinguish one from the other. For example, second graders may be using an application to make a visual organizer as an option rather than drawing it (i.e., instructional/educational technology); however, this same technology could become AT if the child's only means to produce the visual organizer was via the visual organizer application because of support needs that impact writing. Put simply, if a child requires technology to engage in the task/behavior/skill, then the technology may serve as AT, but if the child can do the task/behavior/ skill (as comparable or relative to their peers) when the technology is not present, then the technology may serve as instructional/educational technology (Shepley et al., 2017).

The term *service* encompasses the evaluation, selection, training, and follow-up needed to support the use of the device. The service component of AT is used before, during, and after a specific device is deemed necessary by the team. The service component is key to implementation success. All team members need to have training to be able to support the child using the device to ensure that it is being used properly and when needed. The service component of AT is directly linked to assessment and can be one of the most challenging aspects of AT implementation for teams (Alper & Raharinirina, 2006).

Potential Barriers to Implementation of AT

There is limited research specifically focused on early childhood practitioners and AT (Moore & Wilcox, 2006). Although limited, the available research suggests that AT use has been undersupported and underused by early childhood teams (Dugan et al., 2006; Wilcox, Dugan, Campbell, & Guimond, 2006). Consideration of AT is required by IDEA (2004), but teams may face potential barriers to the adoption and use of AT. One reason may be that early childhood practitioners do not feel prepared to promote AT and provide AT services (Lesar, 1998; Moore & Wilcox, 2006). To compound the issue, teams might be unaware of resources that may support AT implementation (Wilcox, Campbell, Fortunato & Hoffman, 2013). Perhaps this is due in part to a lack of preservice preparation related to AT (Judge, 2006).

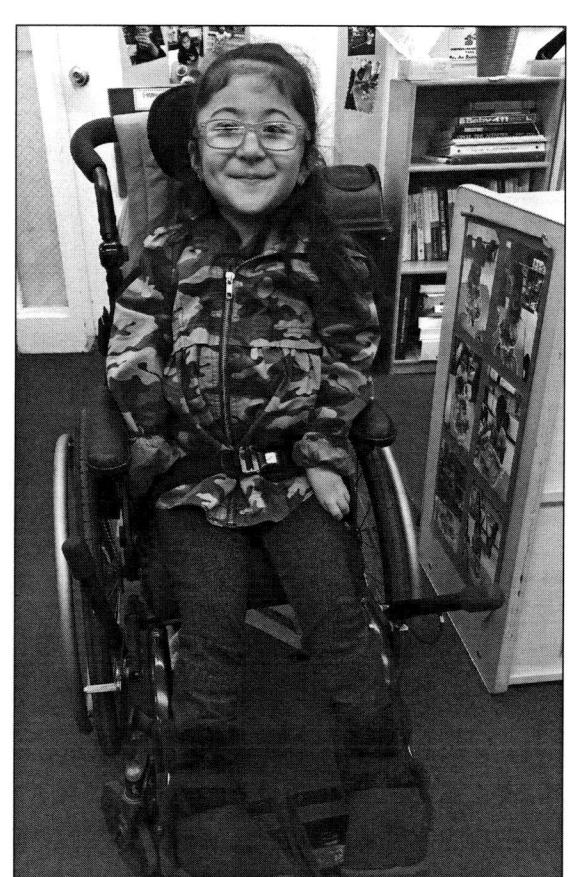

Courtesy of Larry Edelman, Desired Results Access Project, Napa County Office of Education

Families and professionals alike may be unsure of AT resources, acquisition guidelines, and how to best use the AT across natural environments and school contexts (Dugan et al., 2006; Wilcox et al., 2006). Misconceptions about the use of AT (e.g., too young to use, slows development, only for children with complex support needs) may inhibit teams from pursuing options (Dugan et al., 2006; Tebo, 2015).

The Quality Indicators for Assistive Technology (QIAT) provide recommended practice guidelines for teams that serve as an incredible resource for AT; adhering to these guidelines may seem out of reach if a team is new to AT or does not have ready access to an AT specialist. Building a foundation for the team members is important so that everyone can participate in decision-making (QIAT Leadership Team, 2015).

Table 1
Alignment of DEC Recommended Practices With Assessment Cycle

Assessment cycle	Alignment of DEC Recommended Practices	Sample tools and resources
1. Ask questions	• A1 – identify family preferences • A9 – use systematic, ongoing assessment to plan and monitor	**Table 2** • Glossary • Information briefs • State guidelines • Training opportunities
2. Collect and analyze data	• A2 – work as a team to gather information • A3 – use appropriate materials and strategies • A4 – include all areas of development and behavior • A5 – assess in child's dominant language • A6 – use a variety of methods • A7 – assess across multiple environments, activities, and routines • A9 – use systematic, ongoing assessment to plan and monitor	**Table 3** • Quality Indicators for Assistive Technology (QIAT) • Student, Environments, Tasks, and Tools (SETT) Framework • Ohio Center for Autism and Low Incidence (OCALI) • Wisconsin Assistive Technology Initiative (WATI)
3. Take action	• A8 – use clinical reasoning in interpreting results and planning • A9 – use systematic, ongoing assessment to plan and monitor • A10 – use sensitive tools to detect progress • A11 – report results without jargon	**Table 4** • Device selection • Device acquisition

Applying an Adapted Assessment Cycle to the Context of AT

Teams can apply a conceptual model—a slightly adapted, yet familiar assessment cycle (Dichtelmiller, 2011)—to the context of AT if it is deemed an appropriate consideration for the child and their family. This may be a useful way for teams to think about assessment in the context of AT as they assimilate new information (AT) to a potentially familiar assessment process (assessment cycle). This conceptual model consists of asking questions, collecting and analyzing data, and taking action. The steps of collecting and analyzing data were combined because the resources and tools presented assist teams in both the collection of data and in making sense of the information gathered. In addition to the resource and tool connections, this conceptual model can be seen as an ongoing process that closely aligns with the DEC Recommended Practices (see Table 1).

Asking Questions

The first step in the adapted assessment cycle is asking questions (Dichtelmiller, 2011). The culture of the child and family is a vital part of the process when

Table 2
Sample of Resources to Support Teams: Ask Questions

Glossary of AT terms	**Center on Technology and Disability** Commonly used terms and device names/categories https://www.ctdinstitute.org/library/2017-08-28/assistive-technology-glossary
Informational briefs	**Early Childhood Technical Assistance Center (ECTA)** Overview of assistive technology https://ectacenter.org/topics/atech/atech.asp **Pacer Center** Handouts to support the use of AT https://www.pacer.org/stc/tikes/exploring-at.asp **IRIS Center** Collection of information, videos, resources, and modules on the use of AT https://iris.peabody.vanderbilt.edu/resources/iris-resource-locator/
Free online trainings	**Assistive Technology Internet Modules** Free online training modules focusing on all aspects of AT https://atinternetmodules.org/ **Center on Technology and Disability** Free webinars focusing on all aspects of AT https://www.ctdinstitute.org/cafe **CONNECT Module on AT** Online module focused on Early Childhood Education https://www.connectmodules.dec-sped.org/connect-modules/learners/module-5/
State guidelines	**Connecticut State Assistive Technology Guidelines** Provides an overview, guidelines, and resources for AT implementation. https://files.serc.co/sld-dyslexia/2ndary/ CT%20Assistive%20Technology%20Guidelines.pdf

making decisions not only about assessment but also AT use (Parette & Brotherson, 2004). It is imperative that the team use practices that are culturally sensitive and culturally responsive to the child and family. Parette and Brotherson (2004) discussed varying expectations of AT that families may (or may not) hold related to AT and that family-professional partnerships may be put at risk when families and practitioners are not on the same page.

As previously mentioned, teams may not have the training or comfort level to engage in the process. Therefore, teams may have to generate questions and dialogue related to their comfort level and understanding of AT. Resources (see Table 2) related to informational briefs, terminology, laws, benefits, and free trainings may support the teams' readiness and ability to generate questions and dialogue related to AT.

If team members feel comfortable proceeding, they may be overwhelmed with how to begin the process. A starting point for teams is thinking about whether AT is appropriate for the child and their family. Guidance from Tebo (2015) may be particularly helpful for teams: "A general rule of thumb is to consider AT when children are dependent on adult assistance for activities or tasks that their typically developing peers can do independently" (p. 5). Framed as a question, teams might ask: Are there tasks/activities that require adult support for the child when peers are less/not reliant on adult support for the same tasks? Additional questions to facilitate the process may include: How can the child gain greater access to materials and activities? How can we increase independence for the child? How can we support communication? As the process continues, the questions become more focused and specific. Questions to advance the process may include: What AT options are there? What AT is the most effective for the child? What are our purchasing options? The questions generated in this phase of the cycle are unique to the team based on the starting point and the team's readiness to engage in AT assessment.

Collecting and Analyzing Data

Once the team has determined the question(s) to consider, the team can begin the second step of the adapted assessment cycle: collecting and analyzing data. Determining what information to collect and how to collect it may be viewed as a daunting task for the team. To streamline the AT assessment process, team members should establish procedures and guidelines that can support their data collection efforts. There are many tools and resources developed by AT experts to help guide the process. For example, the Student, Environments, Tasks, and Tools Framework, also known as the SETT Framework, is used to promote team decision-making for AT. Another resource is the Wisconsin Assistive Technology Initiative, commonly referred to as the WATI, which developed tools, procedure guides, and materials available for teams going through the AT process.

The resources should be purposely selected based on the questions generated in the "asking questions" step. The application of those resources may vary over time based on the needs of the team. The goal is to systematically collect data across environments and use resources that will be most useful to the team. Guidelines for data collection and analysis procedures should aide in narrowing down considerations and honing in on device options that may be effective. Teams should select the tools and resources that best meet their assessment needs (see Table 3). Developing a

Table 3
Sample of Resources to Support Teams: Collect and Analyze Data

Assistive technology procedures	**Quality Indicators for Assistive Technology (QIAT)** Professional guidelines for AT procedures 　　　https://qiat.org/indicators.html **Ohio Center for Autism and Low Incidence (OCALI)** Resource guides on various AT procedures 　　　https://ataem.org/at-resource-guide
Assessment trainings	**Assistive Technology Internet Modules** Free online training module focused on AT assessment 　　　https://atinternetmodules.org/
Assessment tools	**Student, Environments, Tasks, and Tools (SETT) Framework** Guiding framework and resources for AT assessment 　　　http://www.joyzabala.com/Documents.html **Wisconsin Assistive Technology Initiative (WATI)** AT assessment procedural guides and forms 　　　http://www.wati.org/free-publications/assistive-technology-consideration-to-assessment/ **AT assessment guides by category** 　　　http://www.wati.org/free-publications/wati-student-information-guide-process-forms/

comprehensive and doable system for data collection and analysis will greatly support teams in their ability to take meaningful action. Once a device is selected, ongoing data collection (i.e., generalization, maintenance, social validity) will be necessary to determine the effectiveness of the device and other possible support needs.

Taking Action

After the team has gathered and analyzed data from multiple sources, the next step in the adapted assessment cycle is taking action (Dichtelmiller, 2011). The goal now is to identify, select, and acquire device options based on the interpretations of the assessment data. The selection process can be overwhelming because of a wide range of options or may be frustrating if options are not known. It is possible that teams may not fully use the outcomes of their assessment data to explore a broad range of devices. This could result in teams using specific devices as a one-size-fits-all solution. For example, there might be "go-to" devices in certain AT categories that are used each time the need arises because of limited training, limited access to AT information, or preferences of a team member. Multiple devices that meet the same need in slightly different ways (e.g., different

Table 4
Sample of Resources to Support Teams: Take Action

Device options (categorical)	**Wisconsin Assistive Technology Initiative (WATI)**
	Decision-making guides by category
	   http://www.wati.org/free-publications/
	      assessing-students-needs-for-assistive-technology/

Device options (searchable)	**Tech Matrix**
	Searchable database of AT
	   https://techmatrix.org/
	
	Able Data
	Searchable database of AT
	   https://abledata.acl.gov/
	
	Understood Tech Finder
	Searchable database of applications that includes AT
	   https://www.understood.org/en/tools/tech-finder

Device options (high-tech/ video tutorials)	**ICATER YouTube Channel** Video tutorials on a range of high-tech options https://www.youtube.com/channel/UCsS5iHoCpFJlBwGPvSf64iQ/videos
Loan and reuse programs	**National Assistive Technology Act Technical Assistant and Training Center (AT3)** AT3 directory for state loan, demonstration, and reuse programs https://www.at3center.net/stateprogram

Funding sources	**Assistive Technology Industry Association (ATIA)**
	List of resources and organizations (local, state, national) that support AT funding
	   https://www.atia.org/at-resources/what-is-at/resources-funding-guide/
	
	Pacer Center
	Ideas for using social media to support AT funding
	   https://www.pacer.org/stc/pubs/STC-40.pdf

grips, various sizes of devices, levels of complexity) should be explored to find the best match for the child and their family.

An additional challenge of the AT selection process is that many of the devices are evolving on the high-tech end or are not commercially available on the no-tech/low-tech end. Team members may feel that they do not have the time or expertise to keep pace with the changing world of technology. In addition, commercially available AT may not be developed with the end user in mind, and teams may lack knowledge and resources to adapt their materials, toys, and/or equipment. To help teams sift through information and make more informed decisions, AT experts have developed resources for teams to think about devices that are more closely aligned with their assessment results (see Table 4).

Teams using quality assessment practices and selection techniques may hit additional barriers when it comes time to acquire the device(s). Devices can be expensive and viewed as not worth the risk if the team is not certain the device meets the needs of the child and their family. Opportunities for teams to try out devices with the child and family to collect additional data is a critical feature of the ongoing AT assessment cycle given the rapid nature of growth and development in young children. To support teams through this process, each state has a device "loan" and "demonstration" center that also serves as a lending library for AT. Teams can check out devices to gather more information and determine whether it is the best option for the child and their family. These low-stake trial periods take the pressure off teams to "get it right" the first time.

Once a team has determined a match based on the data collected in the trial period, there may be funding barriers to acquire the preferred device on a full-time basis. Teams should consider the "ownership" of the device, which can be a complex issue. For example, it may be in the best interest of the child if the family is the owner of the device if there is an upcoming transition so there is no interruption in access. Teams will need to use their creative problem-solving skills to establish funding opportunities that can assist in the purchase of the device(s). There are lower cost options to purchase recycled AT (i.e., reuse programs) that may be available through state AT centers. In addition, some organizations (local, state, national) provide funding specifically for AT purchases. Teams may also find success using crowd-funding and other social media platforms to support the purchase of AT. While much of the funding talk is associated with high-tech devices, considerable time and resources are needed to develop quality no/low-tech options. Therefore, resources to assist the development of no/low-tech options can be equally beneficial to teams.

Putting It All Together

Here is a short vignette that demonstrates the conceptual model of the assessment cycle applied to the context of AT.

The early intervention team, consisting of Florence and James (parents), Melanie (occupational therapist), and Jack (special educator), comes together to discuss the strengths and support needs of Lucy (the child) and her family. After discussing the strengths and what continues to work well for Lucy and her family, Jack prompts (ask questions) the team to brainstorm times when Lucy and her family are experiencing challenges within their daily routines. The team works together to narrow down an initial area of consideration to mealtime because of the importance, frequency, and frustration with the task. Florence asks about the use of assistive technology (AT) as a possible fit for Lucy.

At this point, the team discusses some of the perceived benefits and barriers to using AT. The team discusses additional questions (e.g., What's working during mealtime? What's not working during mealtime? Are the challenges related to positioning, muscle tone, and/or specific to certain activities such as eating or drinking?) and agrees to gather more information (collect and analyze data)

> "
>
> Opportunities for teams to try out devices with the child and family to collect additional data is a critical feature of the ongoing AT assessment cycle given the rapid nature of growth and development in young children.

using some of the tools developed by AT experts. The team reconvenes to discuss the information and narrows down some potential options using various resources. Melanie purchases (take action) some low-tech specialized grip handles and nonslip surfaces that can be used across environments rather than high-tech mealtime options (e.g., stabilizing utensils, robotic eating supports) given Lucy's unique strengths and needs.

After a trial period of about two weeks, the team then wants to determine (ask questions) whether the tools are effective and what other steps can be taken to support mealtime. The team members (parents and practitioners) gather information (collect and analyze data) and decide that specialized seating may enhance Lucy's positioning, but they recognize the cost associated with these devices may be prohibitive. Melanie further explores seating options and then reaches out (takes action) to the state AT lending library to try out a seat before making the purchase. After trying the seat for a few weeks with a training and demonstration period, the team wonders (ask questions) whether the seat is the best match for Lucy. James and Florence report (collect and analyze data) that the seat has increased access and comfort during mealtimes. The team begins to explore possible funding sources to support buying (take action) the device. The assessment cycle continues as Lucy's strengths and needs change along with her family over time and across environments.

Conclusion

AT has the potential to "maximize accessibility" for a child, but matching a child and their family with the right AT device is not an easy task given the possible barriers that teams face. Working together to develop an open-minded team with knowledge of AT and shared assessment practices will enable teams to more effectively meet the needs of all children and their families in accordance with the DEC Recommended Practices. Applying a simplified assessment process to the context of AT, combined with purposefully selected tools and resources developed specifically for AT assessment, may provide teams greater access to more fully engage in AT implementation with young children and their families.

References

Alper, S., & Raharinirina, S. (2006). Assistive technology for individuals with disabilities: A review and synthesis of the literature. *Journal of Special Education Technology, 21*(2), 47–64. doi:10.1177/016264340602100204

Dichtelmiller, M. L. (2011). *The power of assessment: Transforming teaching and learning.* Washington, DC: Teaching Strategies.

Division for Early Childhood. (2009, August). *DEC member code of ethics.* Retrieved from https://www.decdocs.org/member-code-of-ethics

Division for Early Childhood. (2014). *DEC recommended practices in early intervention/early childhood special education 2014.* Retrieved from https://www.dec-sped.org/dec-recommended-practices

Dugan, L. M., Campbell, P. H., & Wilcox, M. J. (2006). Making decisions about assistive technology with infants and toddlers. *Topics in Early Childhood Special Education, 26,* 25–32. doi:10.1177/02711214060260010301

Individuals With Disabilities Education Act, 20 U.S.C. § 1400 (2004).

Judge, S. (2006). Constructing an assistive technology toolkit for young children: Views from the field. *Journal of Special Education Technology, 21*(4), 17–24. doi:10.1177/016264340602100403

Lesar, S. (1998). Use of assistive technology with young children with disabilities: Current status and training needs. *Journal of Early Intervention, 21,* 146–159. doi:10.1177/105381519802100207

Moore, H. W., & Wilcox, M. J. (2006). Characteristics of early intervention practitioners and their confidence in the use of assistive technology. *Topics in Early Childhood Special Education, 26,* 15–23. doi:10.1177/02711214060260 010201

Parette, H. P., & Brotherson, M. J. (2004). Family-centered and culturally responsive assistive technology decision making. *Infants & Young Children, 17,* 355–367.

QIAT Leadership Team. (2015). *Quality indicators for assistive technology: A comprehensive guide to assistive technology services.* Wakefield, MA: CAST Professional.

Sadao, K. C., & Robinson, N. B. (2010). *Assistive technology for young children: Creating inclusive learning environments.* Baltimore, MD: Paul H. Brookes.

Shepley, C., Lane, J. D., Ayres, K., & Douglas, K. H. (2017). Assistive and instructional technology: Understanding the differences to enhance programming and teaching. *Young Exceptional Children, 20,* 86–98. doi:10.1177/1096250615603436

Tebo, L. (2015). *A family-centered approach to assistive technology in early childhood* [Online training module]. Columbus, OH: Ohio Center for Autism and Low Incidence.

Wilcox, M. J., Campbell, P. H., Fortunato, L., & Hoffman, J. (2013). A first look at early intervention and early childhood providers' reports of assistive technology reuse. *Journal of Special Education Technology, 28*(3), 47–55. doi:10.1177/016264341302800304

Wilcox, M. J., Dugan, L. M., Campbell, P. H., & Guimond, A. (2006). Recommended practices and parent perspectives regarding AT use in early intervention. *Journal of Special Education Technology, 21*(4), 7–16. doi:10.1177/016264340602100402

Progress Monitoring Within the Embedded Instruction Approach
Collecting, Sharing, and Interpreting Data to Inform Instruction

CRYSTAL BISHOP
DARBIANNE SHANNON
JENNIFER HARRINGTON
University of Florida

It is November, and Justin just transferred to Camille and Wendy's classroom from a different school. He is 4 years old and has been identified as having developmental delays. Camille and Wendy are meeting with Justin's parents, Lita and Guillermo, to learn more about Justin and his family. Lita expresses concern because Justin's previous teacher said he had not yet achieved any of the goals on his individualized education program (IEP). Lita and Guillermo both say they are frustrated because they do not understand how the team at Justin's old school determined whether he was making progress. They thought he had made a lot of progress on the things they and his teachers had been working on with him at home and preschool. Now they are worried about whether he will meet his goals and be ready for kindergarten. They say they want a better way to know whether Justin is "on track" to meet his IEP goals so they can be sure the strategies everyone is using to support him are really helping.

Using data to monitor children's progress toward early learning objectives or goals is an essential component of designing, implementing, and modifying instruction to meet children's developmental needs and to promote early learning (Hojnoski, Gischlar, & Missall, 2009; Wolery & Ledford, 2014). Research has shown that the use of systematic progress monitoring is associated with improved outcomes for students and enhanced accuracy of instructional decision-making by teachers (Fuchs & Fuchs, 2001; Safer & Fleischman, 2005). The importance of collecting assessment data to inform instructional decisions is reflected in the Division for Early Childhood (DEC) Recommended Practices (DEC, 2014) and the National Association for the Education of Young Children's

(NAEYC) position statement on developmentally appropriate practice (NAEYC, 2009). However, research suggests early childhood practitioners do not apply practices associated with progress monitoring and data-informed decision-making as frequently as their colleagues in school-age settings (Hojnoski et al., 2009).

This article includes strategies for making progress monitoring and data-informed decision-making a natural part of instructional activities in authentic preschool environments. We discuss how authentic assessment can be used within the embedded instruction approach, including ways practitioners can team with families to identify learning priorities, plan for and collect data, and interpret data to inform decisions about embedded instruction.

These practices are aligned with Assessment recommended practices focused on obtaining "information about the child's skills in daily activities, routines, and environments such as home, center, and community" (A7); implementing "systematic ongoing assessment to identify learning targets, plan activities, and monitor the child's progress to revise instruction as needed" (A9); and reporting "assessment results so that they are understandable and useful to families" (A11; DEC, 2014, p. 8).

Contextualizing Instruction and Assessment Using the Embedded Instruction Approach

Embedded instruction is an evidence-based and recommended naturalistic instructional approach for providing individualized instruction to children who have identified disabilities or who are at risk for developmental delays (DEC, 2014; Snyder et al., 2018; Snyder, McLaughlin, & Bishop, 2018). Snyder and colleagues (Snyder, Hemmeter, McLean, Sandall, & McLaughlin, 2013; Snyder et al., 2018) developed a four-component framework for organizing the teaching practices associated with the embedded instruction approach. The four key components of embedded instruction are what to teach, when to teach, how to teach, and how to evaluate.

The embedded instruction approach involves the use of contextualized assessment procedures, which are often referred to as authentic assessment. Authentic assessment involves ongoing observations and systematic recording of child behaviors and functional competencies that occur naturally within daily activities, routines, and transitions (Bagnato, Neisworth, & Pretti-Frontczak, 2010). Observations are conducted by familiar adults and provide information about children's strengths and needs with respect to skills needed to enhance their participation and engagement in naturally occurring activities, routines, and transitions across multiple contexts. Authentic assessment can be used to identify priority learning targets (PLTs) for children as part of embedded instruction, to monitor children's progress, and to make data-informed decisions about embedded instruction.

Camille and Wendy explain that by using the embedded instruction approach, they will identify PLTs Justin can achieve in two to four weeks and that can be easily measured so everyone can help collect information to decide whether he is making progress. Justin's parents appreciate that Camille and Wendy want to

> The embedded instruction approach involves the use of contextualized assessment procedures, which are often referred to as authentic assessment.

work as a team with them. The team schedules to meet again in two weeks. This meeting will also include Trevon, who is the speech-language pathologist on Justin's IEP team. The purpose of the next meeting will be to identify Justin's PLTs and to plan how they will collect data to monitor his progress (A9).

Identifying PLTs That Will Inform Progress Monitoring

When supporting young children with or at risk for developmental delays in inclusive settings, teachers should develop functional and strengths-based instructional objectives that can be used to support children's learning and engagement across a variety of meaningful contexts (Bagnato, McLean, Macy, & Neisworth, 2011). A PLT is a behavioral objective that describes an observable, measurable, and generative skill or behavior the teacher wants the child to learn (Snyder et al., 2018). It includes (a) a statement of the behavior the child will learn, (b) the conditions under which the child will demonstrate the skill (e.g., independently, following a model, with familiar adults or peers), (c) the activities in which the child will demonstrate the behavior (e.g., play, meals), and (d) a criterion for determining when the child has learned the behavior (e.g., when the child demonstrates the behavior four times per day for two consecutive weeks). PLTs are aligned with early learning foundations for preschool children, general and targeted curricula objectives, and children's IEP goals (Snyder et al., 2013).

Camille, Wendy, and Trevon collected observation notes about Justin's current skills and potential needs with respect to his IEP goals and the early learning foundations for all children. Two of Justin's IEP goals are:

- *During routine classroom activities, Justin will spontaneously produce three-word utterances to express a variety of communicative intentions, including recurrence (e.g., "more juice please"), initiating social interactions (e.g., "play with me"), and agent-action-object relations (e.g., "you push truck") when requesting objects or actions from adults or peers. He will demonstrate at least three examples from each category (i.e., recurrence, social initiation, agent-action-object) during a language sample collected over two days.*
- *Justin will demonstrate knowledge of quantities up to 10 by counting verbally, counting objects using one-to-one correspondence, and matching numerals to sets of objects. He will demonstrate each skill with 80% accuracy.*

Justin's Priority Learning Targets

- Justin will independently use two words to request an object (e.g., ball please, more crackers) from an adult or peer during meals, indoor play, small groups, and outdoor play. He will make at least three requests per day for five consecutive days.

- Justin will count up to five objects using one-to-one correspondence (e.g., touch and count five blocks to build a tower, count the forks as he helps set the table) following a verbal prompt during meals, indoor play, and classroom small group activities. He will count objects correctly for at least 80% of opportunities three days per week for two weeks.

The team determines Justin consistently uses one word to request objects or food items from adults. Although he appears to enjoy playing with other children, their data show he rarely initiates interactions with his classmates. Lita and Guillermo say Justin only uses words when asking for food or drinks at home. They say they have heard him use two words once or twice in the last two weeks and that he uses one word most of the time. This is progress because at the beginning of the year, he only pointed or gestured to items he wanted.

With respect to counting, Camille and Wendy have collected data showing Justin is consistently able to count verbally to five. He does not yet count more than three objects using one-to-one correspondence. Lita and Guillermo say they are not sure how to help Justin with counting, so they do not practice it much at home and do not have information to share.

The team identifies two PLTs that align with his IEP goals (see sidebar): Now the team needs to consider how they will monitor Justin's progress on these PLTs.

Preparing for Progress Monitoring Within the Embedded Instruction Approach

Progress monitoring within the embedded instruction approach involves gathering data about children's progress on PLT behaviors during ongoing activities, routines, and transitions rather than in a special "testing" situation (A7; Snyder et al., 2013). Using authentic assessment procedures to monitor children's progress provides more accurate information about whether children are learning the behaviors specified in their PLTs than data gathered in a situation that is decontextualized from their typical experiences (Hojnoski et al., 2009; Meisels & Atkins-Burnett, 2000). Collecting data about children's progress on PLTs provides information about small changes toward proximal behaviors that are aligned with their annual IEP goals. This approach to progress monitoring is more sensitive for detecting progress toward annual IEP goals over time than using the criteria stated in the IEP goals. It is also more useful for making data-informed decisions about instruction.

Camille, Wendy, Trevon, Lita, and Guillermo will need to decide *what* data to collect and *how* to collect it, how to *record and summarize* the data, *when* and *how often* to collect the data, and *who* will collect the data (Hojnoski et al., 2009; Snyder et al., 2013; Wolery & Ledford, 2014). The target behavior, conditions, and criterion statements from Justin's PLTs will help the team plan for and collect data to monitor Justin's progress.

Using PLTs to Inform What Data to Collect and How to Collect It

The first consideration for effective progress monitoring is deciding what data should be collected by determining what dimension of behavior is of interest to measure. Four common dimensions of behavior that are measured within the embedded instruction approach include frequency, rate, accuracy, and level of support (Embedded Instruction for Early Learning, 2018). The extent to which the dimensions of behavior are specified impacts the precision with which children's progress can be monitored (Hojnoski et al., 2009; Wolery & Ledford,

2014). In embedded instruction, the dimension of behavior to measure is determined based on the target behavior, the criterion statement, and the conditions specified in the PLT.

Frequency and rate data. Frequency data reflect how many times the child does the target behavior stated in the PLT. These data show how many times the child does a target behavior in a day, over a period of days or weeks, or within or across specific activities. Frequency data can also be used to show how many times a child does a target behavior within a specified interval of time (e.g., per minute, per hour), which reflects the rate of the target behavior per specified unit of time (e.g., three times per 15 minutes). Frequency data are appropriate when the PLT criterion statement indicates the child will do a targeted behavior a specific number of times and when the target behavior is short in duration, with a clear beginning and end (Hojnoski et al., 2009). The criterion statement in Justin's first PLT states he will "make at least three requests per day for five

consecutive days." The target behavior for the PLT is to "use two words to request an object." This behavior can be counted easily, so the team will need to collect frequency data.

Frequency data are collected by recording each time the behavior occurs (Hojnoski et al., 2009). Teams can write tally marks directly on a data-collection form or they can make space in lesson plans or on an embedded instruction activity matrix (Gauvreau & Sandall, 2018; Snyder et al., 2013) to record each time the target behavior occurs. When it is not feasible to record data directly on a data-collection form, in a lesson plan, or on an activity matrix, a token or object can be used to keep count and then data can be transferred to a permanent record as soon as possible after data collection.

Accuracy data. Accuracy data reflect the extent to which a child's behavior matches a targeted performance criterion (Wolery & Ledford, 2014), and they are often specified as a percentage or proportion of correct demonstrations of the target behavior. Accuracy data are appropriate to collect when it is important to know how many times a child attempts to do a target behavior *and* whether the child's behavior matches the targeted performance criterion. The target behavior in Justin's second PLT is to "count up to five objects using one-to-one correspondence." For this PLT, it is important to know whether Justin counts objects correctly using one-to-one correspondence. The criterion statement states Justin will "count objects correctly for at least 80% of opportunities provided three days per week for two weeks." To calculate a percentage, the team will need to collect data about the number of opportunities Justin has to count up to five objects correctly using one-to-one correspondence and whether he counts the

Figure 1
Example of School Data-Collection Matrix

School Matrix		
	Independently uses two words to request an object	**Count up to five objects using one-to-one correspondence following a verbal prompt**
Indoor centers	Planned opportunities: 2 Who: *Trevon, Wendy* How often: *M, Tu, W, Th, F* How: *Data-collection form*	Planned opportunities: 2 Who: *Wendy* How often: *M, W, F* How: *Rubber bands*
Lunch	Planned opportunities: 2 Who: *Camille* How often: *M, Tu, W, Th, F* How: *Data-collection form*	
Small groups	Planned opportunities: 2 Who: *Group facilitator (Wendy/Camille)* How often: *M, Tu, W, Th, F* How: *Data-collection form*	Planned opportunities: 2 Who: *Group facilitator (Wendy/Camille)* How often: *M, Tu, W, Th, F* How: *Data-collection form*
Outdoor centers	Planned opportunities: 2 Who: *Camille* How often: *M, Tu, W, Th, F* How: *Rubber bands*	Planned opportunities: 2 Who: *Wendy* How often: *M, W, F* How: *Rubber bands*

objects correctly. The team can calculate the percentage by dividing the number of times the target behavior occurs by the total number of opportunities and multiplying by 100.

Level of support data. Level of support data reflect the amount of assistance a child needs to demonstrate the target skill. The conditions of a PLT help to inform progress monitoring related to level of support. Justin's first PLT states he will independently use two words to request an object from an adult or peer three times per day for five consecutive days. To know whether Justin is making progress on his PLT, his team will need to know whether he is making two-word requests independently or with assistance. Justin's second PLT indicates he will count up to five objects "following a verbal prompt." The team will need to determine a way to collect data about how much support Justin needs to count up to five objects with one-to-one correspondence. This might involve documenting when the target behavior occurs independently or with a verbal prompt. Another

Figure 2
Example of a Home Data-Collection Matrix

Home Matrix		
	Independently uses two words to request an object	**Count up to five objects using one-to-one correspondence following a verbal prompt**
Breakfast	Who: *Mom* How often: *Sa, Su* How: *Note in class app*	
Lunch	Who: *Mom* How often: *Sa, Su* How: *Note in class app*	
Dinner		Who: *Dad* How often: *Sa, Su* How: *Video in class app*
Play	Who: *Dad* How often: *Sa* How: *Video in class app*	Who: *Dad* How often: *Sa* How: *Video in class app*

strategy might be collecting data specifically about the level of support needed to demonstrate the target behavior (e.g., verbal prompt, gestural prompt, model).

Using Data-Collection Matrices to Plan for Progress Monitoring

School and home data-collection matrices (Figures 1 and 2) are helpful for organizing information about when and how often to collect progress-monitoring data and who will collect progress-monitoring data. They might also include information about the number of opportunities that have been planned for a child to practice target behaviors and the data-collection strategies that will be used. Ensuring every member of the team has access to a data-collection matrix provides a visual reminder of the team's data-collection plan so everyone knows how they will contribute to the progress-monitoring process.

Determining when to collect the data. The team should consider the times of day when the target behavior is needed to participate meaningfully in ongoing activities and times of day when opportunities can be created for the child to practice the target behavior. These activities are important times to provide opportunities for the child to practice the target behavior and to collect data about whether the child is making progress on the PLT. Justin's first PLT indicates he will use two words to request an object "during meals, outdoor play, small groups, and indoor play." His second PLT says he will count up to five objects using one-to-one correspondence "during meals, outdoor play, and indoor play." At a minimum, these will be the times of day when the team needs to collect progress-monitoring data. It might also be appropriate to collect data during other activities to learn whether Justin is generalizing the target behaviors to other times of day (Raver, 2004; Sandall, Schwartz, & Gauvreau, 2016).

Determining how often to collect the data. Collecting data during every activity, routine, or transition each day is not feasible, nor is it necessary to determine whether children are making progress toward their PLTs (Sandall et al., 2016). The criterion statement of the PLT informs how often data should be collected to make data-informed decisions about embedded instruction. Justin's second PLT states he will do the target behavior for 80% of opportunities "three days per week for two weeks."

The team does not have to collect data on this PLT every day to determine whether he is meeting the criterion stated. They can use a probe system where they collect data on three days each week; however, they must have at least two weeks of data before they can determine whether Justin has achieved the criterion stated in the PLT. Justin's first PLT states he will use two words to request an object "three times per day for five consecutive days." The team will need to collect data on this PLT each day for at least five consecutive days to know whether Justin has met the specified criterion.

Determining who will collect the data. When determining who will collect the data, it is important to consider which adults are present during the activities, routines, or transitions when data will be collected. It is also important to consider what other responsibilities each adult has during these times and what other factors might impact the feasibility of data collection. These factors might include the number of people present; the structure of the activity, routine, or transition; the materials or equipment available to collect data; and the comfort or skill level of adults who might be asked to collect data (Gauvreau & Sandall, 2018).

Camille, Wendy, Trevon, and Justin's parents discuss a variety of data-collection strategies they might use to monitor Justin's progress on his PLTs. Camille and Trevon decide to use the paper/pencil data-collection forms to collect data as they embed instruction for Justin (A7). Wendy is not comfortable using a paper and pencil form while she is interacting with children during instructional times, so she decides to transfer one color of rubber band from one wrist to another when she observes the target behavior and a different color when she provides an opportunity but does not observe the target behavior. She plans to transfer her data to the data-collection form at the end of each activity.

Lita and Guillermo often feel rushed to get out the door to school and work in the morning and say their time with each other is limited to a few hours on weeknights. On the weekends, they always set aside time to play at home or to go to the park, and they like to take videos of Justin with their cellular phones during these times so they can share them with other family members. Camille and Wendy mention that the secure electronic application they have been using to share the

> When determining who will collect the data, it is important to consider which adults are present during the activities, routines, or transitions when data will be collected.

Table 1

Guidelines for Making Data-Informed Decisions About Embedded Instruction

Child progress	Next steps
Child has *met the criterion* in the priority learning target (PLT)	• Write a PLT that is the next step toward achieving the IEP goal OR • Determine a new skill for the child to learn and write a new PLT
Child is *making sufficient progress* toward achieving the criterion in the PLT but has not met the criterion	• Continue embedding instruction as planned • Consider minor modifications that might help the child make additional progress
Child is *not making sufficient progress* toward achieving the criterion in the PLT	• Embed learning opportunities in more or different activities, routines, and transitions • Embed more opportunities for the child to practice • Modify instructional procedures

Adapted from "Embedded Instruction for Early Learning: Tools for Teachers Practice Guide," by Embedded Instruction for Early Learning, 2018. Copyright 2018 by the Anita Zucker Center for Excellence in Early Learning, University of Florida. Adapted with permission.

weekly newsletter from school has features for families to write messages to teachers and to upload pictures and videos. They suggest this might be a way to share information about Justin's progress at home (A7). Lita and Guillermo plan to send short messages of things they hear Justin say and to upload one- to two-minute videos from their playtime and dinner-time routines because they usually take videos to share with extended family during these activities. Camille, Wendy, and Trevon make a data-collection matrix they can hang in the classroom. They also make a reminder for Lita and Guillermo to hang on their refrigerator at home. The team schedules a meeting in four weeks to review Justin's progress and decide whether they need to make any changes to how they are embedding instruction (A9, A11).

Making Data-Informed Decisions About Embedded Instruction

Progress-monitoring data should be used to inform decisions about whether to modify the child's PLTs, whether to continue embedding instruction with no or only minor modifications to instructional procedures, or whether to modify instruction to provide more support for children to learn the target behaviors identified in their PLTs (A9; Snyder et al., 2013). Making instructional decisions involves interpreting progress-monitoring data that have been summarized to show how a child is demonstrating a target behavior over time (Gischlar, Hojnoski, & Missall, 2009; Wolery & Ledford, 2014). Teams must look for patterns

Figure 3

Frequency and Accuracy Data for Justin's First Priority Learning Target

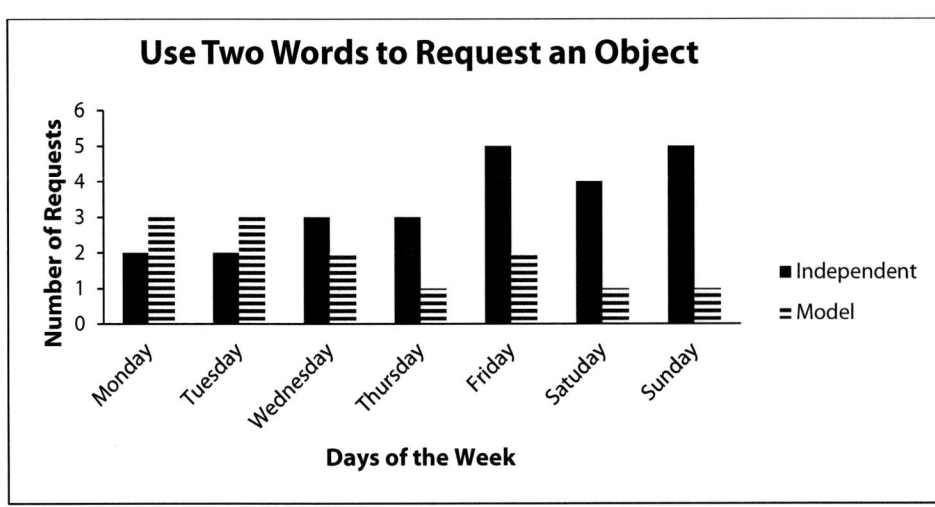

related to the frequency, accuracy, or level of support the child needs to demonstrate a target behavior.

Camille, Wendy, and Trevon display the data the team has collected over time so they can review it with Justin's parents at their upcoming face-to-face meeting (A11). They create graphs to display the information (see Figures 3 and 4). In preparation for their meeting, Camille, Wendy, and Trevon review the data to propose some preliminary recommendations for next steps. As they review the data, they use the guidance provided in Table 1 to consider how they might proceed with embedded instruction (A9).

When they look at the data for the first PLT, everyone is pleased to see Justin has met the criterion; however, they realize they have not collected detailed information about whether Justin is making requests to adults or peers. They make a note to collect information about how Justin interacts with his peers, parents, and sister when he makes requests. As they review the data for his second PLT, the team sees he has not yet met the criterion. When they look back at their data-collection forms, they see there were nine out of 10 days where Justin had three or fewer opportunities to practice counting with one-to-one correspondence. This suggests they might need to consider how they can provide additional opportunities for practice throughout the day.

When Camille, Wendy, and Trevon meet with Lita and Guillermo to review the data they have all collected, they begin by showing the graph illustrating Justin's progress using two words to request an object (Figure 3). They emphasize how much progress he has made. Lita and Guillermo cheer and say they are relieved to see the bars on the graph going up and up and up! Everyone agrees Justin is ready for a new PLT. Lita and Guillermo say that although he is using two words to request more frequently from them at home, he still rarely initiates interactions with his sister, even when he wants something. The team agrees Justin's next PLT should be focused on using two to three words to request an object from a peer.

Figure 4
Frequency and Accuracy Data for Justin's Second Priority Learning Target

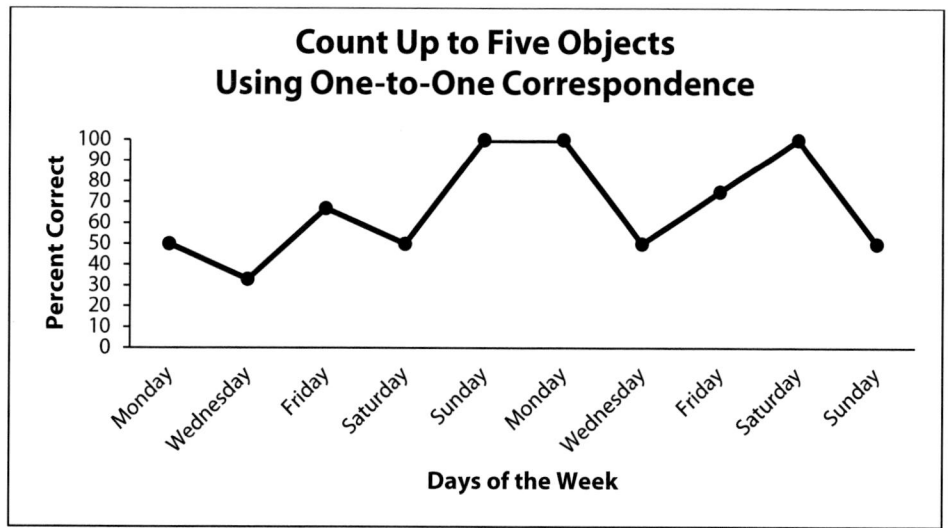

Camille anticipates Justin's parents might feel a little discouraged that he has not also achieved the criterion for his second PLT. Before she shows them the graph (Figure 4), she reminds them that some PLTs take longer to achieve than others and that the reason they look at the data is to help them decide how best to support Justin. She emphasizes there are three days where Justin demonstrated the target behavior in every opportunity he had to practice. Camille shares that she and Wendy have identified additional times to provide Justin with opportunities to practice counting up to five objects with one-to-one correspondence during small-group activities.

Justin's parents say they want to create extra opportunities for him to practice counting when he helps set the table at dinner and when he plays with his toys at bath time. The whole team feels confident that with more opportunities to practice, Justin will be ready for a new PLT soon. In addition to noting changes, they discuss when and how they will embed instruction. The team modifies the data-collection matrix to reflect the new activities where they will embed instruction and collect data (A9). As the meeting ends, Justin's parents thank the team for involving them in the decision-making progress.

Conclusion

The embedded instruction approach to planning, implementing, and evaluating instruction provides a useful framework for using authentic assessment practices to monitor children's progress on targeted skills or behaviors that are aligned with their annual IEP goals and with the early learning foundations for all children.

Collecting data within ongoing activities, routines, and transitions across a variety of contexts where young children learn provides important information about how children are acquiring, maintaining, and generalizing functional skills that support their participation, engagement, and learning. The practical strategies and tools described in this article can be used to plan for, collect, summarize, and interpret data to inform instructional decisions.

Acknowledgments

Work reported in this article was supported, in part, by a grant from the Institute of Education Sciences (R324A070008, R324A150076) to the University of Florida, Patricia Snyder, principal investigator, and from the Office of Special Education (H325D150079) to the University of Florida, Maureen Conroy, principal investigator. The opinions expressed are those of the authors, not the funding agency, and no official endorsement should be inferred.

References

Bagnato, S. J., McLean, M., Macy, M., & Neisworth, J. T. (2011). Identifying instructional targets for early childhood via authentic assessment: Alignment of professional standards and practice-based evidence. *Journal of Early Intervention, 33*, 243–253. doi:10.1177/1053815111427565

Bagnato, S. J., Neisworth, J. T., & Pretti-Frontczak, K. (2010). *LINKing authentic assessment and early childhood intervention: Best measures for best practices* (2nd ed.). Baltimore, MD: Paul H. Brookes.

Division for Early Childhood. (2014). *DEC recommended practices in early intervention/early childhood special education 2014.* Retrieved from https://www.dec-sped.org/dec-recommended-practices

Embedded Instruction for Early Learning. (2018). *Embedded instruction for early learning: Tools for teachers practice guide* [Practice implementation guide]. Unpublished professional development materials. Gainesville: Anita Zucker Center for Excellence in Early Childhood Studies, University of Florida.

Fuchs, L. S., & Fuchs, D. (2001). *What is scientifically-based research on progress monitoring?* Washington, DC: National Center on Student Progress Monitoring. Retrieved from https://files.eric.ed.gov/fulltext/ED502460.pdf

Gauvreau, A. N., & Sandall, S. R (2018). Activity matrices: Tools for planning, organizing, and implementing instruction in early childhood settings. In P. A. Snyder & M. L. Hemmeter (Eds.), *Instruction: Effective strategies to support engagement, learning, and outcomes* (DEC Recommended Practices Monograph Series No. 4, pp. 37–50). Washington, DC: Division for Early Childhood.

Gischlar, K. L., Hojnoski, R. L., & Missall, K. N. (2009). Improving child outcomes with data-based decision making: Interpreting and using data. *Young Exceptional Children, 13*(1), 2–18. doi:10.1177/1096250609346249

Hojnoski, R. L., Gischlar, K. L., & Missall, K. N. (2009). Improving child outcomes with data-based decision making. Collecting data. *Young Exceptional Children, 12*(3), 32–44. doi:10.1177/1096250609333025

Meisels, S. J., & Atkins-Burnett, S. (2000). The elements of early childhood assessment. In J. P. Shonkoff & S. J. Meisels (Eds.), *Handbook of early childhood intervention* (2nd ed., pp. 231–257). New York, NY: Cambridge University Press.

National Association for the Education of Young Children. (2009). *Developmentally appropriate practice in early childhood programs serving children from birth through age 8* [Position statement]. Washington, DC: Author.

Raver, S. A. (2004). Monitoring child progress in early childhood special education settings. *Teaching Exceptional Children, 36*(6), 52–57. doi:10.1177/004005990403600606

Safer, N., & Fleischman, S. (2005). Research matters/How student progress monitoring improves instruction. *Educational Leadership, 62*(5), 81–83.

Sandall, S. R., Schwartz, I. S., & Gauvreau, A. (2016). Using modifications and accommodations to enhance learning of young children with disabilities: Little changes that yield big impacts. In B. Reichow, B. A. Boyd, E. E. Barton, & S. L. Odom (Eds.), *Handbook of early childhood special education* (pp. 349–361). Switzerland: Springer.

Snyder, P., Hemmeter, M. L., McLean, M. E., Sandall, S. R., & McLaughlin, T. (2013). Embedded instruction to support early learning in response to intervention frameworks. In V. Buysse & E. Peisner-Feinberg (Eds.), *Handbook of response to intervention in early childhood* (pp. 283–298). Baltimore, MD: Paul H. Brookes.

Snyder, P., Hemmeter, M. L., McLean, M., Sandall, S., McLaughlin, T., & Algina, J. (2018). Effects of professional development on preschool teachers' use of embedded instruction practices. *Exceptional Children, 84,* 213–232. doi:10.1177/0014402917735512

Snyder, P. A., McLaughlin, T., & Bishop, C. (2018). Maximizing contextually relevant learning opportunities through embedded instruction. In P. A. Snyder & M. L. Hemmeter (Eds.), *Instruction: Effective strategies to support engagement, learning, and outcomes* (DEC Recommended Practices Monograph Series No. 4, pp. 51–64). Washington, DC: Division for Early Childhood.

Wolery, M., & Ledford, J. (2014). Monitoring intervention and children's progress. In M. E. McLean, M. L. Hemmeter, & P. Snyder (Eds.), *Essential elements for assessing infants and preschoolers with special needs* (pp. 383–400). Upper Saddle River, NJ: Pearson Education.

Engaging Families in Meaningful Assessment Practices When Conducting Home Visits

Robyn Ridgley
Middle Tennessee State University

W HEN WORKING WITH FAMILIES AND THEIR CHILDREN IN HOME and community settings, practitioners must encourage families and caregivers to share details about how their child participates and engages in daily routines and activities. Family-centered practices are grounded in the idea that families are experts about their children and should actively participate in sharing information, determining priorities, and making decisions about experiences and interventions (Division for Early Childhood, 2014; Dunst, 2002).

Regular home visits may not provide enough information about how a child performs to identify appropriate outcomes to target, intervention strategies that are effective or not effective, and/or which routines or activities are most motivating and logical for supporting the child's learning. Therefore, practitioners must identify strategies for getting information from families about how children engage during daily routines.

Authentic assessment practices, those embedded in real-life daily activities, guided by professionals, and used by families, can enhance the information families gather and share about their children (Bagnato, Neisworth, & Pretti-Frontczak, 2010). Authentic assessment in which families and professionals work together naturally creates opportunities for cultural sensitivity and unbiased data because information is collected during children's daily lives with their families. The purpose of this article is to provide steps and strategies for helping families find meaningful, authentic, and family-centered approaches for engaging in regular, ongoing data collection that informs the work of early intervention or other home-based supports for young children.

Table 1
Process for Engaging Families With Collecting Data Aligned With the DEC Recommended Practices

Process steps	DEC's Recommended Practices	
	Assessment	Family
1. Explain to the family how data collection can help intervention be more effective.	**A2.** Practitioners work as a team with the family and other professionals to gather assessment information.	**F2.** Practitioners provide the family with up-to-date, comprehensive, and unbiased information in a way that the family can understand and use to make informed choices and decisions.
2. Build a data/information sharing routine into every home visit.	**A6.** Practitioners use a variety of methods, including observations and interviews, to gather assessment information from multiple sources, including the child's family and other significant individuals in the child's life. **A7.** Practitioners obtain information about the child's skills in daily activities, routines, and environments such as home, center, and community. **A9.** Practitioners implement systematic ongoing assessment to identify learning targets, plan activities, and monitor the child's progress to revise instruction as needed.	**F3.** Practitioners are responsive to the family's concerns, priorities, and changing life circumstances. **F4.** Practitioners and the family work together to create outcomes or goals, develop individualized plans, and implement practices that address the family's priorities and concerns and the child's strengths and needs.
3. Identify the specific skills, behaviors, or details for which data should be collected. Capture the skill/behavior in writing and determine exactly what the skill/behavior looks like and does not look like.	**A4.** Practitioners conduct assessments that include all areas of development and behavior to learn about the child's strengths, needs, preferences, and interests.	**F4**
4. Determine daily activities and routines that are logical for collecting data about the skills/behaviors/details.	**A1.** Practitioners work with the family to identify family preferences for assessment processes. **A7**	**F4**

Table 1 (continued)
Process for Engaging Families With Collecting Data Aligned With the DEC Recommended Practices

| Process steps | DEC's Recommended Practices | |
	Assessment	Family
5. Determine how often data should be collected.	A1 A3. Practitioners use assessment materials and strategies that are appropriate for the child's age and level of development and accommodate the child's sensory, physical, communication, cultural, linguistic, social, and emotional characteristics.	F4
6. Identify how to collect and record the data considering efficient methods that do not interfere with interactions and routines.	A1 A10. Practitioners use assessment tools with sufficient sensitivity to detect child progress, especially for the child with significant support needs.	F4
7. Once collected, have families share their data and discuss how it can inform what happens next.	A9 A11. Practitioners report assessment results so that they are understandable and useful to families.	F4
8. Regularly evaluate the process. Discuss whether the methods for collecting and capturing the data work for the family. Also, discuss whether the routines and activities are appropriate for gathering the data.	A1 A2	F3 F6. Practitioners engage the family in opportunities that support and strengthen parenting knowledge and skills and parenting competence and confidence in ways that are flexible, individualized, and tailored to the family's preferences.

Table 1 provides an overview of the process and each step's alignment with the DEC Recommend Practices (2014). Although this article focuses on the Assessment recommended practices, the Family recommended practices also are embedded.

Family First: Getting Families Onboard With Data Collection

The Assessment recommended practices suggest that professionals respond to families' preferences when identifying assessment processes and use multiple approaches to gather assessment information (A1). To identify their preferences, families must be knowledgeable about the choices available for engaging in assessment activities (A2, A6). Sharing with families the varying purposes of assessment (i.e., determine eligibility, learn about the child's current functioning, monitor child progress, report IDEA Early Childhood Outcomes) is the first step in supporting families in identifying their preferences for engaging in specific assessment processes.

The purpose of the assessment often determines the options for involvement in the process. For example, when using a formal assessment tool for determining eligibility, family involvement may include being present during the assessment, indicating whether the child's responses were typical, and providing details about whether the results represent what is typically observed.

Informal assessment processes that are used for determining skills or behaviors a child currently has (i.e., child functioning) usually provide more options for family involvement.

Some informal tools encourage family members to be actively involved in the assessment process by responding to prompts in a family interview, engaging in routine activities with the child to determine how a child performs a skill, reporting what is seen at other times of day or in other environments, or engaging in other ways. These strategies for involvement allow families to provide specific details about the child's skills, behaviors, or approaches to learning; engagement with others; and participation in their daily activities and routines.

When assessment information is collected regularly to see how a child is progressing in his/her learning, family involvement can include (a) serving as the primary observer/data collector, (b) participating in play or other interactions with the child and practitioner to see how the child participates, (c) discussing what the child has done during various daily routines and activities with the practitioner, or (d) reviewing observations and data collected during prior and current home visits.

When discussing the purposes of assessment processes with families, providing clear explanations about why the assessment activities are needed and how family participation can enhance what is known about the child empowers families to engage in the processes. Once families understand the purpose of the assessment activities and the power of their involvement, ongoing conversations about how they can be actively involved for various assessment purposes and processes can occur.

Shanyka has been an early interventionist supporting families in their homes and communities for several years. She recently began supporting Omar, a 2-year-old with cerebral palsy, and his family through weekly home visits. Omar's family wants him to be able to move around their apartment independently. This goal is included in his Individualized Family Service Plan (IFSP), and he receives physical therapy services to help him with his motor skills. He has begun belly crawling to get from place to place. For several weeks when asked how the week has been, Omar's mother and grandmother have shared how Omar has been interested in coming to the kitchen when they cook and spending time in his sister's room when she gets home from school. He is crawling to get to these places on occasion, but mostly he whines until someone picks him up and moves him.

Shanyka talks with them about focusing on this skill during their weekly visits because it seems to be a priority. However, from what they have shared, she is unsure how often he belly crawls, when he crawls, whether he crawls with certain people, or whether his crawling occurs at specific times of day. Shanyka talks with them about collecting information/data over the next week so they will have more details to problem-solve how to encourage him to move independently more frequently. The family understands that because they are with him each day, they can provide the most information about when and how he moves. His mother and grandmother are willing to do this, but they are unsure how.

Necessary Conversations: Building a Progress-Monitoring Routine With Families

Practitioners and family members should work as a team to monitor the progress of children's learning and development (A2, A9). Conversations about progress should occur regularly and become a routine activity for the practitioner and family. When supporting families through home visits, engaging in conversations that focus on the child's progress can be a regular part of each visit. Whether a practitioner is using family-guided routines-based intervention (Friedman, Woods, & Salisbury, 2012), support-based home visits (McWilliam, 2010), a participation-based approach (Campbell & Sawyer, 2007), coaching (Rush & Shelden, 2011), or some other framework for providing home visiting services, gathering information from the family is a necessary component of effective support.

Structuring the home visit to ensure that goals and priorities are reviewed and notable changes discussed is critical to building a "monitoring progress" routine with families. Asking questions such as "How has the week gone?" or "How has Sally been doing this week with (a specific goal or priority)?" are the initial questions that set the stage for learning from the family what has been observed since the last visit. Each and every home visit should predictably include this component. By building this routine, regular progress information is shared, creating opportunities for celebrations, encouragement, and adjustments to routines, strategies, or supports.

Structuring the home visit to ensure that goals and priorities are reviewed and notable changes discussed is critical to building a "monitoring progress" routine with families.

Meaningful Interactions: Deciding When and How to Collect Data

A priority when families interact with their children is to provide meaningful and rich interactions and supports that provide joy to all involved and enrich learning. As early intervention practitioners support families within their daily routines and activities, this priority should be the focus. Within interactions, valuable information about the child's progress and learning can be gathered (A7). It can be challenging to determine how and when to collect progress information so that rich interactions are preserved and authentic, accurate information is gathered.

Identifying the Target

Before one can determine how and when to collect data, the specific skill, behavior, or details to observe need to be identified jointly by the family and practitioner (A4; FACETS, 2014; Stevenson, Grisham-Brown, & Pretti-Frontczak, 2011). For example, Omar's family wanted him to move around their apartment independently. Because he is belly crawling some but not always, Shanyka needed to get more details to know the specific skill to target during their home visits. She needed to know how often he crawled, when he crawled, whether he crawled with certain people, or whether his crawling occurred at specific times of day. This information was going to help her know whether he needed to get more fluent (or better) at belly crawling, whether he needed to be more motivated, or whether some other factor during the day was impacting his crawling. By asking the family whether they knew these details, Shanyka learned more about what needed to be observed or learned (i.e., the target behavior, skills, or details). Jointly, Shanyka, Omar's mother, and his grandmother identified the target or specific skills/behaviors to observe.

When planning for specific data collection for progress monitoring, by reiterating and capturing in writing the targeted skills/behaviors to observe, the family members will be able to focus specifically on those skills/behaviors. Pointing out the behaviors, skills, or details during a home visit; watching a video of other children demonstrating the skill; or providing some other concrete examples facilitates understanding about what should be observed and noted. Sometimes, discussing what the behavior or skill does not look like is important, too. For example, Omar's family will be observing his belly crawling to move from one place to another. They are not observing when he whines even though this behavior is part of what is happening with Omar and his ability to independently move from place to place.

Identifying Routines or Daily Activities

Deciding when to gather information should be guided by natural times that the child demonstrates the skill or the family asks the child to perform the skill (McAfee, Leong, & Bodrova, 2016). Specific daily routines and activities in which the child practices or needs the targeted skill should be identified. Making a list

It can be challenging to determine how and when to collect progress information so that rich interactions are preserved and authentic, accurate information is gathered.

of the routines and activities will provide options of times of day to collect assessment information. Omar's family and Shanyka made a list of times of day in which it would be helpful for him to belly crawl from place to place. These times included in the morning when his sister is getting ready for school, during all meal preparations (breakfast, lunch, dinner), play time, in the afternoon when his sister gets home, during homework time, and TV/hangout time at night.

Once the routines and activities have been identified, discussing with the family member the role he/she plays within the routine can facilitate decisions about how progress information should be collected (A1, A7). If the family member is interacting with the child alone or with another adult or child, observation will need to occur with specific thought given to how information can be recorded efficiently and accurately without interfering with the routine. If the family member is not interacting with the child, he/she can act as the observer and record information in the moment. Omar's family decided that the grandmother would observe and collect the information for the family because she was less involved than Omar's mother in each of the routines.

Determining How Often to Collect Data

The family, with support from the practitioner, should decide the frequency of data collection (A1, A3). Considerations when deciding how frequently to collect data include (a) the feasibility of collecting data within the daily routine (e.g., the routine will not be disrupted, there will be adequate time, data can be collected without jeopardizing the interaction or safety of the child),

(b) where the child is in his/her learning of the skill (e.g., making quick progress so every day is different, slowly learning a new skill, generalizing a skill across routines), and (c) the method used to document data (e.g., anecdotally noting contextual details may take more time than quick tally marks to note presence of a skill).

Collecting information during one routine or daily activity per day for one week may provide enough information to know how the child is doing in acquiring some skills. For example, if a child is learning to crawl and crawls mostly during playtime after dinner, capturing the distances crawled between toys during this time of day may be sufficient for problem-solving how to increase the distance crawled during the next home visit. For other skills, more frequent capturing of data may be needed to know how to respond. If a child is learning to sign "stop" instead of hitting when a child takes her toy or the parent picks her up, capturing each time during the day the child hits or signs provides helpful information in knowing whether the child is using the sign more frequently and hitting less often. If the child is learning to generalize a skill across daily routines, collecting data across multiple routines and days will be needed. Thoughtfully considering the targeted skill or behavior and the purpose of the progress data can help families and practitioners decide how frequently to collect data.

Strategies for Capturing Data

When targeting specific skills or behaviors for children to learn within daily routines and activities, capturing data within those routines can facilitate problem-solving, ensure information is accurate, and highlight progress when progress seems slow. Determining how to capture data within a family's routines and activities should be collaboratively determined between the family member and practitioner (FACETS, 2014). Although methods for capturing do not need to be formal or time intensive, capturing should occur rather than relying on memory and guesses. Capturing the data will ensure important details are noted

and progress detected (A10). Practitioners must talk with families about different approaches for capturing the specific skill identified. Once the approaches have been discussed, the family should identify the method they believe will work best for their family and routines (A1, A2).

Methods used to capture the data should be logical for the skill or behavior targeted. If the skill is discrete (e.g., nodding head to indicate yes, pointing to choose an item, reaching out to be picked up) or the number of times a child performs the skill can be counted, tally mark recording or checklists are efficient and appropriate. If the skill requires more contextual information because it has multiple steps or the quality with which the child demonstrates the skill is important, using text-based approaches (e.g., audio or written notes) for capturing data can be helpful.

Using a paper or electronic form to capture checks, tallies, or steps of a skill may work well for some skills and families. Forms also provide the option for the family to record open-ended details such as noting the routine in which the skill was used or the length of a behavior (e.g., time spent playing with a toy or sibling, distance crawled, length of tantrum). If a form is preferred, the practitioner may need to take the lead on creating the form. Forms can be handwritten in a notebook or on a piece of paper or typed and e-mailed to the family if the family has access to a computer and printer. The purpose of the form is to capture data in an efficient manner; the formality is not important.

Other targeted behaviors, skills, or details are best noted through jottings or anecdotal notes (e.g., how the child initiated an interaction at the playground, words or signs used during a given week). Families can use an inexpensive note-book or pad to record these notes. Talking with families about the important details to include in the jotting or note (e.g., date, context [who, when], specific details about what occurred) can increase the richness of the details.

Some families may prefer to use their phones for capturing data. Using video or audio recording will allow the family to share with the practitioner specifically what the child did during one or many occurrences during a week. Using the notes feature on a phone or electronic tablet can be used for recording anecdotal notes, jottings, or form information. The speech to text feature on many phones facilitates quick recording of information. Inexpensive dictation apps also may support a family's collection of data.

Practitioners should encourage families to identify efficient and preferred methods for capturing progress data (A1). The purpose of capturing is to have more information about the child's functioning to promote problem-solving and decision-making. Families must determine the methods that will work for them within their daily routines and activities. Practitioners must be flexible and re-sponsive to families' preferences.

> Methods used to capture the data should be logical for the skill or behavior targeted.

Omar's mother and grandmother are willing to help gather information about when and how often Omar belly crawls so they can use this information to plan how to get him to crawl more frequently. Because they really have not noticed a pattern in his crawling, they have decided to note when he crawls every day for the next week. They have a notepad that they use for making grocery lists that will work for writing down when he crawls. Shanyka talks with them about what would be helpful to write each time. Shanyka asks, "Do you know whether he is more likely to crawl when his sister is around or if no children are home?" They are unsure. She follows up with "Does Omar crawl to get closer to specific people or activities when everyone is scattered about the apartment or does he crawl more when everyone is gathered in one place?" Omar's mother believes he crawls more when they are gathered in one room. Shanyka responds, "If everyone is in one room, then having a shorter distance to travel may encourage Omar to crawl."

This conversation continues, and they decide together that the following infor-mation should be written on the notepad each time he crawls for the next week: date, time, what, who, how far. The mother writes this at the top of the notepad. She and the grandmother plan to write on the chart the actual date and time that Omar crawls, the daily routine or activity happening at the moment (e.g., play in living room, cooking dinner, homework time), who is present, and the approximate distance that he crawled (e.g., length of coffee table, from front door to sofa). Ev-eryone thinks this is doable. Shanyka assures them it will be okay if they forget on some days or miss some of the crawling during one day. However, getting as much information as feasible will be helpful.

Sharing and Reflecting: Summarizing Progress Data

When families have been involved in actively observing and collecting informa-tion about their child's progress, the information shared during the initial part of the home visit is richer. Families can share the information they have gathered during the week by reviewing the data captured through notes/jottings, audio, video, other recordings, and observations. This creates the opportunity to discuss with the family what occurred during the daily routine or activity in which the data were collected, what the data tell about the child, the strategies used by the family member when interacting with the child during the routine, and other factors that may have impacted the child or family member. Follow-up questions may be needed to fill in details not captured. If appropriate, the data could be graphed, narratively summarized, or stored in another way that will allow the family and practitioner to analyze the child's progress across time to see incremental changes (or lack thereof). The family member and practitioner can engage in discussions about next steps or responses. Important information about the families' interactions and expectations that are often tied to family culture can be learned, discussed, and included in next steps. Specific decisions about intervention strategies, coaching approaches, and environmental arrangements can be made based on the data.

An important component of sharing and summarizing data is reflecting on the routines and daily activities in which data were collected and the methods used to collect and record data. Families should be asked whether the routines and activities were the most logical for collecting data. They can be encouraged to discuss whether the collection and capturing of data worked for them. If it did not, the family and practitioner can problem-solve how the process could be improved. There also may be times in which families planned to collect data but it did not happen because of forgetfulness, busyness, or lack of desire. When this is the case, practitioners should acknowledge these factors without judgment and discuss alternatives. It could be that a different approach could be used. For example, instead of taking notes, the family agrees to video record using their phones during the routine. During the home visit, the family and practitioner will watch the video recordings and note the child's use of the skill or behavior together. Progress data are still collected, discussed, and used, but the manner in which it was gathered is adjusted to respond to the family's situation. Table 2 provides the essential elements for a progress-monitoring routine during regular home visits.

> An important component of sharing and summarizing data is reflecting on the routines and daily activities in which data were collected and the methods used to collect and record data.

The next week, when Shanyka arrived at Omar's home, Shanyka asked how the week had gone. Omar's mother shared some family updates, then got the notepad with the information about Omar's belly crawling. She said they only collected data on four days. Some days they forgot, and on other days they were too busy. Shanyka assured them that the data collected helps them know more about how to encourage Omar to crawl, even though it was not collected every day. They looked at the notes together, sitting side by side on the sofa. Shanyka said, "Let's see what we notice as we look at these notes." They quietly look together. Shanyka said, "Let's look at the times of day and what was happening to see if there is a pattern. Does he crawl at the same time of day on more than one day?"

Omar's mother said, "On three days, I see he crawled during sister's breakfast and sister's homework times." Shanyka said, "He also crawled on two days before lunch when you were in the kitchen. During all of these times, he was in the living room and you were in the kitchen. You can see him, right?" Omar's

Table 2
Essential Elements for Progress Monitoring Routines With Families

Essential element	Examples
Ask open-ended questions about how things have gone generally or related to the targeted skill.	• How has Omar been doing this week with scooting? • How has the week gone?
Review information captured by the family, having the family narrate or share details about the interactions. Ask follow-up questions to get more information, as needed.	• When does Omar scoot during the day? • When Omar is in the living room and you are in the kitchen, how is everyone positioned? • Who else was around when he scooted?
Summarize the information for the family using a strategy that can be referenced in future visits.	• Create a graph • Write a narrative note on your visit form
With the family, decide what needs to happen next.	• Intervention strategy to use • Environmental arrangement to implement • Provide more practice, collect more data
Reflect on the data-gathering process.	• Were the routines and activities logical for collecting data? • Did the family like and feel comfortable using the methods to capture data? • Did the family have time and desire to capture data?

mother replied, "Yes, I can see him. I also talk to him a lot when he is in the other room. When his sister is eating and doing homework, he can see her and may be trying to get to her."

Shanyka and his mother discuss that Omar only seemed to crawl from the coffee table to midway to the entrance of the eating area, which was about three feet. From this information, they are beginning to think that Omar is motivated to crawl when his sister is near and when his mother is talking to him from the other room. They decide that two strategies will be used to encourage Omar to crawl more often and farther. Every time that Omar is in a room within hearing distance of an adult and he cries or whines to indicate he wants to move there, the adult will talk to him and encourage him to "come see them." Second, once Omar has reached his typical distance, the adult or his sister will move closer to Omar, get down on the floor, and say, "Come on, Omar, you can come in here with me." They decide to try both of these strategies over the next two weeks.

Shanyka asks Omar's mother whether she would be willing to keep recording his crawling. She says she will, but she does not want to feel the pressure of having to do it every day. They talk about what would be reasonable and would provide enough information to know how things are going. They decide that the family will *collect data across two days during the school week and one day on the weekend. The family will decide which days will work best for them.*

Having rich conversations with family members and caregivers about the purpose and benefits of collecting data and how data can be collected within daily routines and activities in efficient and appropriate ways empowers families to make decisions about their involvement in gathering information about their child's growth and development. The resulting data collected by families provides details that otherwise would not be available to inform the support provided to children and families during ongoing home visits. Reflecting on the processes used and the data collected encourages families to continue to participate in data collection that is meaningful for their families and fits within their daily routines and activities. This process also highlights progress made and establishes the foundation for home visits that use data to guide the ongoing work with families.

References

Bagnato, S. J., Neisworth, J. T., & Pretti-Frontczak, K. (2010). *LINKing authentic assessment and early childhood intervention: Best measures for best practices* (2nd ed.). Baltimore, MD: Paul H. Brookes.

Campbell, P. H., & Sawyer, L. B. (2007). Supporting learning opportunities in natural settings through participation-based services. *Journal of Early Intervention, 29,* 287–305. doi:10.1177/105381510702900402

Division for Early Childhood. (2014). *DEC recommended practices in early intervention/early childhood special education 2014.* Retrieved from https://www.dec-sped.org/dec-recommended-practices

Dunst, C. J. (2002). Family-centered practices: Birth through high school. *Journal of Special Education, 36,* 141–149. doi:10.1177/00224669020360030401

FACETS. (2014, September). *Monitoring progress on family guided routines based intervention.* Retrieved from http://fgrbi.fsu.edu/handouts/approach3/Tip%20SheetMonitoring2014.pdf

Friedman, M., Woods, J., & Salisbury, C. (2012). Caregiver coaching strategies for early intervention providers: Moving toward operational definitions. *Infants & Young Children, 25,* 62–82. doi:10.1097/IYC.0b013e31823d8f12

McAfee, O., Leong, D. J., & Bodrova, E. (2016). *Assessing and guiding young children's development and learning* (6th ed.). Upper Saddle River, NJ: Pearson.

McWilliam, R. A. (2010). *Routines-based early intervention: Supporting young children and their families.* Baltimore, MD: Paul H. Brookes.

Rush, D. D., & Shelden, M. L. (2011). *The early childhood coaching handbook.* Baltimore, MD: Paul H. Brookes.

Stevenson, W. A, Grisham-Brown, J., & Pretti-Frontczak, K. (2011). Authentic assessment. In J. Grisham-Brown & K. Pretti-Frontczak, *Assessing young children in inclusive settings: The blended practices approach* (pp. 16–36). Baltimore, MD: Paul H. Brookes.

Resources to Support Assessment Practices

CAMILLE CATLETT
University of North Carolina at Chapel Hill

ASSESSMENT, AS DESCRIBED IN THE 2014 DEC RECOMMENDED PRACtices, "is the process of gathering information to make decisions. Assessment . . . is a critical component of services for young children who are at risk for developmental delays/disabilities and their families" because it is essential for identifying children with developmental challenges and informing intervention (DEC, 2014, p. 8). Each article in this monograph highlights innovative, evidence-based approaches to implementing the 11 Assessment recommended practices.

This annotated collection offers additional resources for learning about and implementing the assessment practices. It starts with resources specifically developed to address the Assessment recommended practices. This is followed by general resources that are cross cutting and provide information about assessment of young children. The third, fourth, and fifth set of resources include those based on the purpose of the assessment such as screening, eligibility determination, program planning, progress monitoring, or program evaluation and accountability. The sixth set of resources offers written and audio/visual materials to support assessment of young dual language learners (DLLs). The seventh set of resources covers compendia of measures used in assessment of young children. The final set includes books and other materials that may be considered sound investments.

While there is a clear overlap of resources among these topics, we have tried to categorize the tools and materials based on the primary goals of the resource. The resources consist of web-based and printed materials that are easily available. With the exception of the final section (Sound Investments), which describes classics for any assessment library, all resources are available online at no cost.

1. Resources Addressing the Recommended Practices

Assessment Checklists

Four checklists are available from the Early Childhood Technical Assistance (ECTA) website to support practitioners and families to learn about and incorporate the Assessment recommended practices. The checklists may be used to observe and rate assessment practices, plan for interactions that reflect recommended practices, or reflect on assessment practices with an eye toward improvement. The checklists include:

- **Informed Clinical Reasoning Checklist**
  https://ectacenter.org/~pdfs/decrp/ASM-1_Informed_Clinical_Reasoning_2018.pdf
- **Engaging Families as Partners in Their Child's Assessment Checklist**
  https://ectacenter.org/~pdfs/decrp/ASM-2_Engaging_Families_Partners_2018.pdf
- **Authentic Child Assessment Practices Checklist**
  https://ectacenter.org/~pdfs/decrp/ASM-3_Authentic_Child_Assessment_2018.pdf
- **Building on Child Strengths Practices Checklist**
  https://ectacenter.org/~pdfs/decrp/ASM-4_Building_on_Child_Strengths_2018.pdf

Assessment Practice Guides for Practitioners

Each practice guide features a recommended practice, describes how to do the practice, offers an illustrative vignette and a short video of the practice, and lists suggestions for additional resources. Five Assessment Practice Guides for Practitioners are available (i.e., engaging in informed clinical reasoning, engaging families as assessment partners, authentic child assessment, building on child strengths, and identifying child strengths) in web and mobile device formats.

https://ectacenter.org/decrp/topic-assessment.asp

Assessment Practice Guides for Families

Each practice guide features a recommended practice, describes how to do the practice, offers an illustrative vignette and a short video of the practice, and lists suggestions for additional resources. Five Assessment Practice Guides for Families are available in web and mobile device formats, and in English and Spanish.

https://ectacenter.org/decrp/topic-assessment.asp

DEC Recommended Practices Module: Assessment

Completion of this module will enable learners to (1) explain what assessment practices are and describe how they support children's short-term and long-term goals and (2) describe key assessment principles to make optimal data-driven decisions related to intervention practices. The module introduces and illustrates the Assessment recommended practices. Companion learning guides provide additional resources for faculty and professional development providers to use in addressing the content of the module.

> https://rpm.fpg.unc.edu/module-7-assessment
> https://rpm.fpg.unc.edu/instructor-area/module-7-learning-guides

Dual Language Learners: Screening and Assessing Young Children

This 30-minute activity features a video and discussion questions that align with the Assessment recommended practices.

> https://iris.peabody.vanderbilt.edu/wp-content/uploads/pdf_activities/group/
> IA_DLL_Screening_Assessing.pdf

2. General Assessment Resources

Early Childhood Curriculum, Assessment, and Program Evaluation: Building an Effective, Accountable System in Programs for Children Birth Through Age 8

What should children be taught in the years from birth through age 8? How would we know if they are developing well and learning what we want them to learn? And how could we decide whether programs for children from infancy through the primary grades are doing a good job? Answers to these questions—questions about early childhood curriculum, child assessment, and program evaluation—are the foundation of this joint position statement from the National Association for the Education of Young Children (NAEYC) and the National Association of Early Childhood Specialists in State Departments of Education (NAECS/SDE). A companion statement, "Promoting Positive Outcomes for Children With Disabilities: Recommendations for Curriculum, Assessment, and Program Evaluation," addresses specific considerations for children with disabilities.

> https://www.naeyc.org/sites/default/files/globally-shared/downloads/PDFs/
> resources/position-statements/pscape.pdf

Promoting Positive Outcomes for Children With Disabilities: Recommendations for Curriculum, Assessment, and Program Evaluation

The Division for Early Childhood developed this document to be read and used in conjunction with the NAEYC-NAECS/SDE position statement (*Early Childhood Curriculum, Assessment, and Program Evaluation: Building an Effective, Accountable System in Programs for Children Birth Through Age 8*), which puts forth general recommendations and guidance intended to apply practices for all young children, including those with disabilities. The recommendations are not alternatives, nor do they contradict the NAEYC-NAECS/SDE recommendations. Rather, they extend, more specifically apply, and further explicate the recommendations in the more general position statement. By reading and implementing both sets of recommendations, practitioners and policy makers will have the benefit of complementary perspectives and expertise.

> https://www.decdocs.org/position-statement-promoting-positi

Early Childhood Assessment: Why, What, and How

This downloadable book identifies the important outcomes for children from birth to age 5 and the quality and purposes of different techniques and instruments for developmental assessments. Individual chapters address screening, measuring quality in early childhood environments, and assessing all children, which includes those who are dual language learners and children with disabilities.

> https://www.nap.edu/catalog/12446/
> early-childhood-assessment-why-what-and-how

Authentic Assessment in Early Intervention (Module)

This module provides an overview of authentic assessment in early intervention, including what it is and why it is important. Individuals who complete this module will have an understanding of who participates in authentic assessment, where it may happen, when it can be done, and within what early intervention processes it can occur. The module includes numerous opportunities for reflection as well as tools to support both the online learner and the administrators/supervisors who support and prepare early intervention practitioners/service coordinators. It includes links to a variety of tools and resources.

> http://universalonlinepartceicurriculum.pbworks.com/w/page/123567288/
> Authentic%20Assessment%20in%20Early%20Intervention

Authentic Assessment in Early Intervention (Video)

In this video, physical therapist Megan Klish Fibbe describes and illustrates how authentic assessment practices enhance her early intervention work with children and their families, including the use of observation, conversations with families, and video.

> https://youtu.be/CjE3tSxhDDg

Authentic Assessment in Infant-Toddler Care Settings

This policy brief describes what authentic assessment is, the role observation plays in authentic assessment, the use of information from observations to develop curriculum, outcomes from authentic assessment, and the need to include authentic assessment training in professional development activities for early childhood practitioners who work with infants and toddlers.

> http://muskie.usm.maine.edu/Publications/CYF/Authentic-Assessment-Child-Care.pdf

Results Matter Video Library: Practicing Observation, Documentation, and Assessment Skills

The videos in this collection are perfect for practicing observation, documentation, and assessment skills. Each has a description of the ages and activities of the children. All clips may be watched online or downloaded for free.

http://www.cde.state.co.us/resultsmatter/RMVideoSeries_PracticingObservation

Asking the Right Questions in the Right Ways

While this classic article purports to be for speech-language pathologists and audiologists, it is a terrific resource for anyone who will be gathering information from family members about their children and home practices. Using the examples of the descriptive and structural questions, paired with the insights about social connections, will make anyone a better partner in the information-gathering process.

https://leader.pubs.asha.org/article.aspx?articleid=2292396

Research Synthesis on Screening and Assessing Social-Emotional Competence

This 2008 synthesis provides information for early care and education providers on using evidence-based practices in screening and assessing the social-emotional competence of infants, toddlers, and young children. The synthesis is organized around common questions related to screening and assessing social-emotional competence. It begins with a discussion of what is meant by social-emotional competence and then describes general issues and challenges around screening and assessment. The authors then discuss the roles of families, culture, and language in screening and assessing social-emotional competence, and they end with a list of resources and some examples of social and emotional screening and assessment tools.

http://csefel.vanderbilt.edu/documents/rs_screening_assessment.pdf

3. Screening and Determining Eligibility

Screening, Assessment, and Evaluation

This web page provides a variety of resources from different sources on screening, evaluation, and assessment, which are distinct processes with different purposes under the provisions of Part C and Part B of the Individuals With Disabilities Education Act. It includes citations of the federal regulations related to determining eligibility and examples of guidance materials developed by states.

https://ectacenter.org/topics/earlyid/screeneval.asp

Identifying Specific Disabilities and Children at Risk

This web page includes an extensive collection of resources addressing the identification of specific disabilities (e.g., autism spectrum disorder, communication disorders, Fragile X). It also includes resources addressing identification and referral of children experiencing abuse and neglect, mental health issues, or prenatal substance abuse.

> https://ectacenter.org/topics/earlyid/idspecpops.asp

Infant and Toddler Development, Screening, and Assessment Module

This online module provides child care consultants with information about screening and assessment of infants and toddlers. Content and activities address development, family engagement, observation/screening/ongoing assessment, and red flags.

> https://www.zerotothree.org/resources/72-infant-and-toddler-development-screening-and-assessment#downloads

4. Program Planning and Monitoring of Progress

What Does It Mean to Use Ongoing Assessment to Individualize Instruction in Early Childhood?

This brief presents a conceptual framework for curriculum-embedded approaches to ongoing child assessment. The conceptual framework shows how teachers can use ongoing assessment for individualization.

> https://www.mathematica.org/our-publications-and-findings/publications/brief-what-does-it-mean-to-use-ongoing-assessment-to-individualize-instruction-in-early-childhood

Using Child Assessment Data to Achieve Positive Outcomes

In this video, administrators and teachers illustrate how they use authentic child assessment data to inform classroom-level instruction, support teachers, and meet the needs of individual children and their families.

> https://www.youtube.com/watch?v=PtR24V8z9_w&feature=youtu.be

Appropriate and Meaningful Assessment in Family-Centered Programs

This 2013 article discusses elements that make up continuous assessment, including ways teachers can collect, document, organize, and maintain information; the importance of reflecting on this information in collaboration with colleagues and families; and how to use this information for setting goals and planning for individual children and groups.

> https://cms.azed.gov/home/GetDocumentFile?id=59e6256d3217e1076c0f5680

Early Childhood Assessment: Implementing Effective Practice

This paper will help readers understand the big ideas early childhood thought leaders believe should guide assessment decisions for the youngest school-aged students (prekindergarten to third grade), discover what the research shows to be effective in terms of assessment in the early grades, and come away with a clear sense of next steps they can take to apply the research and best practices to their assessment planning processes.

> http://info.nwea.org/rs/nwea/images/EarlyChildhoodAssessment-
> ImplementingEffectivePractice.pdf

Tailored Teaching: The Need for Stronger Evidence About Early Childhood Teachers' Use of Ongoing Assessment to Individualize Instruction

This brief reviews the literature on ongoing assessment for researchers and practitioners.

> http://www.mathematica-mpr.com/our-publications-and-findings/publications/
> brief-tailored-teaching-the-need-for-stronger-evidence-about-early-childhood-
> teachers-use-of-ongoing

What Do We Know About How Early Childhood Teachers Use Ongoing Assessment?

This brief has findings from a review of the literature on ongoing assessment in early childhood, including what we know, what we still need to learn, and recommended practices for using assessments to support learning and development.

> https://www.mathematica.org/our-publications-and-findings/publications/
> brief-what-do-we-know-about-how-early-childhood-teachers-use-ongoing-
> assessment

5. Program Evaluation and Accountability

Measuring Children's Progress From Preschool Through Third Grade

This paper discusses the measurement of child outcomes in the context of evaluating the effectiveness of preschool programs for children. The paper discusses the importance of focusing on the whole child rather than just the language and cognitive domains and explores what is known about the current assessment methods used with young children.

> https://www.mathematica-mpr.com/-/media/publications/pdfs/
> measchildprogress.pdf

6. Assessing Dual Language Learners

Culturally and Linguistically Diverse Young Children With Disabilities

When assessing young children for early intervention or special education services, practitioners need to be sensitive to the cultural and linguistic variations that exist in our society. Appropriate procedures need to be in place to determine which language will be used to conduct assessments and to ensure that appropriate assessment/screening tools are being used. It is critical to obtain a nonbiased picture of the child's abilities to determine whether certain patterns of development and behavior are caused by a disability or are simply the result of cultural and linguistic differences. This annotated web collection of resources addresses these issues.

> https://ectacenter.org/topics/earlyid/diverse.asp

Dual Language Learners With Disabilities: Supporting Young Children in the Classroom

This module offers an overview of young children who are dual language learners. It highlights the importance of maintaining the home language(s) of children at the same time they are learning a new or second language, discusses considerations for screening and assessment, and identifies strategies for supporting them in inclusive environments.

> https://iris.peabody.vanderbilt.edu/module/dll/

Bilingualism and Assessment in Early Childhood Special Education

In this vlog, Greg Cheatham (University of Kansas) discusses bilingualism and assessment and offers tips on working with families who have home languages other than English.

> https://militaryfamilies.extension.org/2017/04/26/fdei-ask-the-expert-vlog-bilingualism-and-assessment-in-early-childhood-special-education/

Screening DLLs in Early Head Start and Head Start: A Guide for Program Leaders

This guide reviews current understandings of the development and importance of screening in supporting DLLs. It includes tools that can help Head Start and Early Head Start program leaders make informed and intentional decisions about selecting valid screening instruments and implementing high-quality screening practices for young DLLs. This is helpful when valid screening tools are not available in the languages of the children being served. While the emphasis in this publication is Head Start and Early Head Start, the content has broader applicability and relevance.

> https://eclkc.ohs.acf.hhs.gov/child-screening-assessment/article/screening-dual-language-learners-early-head-start-head-start-guide-program-leaders

Gathering and Using Language Information That Families Share

This resource shares evidence-based strategies for thoughtfully gathering information from families with home languages other than English.

> https://eclkc.ohs.acf.hhs.gov/sites/default/files/pdf/gathering-using-language-info-families-share.pdf

Where We Stand on Assessing Young English Language Learners

The recommendations in this synthesis, along with specific indicators of effective practice, are intended to help policymakers, program administrators, teachers, and others improve screening and assessment practices for young children who are dual language learners.

- **English**
  http://www.naeyc.org/files/naeyc/file/positions/
  WWSEnglishLanguageLearnersWeb.pdf
- **Spanish**
  http://www.naeyc.org/files/naeyc/file/positions/
  ELLSpanishWWS.pdf

7. Compendia of Measures

Birth to 5: Watch Me Thrive! A Compendium of Screening Measures for Young Children

The purpose of this compendium is to identify a set of first-line screening tools that meet certain quality parameters. Federal partners have identified 11 screening tools that meet quality criteria for tool accuracy, inclusion of family input, and inclusion of the social and emotional domain of development.

> https://eclkc.ohs.acf.hhs.gov/sites/default/files/pdf/screening-compendium-march2014.pdf

Early Childhood Developmental Screening: A Compendium of Measures for Children Ages Birth to Five

This user-friendly compendium defines developmental screening and explains how it differs from child assessment. It reviews commonly used developmental screening tools, providing key information to aid practitioners in selecting the appropriate tool for their population, including reliability and validity, background, cost, time to administer, needed training for assessors, family input, and use with special populations.

> https://pdg.grads360.org/services/PDCService.svc/
> GetPDCDocumentFile?fileId=17013

Understanding and Choosing Assessments and Developmental Screeners for Young Children Ages 3–5: Profiles of Selected Measures

This document, originally designed for Head Start readers, offers valuable information for anyone who is selecting screening and assessment instruments. It reviews reliability and validity information for specific tools and describes how to evaluate and select tools for specific populations or purposes (for example DLLs).

https://www.acf.hhs.gov/sites/default/files/opre/screeners_final.pdf

Early Childhood Measures Profiles

This report describes a profile of instruments used to measure developmental domains in early childhood, including language, literacy, math, approaches to learning, ongoing observation measures, general cognitive measures, social-emotional measures, and measures used in Early Head Start analyses.

https://www.childtrends.org/publications/early-childhood-measures-profiles

Executive Function Mapping Project Measures Compendium: A Resource for Selecting Measures Related to Executive Function and Other Regulation-Related Skills in Early Childhood

This May 2018 resource was designed to assist researchers and early child assessment and evaluation practitioners to identify the range of measures available to assess executive function and other regulation-related skills in young children. Summary tables listing all the measures by age, skills, and tasks are provided.

https://www.acf.hhs.gov/sites/default/files/opre/e_mapping_measures_full_document_pjg_508_bluelinksfinal.PDF

8. Sound Investments

Bagnato, S. J., Neisworth, J. T., & Pretti-Frontczak, K. (2010). *LINKing authentic assessment and early childhood intervention: Best measures for best practices* (2nd ed.). Baltimore, MD: Paul H. Brookes.

How can early childhood professionals make informed decisions while selecting assessment materials that meet recommended practices? One answer is to use this book with professional ratings and reviews of 80 authentic, widely used assessment tools for children birth to age 8. It provides ratings of the qualities of assessment materials based on "consumer reports" and ratings from a survey of more than 1,000 professionals, detailed reviews from a panel of assessment experts, and ratings drawn from the authors' extensive expertise. Cost: $49.95

Grisham-Brown, J., & Pretti-Frontczak, K. (2011). *Assessing young children in inclusive settings: The blended practices approach.* Baltimore, MD: Paul H. Brookes.

The major focus in this book is on how to conduct authentic assessments during children's natural routines and play activities and then how to use assessment to inform effective programming. The text gives readers vignettes of common dilemmas teachers may encounter, classroom examples featuring diverse children, and practical aids such as assessment checklists and excerpts from select tools. Cost: $39.95

Losardo, A., & Notari Syverson, A. (2011). *Alternate approaches to assessing young children* (2nd ed.). Baltimore, MD: Paul H. Brookes.

This book focuses on six alternative assessment methods: naturalistic, focused, performance, portfolio, dynamic, and curriculum-based language. In addition to exploring the advantages and limitations of each approach, the book offers strategies for effectively linking assessment with intervention and building consensus with families. Cost: $39.95

Macy, M., & Bagnato, S. J. (2013). The authentic alternative for assessment in early childhood intervention. In D. H. Saklofske, C. R. Reynolds, & V. L. Schwean, (Eds.), *The Oxford handbook of child psychological assessment* (pp. 671–681). London, England: Oxford University Press.

This chapter promotes authentic assessment as the evidence-based alternative for young children to prevent the mismeasure of young children with disabilities.

Reference

Division for Early Childhood. (2014). *DEC recommended practices in early intervention/early childhood special education 2014*. Retrieved from https://www.dec-sped.org/dec-recommended-practices

Editorial Team

Editors

Mary McLean, *University of Florida*
Rashida Banerjee, *University of Denver*
Jane Squires, *University of Oregon*
Kathleen Hebbeler, *SRI International*

Resources Within Reason

Camille Catlett, *University of North Carolina at Chapel Hill*

Reviewers

Harriet Able, *University of North Carolina at Chapel Hill*
Kathleen Artman-Meeker, *University of Washington*
Karyn Aspden, *Massey University*
Ruby Batz, *University of Oregon*
Crystal Bishop, *Anita Zucker Center for Excellence in Early Childhood Studies*
Patricia Blasco, *Oregon Health & Science University*
Sue Carbary, *Bank Street College of Education*
Judith Carta, *University of Kansas*
Tricia Catalino, *Hawai'i Pacific University*
Lynette Chandler, *consultant*
Deborah Chen, *California State University, Northridge*
Ching-I Chen, *Kent State University*
Dana Childress, *Virginia Commonwealth University*
Cinda Clark, *University of Florida*
Jennifer Cunningham, *University of Washington*
Carmen Dionne, *Université du Québec à Trois-Rivières*
Glen Dunlap, *University of Nevada, Reno*
Chelsea Guillen, *University of Illinois at Urbana-Champaign*
Jen Harrington, *University of Florida*
Corinne Hill, *Virginia Commonwealth University*
Hollie Hix-Small, *Portland State University*
Robin Hojnosi, *Lehigh University*
Jin Hee Hur, *University of Florida*
Snezana Ilic, *University of Belgrade*

Laurie Jeans, *St. Ambrose University*
Justin Lane, *University of Kentucky*
Bernadette Laumann, *University of Illinois at Urbana-Champaign*
Rebecca Lieberman-Betz, *University of Georgia*
Angela Losardo, *Appalachian State University*
Mary Moran, *independent consultant*
Rebecca Parlakian, *Zero to Three*
Ozden H. Pinar Irmak, *University of Massachusetts Boston*
Debra Prykanowski, *Appalachian State University*
Megan Purcell, *Purdue University*
Cordelia Rosenberg, *University of Colorado*
Dathan Rush, *Family, Infant and Preschool Program*
Susan Sandall, *University of Washington*
Amy Santos, *University of Illinois at Urbana-Champaign*
Alana Schnitz, *Juniper Gardens Children's Project*
Celeste Schultz, *University of Illinois at Chicago*
Sheila Self, *California Department of Education*
M'Lisa Shelden, *Wichita State University*
Patricia Snyder, *University of Florida*
Elizabeth Steed, *University of Colorado Denver*
Sondra Stegenga, *University of Oregon*
Sloan Storie, *University of Oregon*
Judy Swett, *PACER Center*
Jenna Weglarz-Ward, *University of Nevada, Las Vegas*
Pei-Fang Rachel Wu, *National Taichung University of Education*
Huichao Xie, *National Institute of Education, Singapore*
Naomi Younggren, *DoD EDIS Early Intervention*

Index

Notes

Page numbers for figures are in *italics* followed by the letter *f*.

Page numbers for tables are in *italics* followed by the letter *t*.

Page numbers for vignettes (descriptive examples of the topic) are in *italics* followed by the letter *v*.

Names of vignette subjects are in *italics* followed by the topic of the vignette in brackets [ ], for example, *Andie* [EF assessments].